...AND WELL TIED DOWN

...AND WELL TIED DOWN

CHILE'S PRESS UNDER DEMOCRACY

Ken León-Dermota

PRAEGER

Westport, Connecticut
London

50410150

Library of Congress Cataloging-in-Publication Data

León-Dermota, Ken.
  --and well tied down : Chile's press under democracy / Ken León-Dermota.
    p. cm.
  Includes bibliographical references and index.
  ISBN 0-275-97590-8 (alk. paper)
    1. Press—Chile—History—20th century. 2. Press and politics—Chile—History—20th
century. I. Title.
  PN5044.L46 2003
  079'.83'09045—dc21   2002030719

British Library Cataloguing in Publication Data is available.

Library of Congress Catalog Card Number: 2002030719
ISBN: 0–275–97590–8

First published in 2003

Praeger Publishers, 88 Post Road West, Westport, CT 06881
An imprint of Greenwood Publishing Group, Inc.
www.praeger.com

Printed in the United States of America

The paper used in this book complies with the
Permanent Paper Standard issued by the National
Information Standards Organization (Z39.48-1984).

10 9 8 7 6 5 4 3 2 1

For Beatriz Elena and Eddie,
without whose inspiration and patience
Daddy would never have gotten the book done.

Contents

Preface

Chile's story is nothing if not dynamic. Chile hosted the only leftist revolution to be elected to power anywhere in the world—immediately followed by the last of the hemisphere's anti-Communist military dictatorships. From a closed, socialist economy, Chile jumped to the head of the class among the open economies of the world, anticipating both Ronald Reagan and Margaret Thatcher in imposing free-market economies. In all the standard indicators—literacy, medical care, education, corruption, and infrastructure—Chile became the exception among Latin American nations and was looking more like a Mediterranean country by the end of the twentieth century. Chile's image in the world community is that of a country that has recovered its democratic tradition after a 17-year hiatus, and except for some niggling problems with trying to bring the former dictator to justice, its important institutions are largely intact. In 2001, the so-called "Press Law" rescinded the most onerous infringements on free expression, many of which dated from the 1930s and 1940s.

So you ask, what is there to write a book about?

As a teaching fellow at the University of Chile and the Diego Portales University, I came in touch with journalists at all levels of the masthead and at every latitude along Chile's stringbean geography. Their unanimous complaint: Journalism in Chile just isn't what it used to be. It's easy for the outsider to be misled: The newsstands carry many well-printed newspapers, the radio dial is filled with stations, and the broadcast media have attracted large amounts of foreign investment. However, a closer reading tells you that the level of journalism in Chile is below that of its neighbors, many of which are truly underdeveloped. Chilean journalism is not pulling its own weight as a democratic institution. However, it wasn't always that way.

Reading back issues of the underground periodicals that opposed the dictatorship convinced me that Chileans were no slouches when it came to journalism. These publications were filled with astounding investigations, stories with revealing background and forceful structure, written with the irony, wit, and sarcasm that are nowhere to be found in Chilean journalism today. How could journalism written under a dictatorship possibly be *better* than the sawdust copy in today's newspapers? In addition, why did *all* of the resistance publications that thrived under Pinochet mysteriously disappear once democracy came around?

As I assembled files of news clippings from today's newspapers, patterns began to emerge: There is no investigative journalism in Chile; there are virtually no dissenting opinions about the state of the economy; no periodical does an ongoing analysis of Chile's controversial health or pension systems; native people, workers, and the poor are portrayed as rabble when they are portrayed at all; television programming looks to be vetted by the Vatican; the news is devoid of analysis, walk-ups, think pieces, backgrounders, and commentary—it is full of just hard news, features, and opinion.

This is democracy? Spain and Peru have vibrant media that take up sides and challenge their leaders and each other. Colombians and Argentines do sophisticated investigations and add value to the marketplace of ideas even under threat of violence. If Chileans could do all this during the dictatorship, who's stopping them now? Many suspect that it is the media owners.

Chilean journalists confided that they didn't really know the owners of the news media thoroughly. So I met with communications minister Claudio Huepe. He didn't know, either. Huepe and his research staff knew the names of the principals, of course. However, they could not unearth the owners' other business interests. I was intrigued. The owner of one half of Chile's newspaper duopoly, the *El Mercurio* chain, coordinated U.S. backing leading up to the 1973 coup and assembled the University of Chicago-trained economists who would eventually run the dictator's economy. What fascinated me most was that several of these same economic advisors wound up owning the *other half* of Chile's newspaper duopoly.

Minister Huepe said that further investigation into the holdings of the media owners was stymied by the fact that during the dictatorship, these same economic advisors, nicknamed the "Chicago Boys," had created a secret corporate registry that shields the names of the shareholders from public scrutiny. My investigation discovered the reason: A group of these economists used their control of a state-owned bank to set themselves up in the newspaper business. Putting his former ministers and friends in charge of the news media was part of Pinochet's insurance that, once out of office, he would stay out of prison, avoid investigations of martial corruption and stunt the growth of Chile's nascent democracy. Of the seeming variety of newspapers and magazines, all of the important ones somehow wound up in the hands of Pinochet's friends and collaborators.

The rumor among journalists had it that a set of judicial files somewhere would reveal this conspiracy. Some said the files had "disappeared"—like others of Pinochet's victims—but I eventually became the first journalist to examine them. We now know the details of an international banking conspiracy that used state monies to bail out the very newspapers that now refuse to investigate their owners' participation in the plot. The owners of these media control the practice of journalism and manipulate public perceptions so as to perpetuate the ideals of the dictatorship, even under democracy.

Research reveals that some of these same media owners participated in dismantling the public university system and then wrote legislation that permitted them to set up their own private universities. Each of them has a journalism school. In addition, the media moguls established their own think-tanks—whose findings are then reported in their newspapers. This takeover of Chile's institutions is the work of a knot of businessmen, religious fundamentalists, and media owners who wish to impose antidemocratic social organizations, unselfconsciously borrowed from fascist Spain, by manipulating news and opinion in times of democracy.

My impression of Chile as a modern liberal democratic country dissolved. The Chicago economists were supposed to have created a free-market economy in Chile. However, nothing could be further from the truth. Some of them, as owners of the news media, black out information that could threaten their own investments. Other media owners who backed the "Chicago Boys" edit news for ideological and religious content. There is neither a free market nor a marketplace of ideas in Chile. There is a nominal democracy and the 2001 Press Law does grant greater freedom of expression. However, both will remain dead letters as long as Chile's media duopoly deprives citizens of vital information about their economy and their democracy while ignoring their needs. The media in Chile are the polar opposite of *public interest journalism*; they are bastions of *self-interest journalism*.

The most significant obstacle to a free and open press in Chile is not the law, which is indeed restrictive, but the concentration of ownership on one extreme of the political spectrum and the willingness of the owners to use those media to propagate their narrow views. Before the dictatorship, Chile's media represented myriad points of view. Immediately after the coup, any medium whose owners did not support the military was either shut down or bought out. But as the dictatorship dragged on, a crop of resistance publications sprang up, representing a diversity of political perspectives. Unfortunately, every one of them died once Chile returned to democratic rule, leaving nearly all the important national media in the hands of Pinochet collaborators. This book tells the story of how that happened.

The study of Chile's news media is not a narrow pursuit for journalism scholars but encompasses Chile's politics and economy; it is the tale of Chile itself—one of the few countries whose story may be told through its media.

El Mercurio, the oldest newspaper in the Spanish language, is the foremost determiner of Chile's destiny. As President Ricardo Lagos said on the Santiago edition's one hundredth anniversary, "It is impossible to understand the history of Chile without *El Mercurio*." Today, Chile's news media are at the epicenter of a movement among Chile's richest and most powerful men who are skillful at using the communications media to continue building the *nueva institucionalidad*—a code word for the anti-democratic institutions they founded during the dictatorship and which has only strengthened during the past decade of democracy.

Their homegrown authoritarian ideology seeks to impose a "natural" hierarchy of aristocrats to rule over commoners, which is justified by extremist readings of papal messages that are presented as immutable truths. The economic program, a far-right interpretation of neoliberals Milton Friedman and Friedrich von Hayek of Chicago University, became the unlikely ally of the religious right. What they have in common is both a longing for social control in Pinochet's absence and the willingness to control opinion and information in order to make this happen. Their shared affection for authoritarianism and intolerance of dissident ideas or minority views seeks the exclusion of citizen participation in public policy debate in lieu of which self-appointed authorities on the economy and morality may simply dictate what is right and wrong. Their presidential candidate, a Chicago Boy, religious fundamentalist, and former *El Mercurio* editor, nearly won the presidency in 2000.

An analysis of Chile without an examination of its news media is incomplete. Just as the apparent diversity of titles in Santiago's newsstands is a red herring, the casual observer may point to the election of a Socialist president (Ricardo Lagos, in 2000) as evidence that the right is out of power. However, the fact that Lagos—backed by his coalition's majority in Congress—has been effectively prevented from making significant policy changes is a testament to the elite's strength, not its weakness. Central to that strength are the "powers-in-fact" within the business community, religious fundamentalists, the military, and news media owners. This alliance rivals the strength of the government, says the Chilean dean of American University's law school: "In Chile, the *government* is in the opposition."

If the powerful succeed in undermining even the nineteenth century Enlightenment standards of tolerance and participatory democracy, Chileans cannot enjoy journalistic, democratic, or economic freedom. Financier-*cum*-philosopher George Soros says the greatest threats to democracy are no longer Communists or fascists, but what he calls "market fundamentalists" for whom economic expansion is an end in itself. The neoliberal Chicago economists are the archetype, justifying the sacrifice of democracy and pluralism to those ends. Soros says the revival of *laissez-faire* capitalism with its tendency to monopolize power is the principal threat to Karl Popper's vision of an "Open Society"—one where religious, moral, and racial animosities are diluted by giving competing ideologies access to the marketplace of ideas. However, Chile's media owners go beyond the passive role that Soros depicts. Instead, they actively censor or shout down competing views, many of which may be held by the vast majority of Chileans, while exacerbating the racial, class, and political cleavages that have plagued Chilean history. As a result, the news media are out of step with the average Chilean who is more open, liberal, tolerant, and curious—as is the average Chilean journalist.

It is my hope that the story of the news media in a population of less than 16 million will serve as a lesson in the world beyond Chile, where the news media are concentrated in ever fewer hands and are pressed into the service of the conglomerates that control them.

Two notes on methodology: First, this book emphasizes news over other journalistic genres. "News," as used here, refers specifically to the coverage of events within the current news cycle (once daily for newspapers or evening television newscasts, with hourly cycles for radio and nearly continuous cycles for Internet coverage) and that is found on *news pages* or broadcast during *news segments*. Any published pieces covering events, trends, or ideas found in periodicals and their various supplements that is expected to be of continued value beyond the medium's news cycle is referred to as a "feature," "editorial," "analysis," "op-ed," or something other than "news." Likewise, television and radio *news segments* are segregated from "talk," "interview," "feature," "opinion," "documentaries," and so on.

Because of the immediacy of news, the reader has a heightened expectation that what he or she is reading or hearing is an "objective" version of what occurred. Therefore, *news* is more potent as opinion-forming information than are editorials, which readers take with a grain of salt because the reader is conscious of the writer's attempt to sway him or her.

Second, distortions of news in Chile are achieved for the most part not by the addition of modifiers, qualifiers, or slanted background material. Rather, bias is achieved simply by leaving out people, ideas, or entire stories, making the job of measuring bias that of finding a ratio between what (or who) does and does not appear. This book, then, measures "coverage"—whether persons, groups, or their issues are covered or not. Such a measure is more objective because it is binary (covered/not covered) rather than a measure of degree (very biased/somewhat biased/objective), thus making quantification more meaningful.

Acknowledgments

My wife, Beatriz Elena León Sánchez, gave legal, practical, and emotional support, as did our friend Marcela Lobos. Professor Carol Wise, of the Johns Hopkins University School of Advanced International Studies, gave key advice on structure. University of Chile Professor Rafael Otano opened up his memory, his files, and his library. Graduate student Bernardita Ramírez handed me her thesis in the hopes that part of it would see the light of day in this book; it has.

Other researchers who shared their work are Paulo Ramírez, Sergio Godoy, and Manuel Salazar. Students who helped out include Marcela Nagel and Pilar Forrero Molina, both of whom will one day be great journalists. Auditor Ernesto Lobos helped me crunch numbers. Several public servants went out of their way to assist me, including Franco Compás and Karín, who commented under her breath, "It's about time someone investigated this."

Others who shared their sources and resources include Nibaldo Mosciatti and Tomás Mosciatti, Alejandra Matus, Washington Aris, Pedro Anguita, Carmen Allendes, Tomás Mac Hale, Alvaro Bardón, Federico Joannón, Sebastian Brett, Malcolm Coad, Virginia Bouvier, Homero Ponce, José Miguel Infante, Sybilla Brodzinsky, Mike Zellner, Jack Otero, Elizabeth Hutchison, Eduardo Silva, and Mónica González—who edited the Spanish version of this book, *Chile Inédito*.

Felipe González, Richard Foster, Sergio Godoy, Anny Rivera, Andrés Sanfuentes, David Stemper, Washington Aris, and Roger Atwood each read a section of the manuscript and pointed out many atrocities before they saw ink. Any surviving errors are mine alone.

Thanks also go to the 120 consultants, educators, businessmen, newsstand owners, and journalists who consented to be interviewed, especially the four journalists spoke on condition of anonymity for fear of reprisals from the news duopoly.

The cost of my 51-week teaching fellowship in Chile was defrayed by the John S. and James L. Knight Foundation with funds administered by the International Center for Journalists in Washington. They are in no way responsible for the book or its content, but it is my hope that this was a good investment in knowledge.

Ken León-Dermota, Washington, D.C.

Chapter 1

The "Concentration of the Media"

El Mercurio fulfilled a very important role during the UP.
It was the bourgeoisie's assurance that Chile would not become another Cuba.

—former *El Mercurio* general manager Fernando Léniz[1]

On August 3, 1939, the French World War I troop transport ship *Winnipeg* set ashore in Chile 2,100 refugees from the Spanish Civil War. Among them was a Catalan civil engineer named Victor Pey. He fit easily into Chile's whirling political and social movements because many were transplanted from Europe, such as labor movements, a large Communist Party, the National Front, and, decades later, Christian Democracy.

Pey, tall and charming, wasted no time making friends on the left. He befriended the owner of the nation's largest-circulation, populist newspaper, *Clarín*. Pey also befriended a senator named Salvador Allende, who had made three unsuccessful bids for the presidency. By 1969, Allende's fourth attempt got a boost from a lower voting age and suffrage for illiterates. Allende, who spoke better in living rooms than in outdoor political rallies, also did well on the small screen. The 1970 election was the first in which home television sets were numerous enough to become a factor. More accustomed to rousing crowds were Allende's opponents, Christian Democrat Radomiro Tomic and rightist Jorge Alessandri, whose television close-ups gave the impression of an old and weary candidate who reluctantly sought a second term.

Allende ran as the candidate for the Popular Unity (UP) movement, which was made up of his own Socialist Party, Radicals, Social Democrats, API (Independent Action Party), Unitary Popular Action Movement (MAPU), and the Communist Party (PC). The UP won the September 4th election with 36 percent of the vote. But without a majority, the Chilean Constitution of 1925 called for a joint session of Congress to confirm the election. Before doing so, legislators wanted some clarification about the UP's radically socialist platform, which said that, as part of the nationalization of basic industry, the communications media "are fundamental in the formation of a new culture and a new man. To this end, they must be educationally oriented and freed from their commercial character" by placing them in the hands of social organizations and out of reach of "nefarious monopolies."

Allende and the UP allayed the fears of Christian Democrats by cobbling together a bill that banned the expropriation of mass media without the approval of Congress and proscribed government interference with the media's supply of paper, ink, and other supplies and equipment. Once Christian Democrats and UP members of Congress passed this Statute of Constitutional Guarantees, they approved Allende's presidency 153 to 35.

The deal was easier for Allende to accept than anyone imagined, because he held a card that almost no one knew of. The powerful Hirmas family had promised Allende the majority of shares in Chile's highest-rated radio network. Brothers Alfredo and Miguel Hirmas had investments in textiles, garments, and agriculture. They had heard the revolutionary UP political program—over their own radio network—that called for the expropriation of essential industries. So, they decided to make a peace offering to the Marxist government: They handed Allende 51 percent of Radio Portales.[2]

The network's share of the audience was enormous in a country where television still didn't reach much of the countryside: Of every three radios playing in Chile, one was tuned to Radio Portales.

Once in office, Allende installed a hot line to the Radio Portales newsroom to comment on news stories—either to his employees or on the air. Radio Portales was Allende's megaphone. It was also the hub of the "obligatory networks"—when Allende commandeered the networks in the country and required them to carry his message. Allende used obligatory networks to a greater extent than his predecessors ever did, commandeering stations for weeks during the 1972 trucker's strike that marked a high point in resistance to his regime. As opposition grew, Radio Santiago, Radio Minería, and Radio Bío Bío, a family-owned network, found the courage to drop out of the obligatory networks and were closed for days at a time as punishment.

When the Christian Democrats had had enough of the UP's expropriations, they joined the rightist National Party in opposing Allende, both with the aid of their respective radio networks. Radio Balmaceda defied the government and was nearly denied a license renewal until Christian Democratic legislators prevailed upon the UP. The Socialist Party then purchased Radio Corporación from the Edwards combine, owners of *El Mercurio*, to get Allende's message across.

Allende's message was that Chile would show the world the peaceful road to socialism. Chile would do what Cuba had done a decade earlier, but without violence; it would accomplish what France had not in May of 1968. This would be *la vía chilena*—the Chilean road to socialism. Unfortunately, some didn't heed the message.

The Leftist Independent Movement (MIR), which included members of Allende's own Socialist Party, launched violent attacks with the avowed purpose of triggering a military takeover. That takeover would lead to a popular uprising and the definitive overthrow of the bourgeoisie, said MIR, which stockpiled guns and set about training a worker militia to that end.

In any case, the working class was buoyed by Allende's victory and unleashed centuries of pent-up fury at the Chilean aristocracy. Workers occupied *La Mañana* newspaper of Talca for eight months. The union at *El Sur* in Concepción simply took over the presses and published its own newspaper in which it called the bosses puppets of the CIA.[3] Radical unions struck small businesses for higher wages, eroding Allende's support within the middle class—which was already angry at the government's inefficient food distribution system.

The UP used strikes as an excuse to nationalize factories under an obscure law passed during the 1932 "Socialist Republic" that allowed expropriation of businesses that weren't meeting demand. The UP also went on a buying spree of large industries and redistributed much of the land belonging to *latifundios* among the peasants.

Perhaps Allende moved too quickly in socializing Chile—or maybe not quickly enough. Faster expropriation would have appeased some radical leftists and would have removed the economic power base from the industrialists. Moving more slowly might have avoided the disorderly system of expropriations that maximized uncertainty within the business community and prevented firms from conducting any sort of planning that could possibly have helped them deal with the socialist economy. In any case, what sealed Allende's fate was the UP's attempt to nationalize *El Mercurio*'s newsprint supply. Tactically, he might have been better off seizing *El Mercurio* itself, as we shall see.

"Trench Journalism"

In an increasingly polarized country, each medium chose a side—either as a part of the new chapter in the history that Chile was going to write or as a "mummy" buried in the past. Radio leaped into the "trench journalism" that was part of the roiling class war. Stations gave voice to nearly every tendency all along the political spectrum as did the newspapers. At the time, there were 46 daily newspapers in Chile, 11 of which were located in Santiago. The Communist Party's *Puro Chile* threw in its lot with Allende. MIR's *Punto Final* vowed to launch a class struggle without quarter. "Trench" journalism meant that there was a medium to defend just about any point of view—except neutrality.

Television was not excepted from the fray. The state-owned Televisión Nacional was the only network with nationwide coverage. Its "*A tres bandas*" was intended to present views from left, right, and center, but eventually narrowed its political sampling before going off the air entirely. Catholic University's station was allowed to operate with some degree of independence. Its news director, Father Raúl Hasbún, used Channel 13 as a bully pulpit to oppose the UP and Marxism "based on a hatred of God," as he put it.

The most vitriolic voice was that of *Clarín*. Dictator Carlos Ibáñez had expropriated *La Nación* from owner Eliodoro Yáñez who had dared to oppose him. During his second presidency, Yáñez used *La Nación*'s print shop to get the daily *Clarín* up and running in 1954. Once Ibáñez left office, he no longer needed the newspaper, so he sold out to his business partner, Darío Sainte-Marie. Bolivian by birth, Sainte-Marie found himself outside the inner circle of Chilean politics. So, he lobbed petards from the sidelines, wounding with his pen and using *Clarín* as a butcher would, to render up the spilled entrails of the victims. Because political coverage didn't sell many copies, he built up circulation with photos of scantily-clad women and used street slang in his sensational headlines. *Clarín* used all the advertising that would fit, despite the fact that it rejected ads from the right wing National Party and the Christian Democrats. *Clarín* backed Allende and was hardest on right-wing politicians. *Clarín*'s editors bragged of having destroyed political careers.

Sainte-Marie had maneuvered his daily newspaper into perilous waters, drawing fire from practically all sectors. After all, *Clarín* became the largest-circulation newspaper in Chile in part by slinging mud in all directions at once. Under the poison-pen name Volpone, Sainte-Marie took potshots at politicians—their private lives and their ethnic backgrounds. His invective drew the staid *El Mercurio* into the fray, with editorial writer René Silva Espejo answering Volpone tit-for-tat—that is, until it reached the name-callin', mud-rasslin' level. *El Mercurio* refused to dirty its patrician hands.

To answer Volpone—and to smear Allende, the National Party launched its own populist newspaper and *El Mercurio* chipped in a second-hand press to print *Tribuna*. This paper lampooned Allende as an irresponsible drunk. ("Yankee Agent Discovered Here on Mission to Kill Allende; His Name is Johnny Walker.")

Tribuna wasn't as crass—or creative—as Volpone, however. One of *Tribuna*'s shareholders was Senator Pedro Ibáñez, who was photographed in a pose that gave the appearance that he was picking his nose during a legislative session. When *Clarín* published the photo (with a caption we won't bother to translate), the senator brought charges against the editor who spent 22 days in jail.[4]

Eventually, Sainte-Marie was hamstrung by his own hubris. On top of this controversy, the MIR-led union at *Clarín* was demanding direct control over two pages of the paper. Victor Pey saw a win-win-win situation: If Pey purchased *Clarín*, he could help Allende and get Sainte-Marie off the hook. Sainte-Marie sold out and Pey enjoyed control from March until September of 1973 when the military seized *Clarín*.

The coup

On September 11, 1973, Chilean President Salvador Allende Gossens picked up a special telephone that he had had installed in the executive offices at La

Moneda. It was an old hand-crank model for use during emergencies; strikes had cut power to La Moneda recently.

The armed forces had taken up positions around La Moneda. The military had secretly patched the defense ministry to Radio Agricultura, Radio Minería, and to a clandestine network of short wave radio operators as the military's communications network. At 8:32 A.M., a defense ministry feed over Agricultura told Allende to relinquish power to the armed forces, said that workers would not suffer, and that all UP media that did not cease operations immediately "will receive air and land punishment."[5] Transmitters of most leftist radio stations, including Portales, Corporación, and Magallanes had been bombed or rocketed in "Operation Silence," which had begun before dawn. Networks whose installations were in urban areas and could not be bombed, such as Radio Sargento Candelaria and Balmaceda, were quickly occupied.

Allende's magneto telephone reached the only friendly station still on the air. Radio Magallanes had switched to an emergency transmitter. The engineer who recorded Allende's final message left open a studio microphone that captured the voices of personnel in the background, leading to speculation as to the veracity of the recording that somehow survived the military's trashing of Magallanes's studios:

Surely Radio Magallanes will be silenced and you will not hear the calm timbre of my voice. It doesn't matter; you will still hear me. I will always be with you. At least my memory will be that of a dignified man who was loyal to his country. The people should defend themselves, but not to the death. The people should neither be crushed nor mowed down but neither should they be humiliated. Workers of my country, I have faith in Chile and in her destiny. Other men of Chile will overcome this gray and bitter moment when treason seeks control. Go forward, knowing that much sooner than later the grand avenues will open once again, making way for the free man to build a better society.

From their studios at the intersection of Estado and Agustinas, Radio Magallanes reporters heard the air force Hawker Hunters swoop in and rocket La Moneda.[6] They found out later that Allende committed suicide with a rifle given to him by Fidel Castro.

Soldiers machine-gunned the controls at Magallanes. The armed forces would seize 40 radio stations and a dozen publications, most of which would never be returned to their owners. The military banned all political parties and confiscated their property, much of it in the form of print and radio news installations. The most divisive period in Chilean politics and the cacophonous journalism that cheered it on was followed by an eerie silence.

The first news some Chileans received in the wake of the coup was that their names had appeared on lists posted on the walls of military headquarters. Chileans who had never feared their government reported to the military and found themselves exiled, imprisoned, tortured, or shot. Victor Pey had been through this once before in Franco's Spain. When he literally saw the writing on the wall, the Venezuelan embassy gave him papers that safely landed him in Caracas. When he returned to Chile 17 years later, the democratic government still refused to return his newspaper, *Clarín*.

The order of battle

Judging by the news organizations on its side, the UP government had held the upper hand when it came to mass communications because the government had the sympathy of about two-thirds of the nation's media.[7] However, the sword proved mightier than the pen. Chile's system of "national front" politics became unstable when the Popular Unity was elected independent of the traditional moderating force of the Radical Party. When the military toppled that government, it crushed the party system as well as the news sources that represented myriad points of view. Only one point of view prevailed throughout the dictatorship and afterwards: That espoused by the military-run television networks and by *El Mercurio*, which called itself "the dean." See Table 1.1 for the order of the battle.

THE DEAN

The "Dean of the Press" in Chile cannot affiliate itself with those who agitate, who wish to exhilarate the emotions, but among those forces of order which must always be on the side of all that which assures social, political, economic, and administrative stability.
                                               —*El Mercurio* editorial, June 1, 1900

The year 1955 changed the direction of *El Mercurio* and thus, the direction of Chile. Agustín Edwards Budge died. His conservative son, Agustín Edwards Eastman, would take over the business empire by 1963. The fifth Agustín Edwards was aloof, authoritarian, and removed from the interests of the average Chilean; Agustín Edwards Eastman sought to reimpose aristocratic rule and values in Chile under a capitalist system.

El Mercurio took particular interest in recommendations made by a U.S. consulting firm that the government hired in 1955 to help deal with inflation and the foreign credit squeeze. The Klein-Sacks mission, as it came to be known, recommended incipient free-market reforms to Chile's highly-socialized economy, such as delaying automatic wage indexation to inflation, phasing out subsidies, and permitting the market to determine exchange rates and prices.[8]

The other *norteamericanos* who arrived in Chile that year were from the University of Chicago as part of "Project Chile," an exchange program funded by the U.S. International Cooperative Administration, predecessor to the Agency for International Development. Chicago University professors Theodore Schultz and Arnold Harberger led the delegation to Chile. Meeting them at the airport were Catholic University students Sergio de Castro

Table 1.1

Order of Battle, Santiago Newspapers

1973	1974	1984	Newspaper	Owner - 1973	Owner - 2000	Bias	1990	2000
✓	✓	✓	El Mercurio	Edwards	Edwards	Opposed	✓	✓
✓	✓	✓	El Mercurio regional newspapers	Edwards	Edwards	Allende, supported	✓	✓
✓	✓	✓	La Segunda	Edwards	Edwards	Pinochet	✓	✓
✓	✓	✓	Las Ultimas Noticias	Edwards	Edwards		✓	✓
✓		✓	La Tercera	Picó-Cañas	Chicago Boys/ Pinochet collaborators		✓	✓
		✓	La Cuarta	—		Pro-Pinochet	✓	✓
✓			Tribuna	Partido Nacional	—	"Trench" publications opposed		
✓			La Prensa	members PDC	—	Allende		
✓	✓	✓	La Nación	51% gov., 49% priv.	70% gov., 30% priv.	State-owned	✓	✓
✓			Ultima Hora	Manuel Becerra	—	UP		
✓			Clarín	Victor Pey	Victor Pey	UP		
✓			Chile Hoy	Independent left	—	UP		
✓			Punto Final	MIR	MIR*	Left, non-UP	✓	✓
✓			El Rebelde	MIR	—	UP		
✓			Causa	Marxist-Leninist	—	UP		
✓			Enfoque	Communist	—	UP		
✓			El Siglo	Communist Party	Communist Party*	UP	✓	✓
✓			Puro Chile	Communist Party	Communist Party*	UP		✓
✓			Ramona	Communist Youth	—	UP		
			Fortín Mapocho	Lavandero	—	"Trench" papers opposing	✓	
			La Epoca	PDC	—	Pinochet	✓	

*Denotes the publications that were dailies before the coup and are today weeklies.
✓Indicates years in which newspaper was publishing.

and Ernesto Fontaine, whose English had been polished at the Grange School.[9] Eventually a hundred graduates would study at Chicago, many of them under Nobel laureates Milton Friedman, Gary Becker, Friedrich von Hayek, and Robert Lucas.[10]

The University of Chicago economics faculty was one of the few interested in free-market economics in the decades after Keynesian governmental intervention was widely credited with having brought the world out of the Great Depression. The university had "kept alive the vision of a fundamental truth for a small circle of the initiated during the dark years of Keynesian despotism."[11] Not until Reagan's presidency would the United States embrace the free market. Margaret Thatcher would slam a copy of Hayek's *The Constitution of Liberty* down on a table at the Conservative Party's research department, exclaiming "This is what we believe!"—but only after Chile had done so.

The Chicago-trained economists shared Edwards's disdain for Chile's socialism and the structuralist analysis of the Economic Commission for Latin America and the Caribbean (ECLAC), the UN's economic mission in Santiago. Edwards grew so enamored of the Chicago exchange program that he donated a new campus for it at Catholic University. Edwards also set up Centro de Estudios Socio-Económicos (CESEC) in 1963 to bring the think-tank concept to Chile. CESEC provided ammunition for the "Campaign of Terror" that opposed Allende in *PEC, Qué Pasa,* and *El Mercurio*.[12] Chicago graduates staffed CESEC to prepare a free-market economic policy in case Alessandri had won the 1970 presidential election, and it was disbanded when he didn't.

The Chicago brand of economics is called free market or neoliberal economics. Its belief that nothing must interfere with the setting of prices by the law of supply and demand rivals Marxism in the faith of its followers and in the scientific claims of the theories. The neoliberal economy seeks to be a unified theory of economics that, in the absence of interferences in the marketplace such as subsidies or deficit spending, prices will reach a state of "equilibrium," in an economy without inflation, high unemployment, or recessions.

Whereas previous schools of economics proposed central bank intervention as the antidote to economic instability, Friedman led economists who believed that economies tend to move toward stability; it was government meddling that often set off larger fluctuations in the economy. The most radical of these "monetarists" would remove the government's hand from the money supply altogether: Hayek advocated the privatization of central banks.

Interferences with the economy's intricate clockwork are labeled as "exogenous" factors which unbalance the delicate "equilibrium," said the neoliberals, who reduced their proofs to mathematical formulae that were value-neutral and nonpolitical. One Chilean economist, Ricardo Ffrench-Davis, was criticized by a Chicago professor for observing that free-market theories weren't valid for less-developed countries where markets didn't function freely. Numbers were numbers, claimed the neoliberal professors, despite the country in which the calculations were performed.

Exempting neoliberal theories from the scrutiny of real-world observations reminds financier George Soros of "Ptolemy's efforts to explain the movement of heavenly bodies by drawing extra circles when the planets failed to follow their prescribed course[s]."[13] The Chicago grads touted themselves as the high priests with mastery of these secrets.

These men who were dubbed the "Chicago Boys" eventually controlled the Catholic University economics department including the deanship, pushing aside more moderate voices.[14] However, it was *El Mercurio* that gave their ideas currency by publishing their columns in the mid-1960s. Edwards launched an economic section in 1968, putting the Chicago Boys in charge of providing economics lessons to Chile's business community—while managing editor Arturo Fontaine complained that their jargon sounded as though it had been translated from English. *El Mercurio* also disseminated the writings of the Chicago Boys on the editorial pages and eventually gave them a stand-alone magazine. In the process, they honed the communication skills that they would use throughout the dictatorship and to the present day.[15]

The Gremialists

I am in complete agreement with *El Mercurio* editorials in all issues upon which I have formed an opinion. As for those for which I have no opinion of my own, I adopt that of *El Mercurio*.
—Jaime Guzmán, quoted in *El Mercurio's Revista del Domingo*, Anniversary Edition, June 1, 1980.

The Chicago Boys were influenced and adopted by a quasi-fascist movement, which had sunk roots at Catholic University, led by law professor Jaime Guzmán. In 1961, a young Guzmán visited Spain—the last holdover of fascism in postwar Europe. General Francisco Franco had installed a pro-Vatican regime that, Guzmán wrote in a letter to his mother, reminded him of another epoch: "[T]here was a Middle Age better than our modern world because in those times the world was theocentric."[16] As far as Guzmán was concerned, Franco was the "savior" of Spain, where "today there is absolute liberty." In 1958, Franco had placed the economy in the hands of neoliberal technocrats, many of whom belonged to the Roman Catholic lay organization Opus Dei. By 1967, Franco's "organic law" granted limited suffrage, relaxed censorship, and placed civil society organizations under the auspices of the state corporatist model.

A corporatist model had long been a staple of Chilean conservative thought. Guzmán's philosophical predecessor, Jaime Eyzaguirre, proposed corporatism as an alternative to the social disintegration brought on by the liberal social order. To shore up what he saw as a crisis in Chile's "natural" authoritarian and oligarchic order fostered by "unnatural" liberal party democracy, Eyzaguirre posited the three foundations of rightist thought as Hispanism, Catholic traditionalism, and corporatism.[17] These became three facets of Guzmán's *gremialista* corporatism, which prescribed government intervention in the economy.

Guzmán was no socialist, but saw that a liberal, capitalist society allowed men to stray from God, unlike feudal social organization. However, he also saw the possibility that a corporatist system such as Franco's "organic" society could provide the necessary social controls. Under it, state-sponsored groups organized vertically would supplant trade associations, labor unions, and associations of shopkeepers, manufacturers, lawyers, doctors and the like which are called *gremios*, the Spanish word for guilds.

Guzmán's *gremialistas* sought to build large industrial and agrarian associations to operate independently of the state and represent their members before the state. Such "intermediary organizations" include professional organizations, vertical labor unions, community groups, and the family as part of the nation's "common goods," concepts Guzmán borrowed from Franco and from Antonio Salazar's regime in Portugal. Although Spanish fascism de-emphasized religion over time, Chilean *gremialismo* remained devoutly religious, as Chile's aristocracy has always been and remains to this day.[18]

The Chicago Boys who returned to teach at Catholic University were at first at odds with the *gremialista* attachment to the Roman Catholic Church and to government intervention in the economy. The Chicago Boys were not as a rule strict moralists, influenced as they were by the Chicago school's positivism and the philosophy that market forces would become "the sole determinant of all that was socially desirable." Such thinking would provide Friedman with the justification for legalizing drugs.

The Chicago Boys also had difficulty with Guzmán's corporatist model. Guzmán resolved this difference by amending his authoritarian model to include the pontifical understanding of *subsidiarity*: The state should confine itself to temporal matters particular to it and to which it is uniquely suited, such as defense and international relations. "Intermediary organizations"— such as the family, labor unions, the church, professional associations, or the business community—would be allowed to participate in public life. However, they could not participate in politics.

Guzmán's embrace of subsidiarity in a 1969 *Portada* article brought *gremialismo* close to Hayek's separation of public and private sectors:[19] Subsidiarity broke the public-private union of corporatism. The intermediary organizations mirrored Hayek's notion that the Protean nature of a neoliberal society made it impossible to plan the organization of the private sector, which would generate a "spontaneous order" instead.[20]

Ideology drew them together and Catholic University put them on the same campus; however, one event sealed the relationship among the Chicago Boys, the *gremialistas,* and *El Mercurio.*

THE TAKEOVER

It is worthwhile examining the reasoning behind the President's choice of this economic policy that he backed as long as was politically feasible. The economists who had studied at the University of Chicago and at Catholic University as well as the *gremialistas* from that same university, led by Jaime Guzmán, offered the most intransigent opposition to Popular Unity, to socialism and to the values, norms and practices that guided Chilean politics during the last 50 years. They form, in reality, a new right, a resurrection of the principles inherent to liberalism as well as a revival of [Diego] Portales's authoritarianism, to which their mentors attributed Hispanic and monarchist roots. The two currents of this new right coexist separately but come together to join as one in periods of crisis. President Pinochet, a skilled politician, needs to found the military regime upon renewed principles. It is not enough for him to abide by the trends and policies that are a continuation of what ended in September 1973.
                        —Arturo Fontaine Aldunate, former editor in chief of *El Mercurio*[21]

In 1967, Guzmán founded the *Gremialista* Movement in Catholic University's law school as a campus organization. Guzmán touted *gremialismo* as an apolitical alternative to the growing politicization of the university campuses that reflected the mass party politics in the rest of Chile. The *gremialistas* were the antithesis of the participatory democracy, which they felt had gotten out of hand, to wit: Socialism, Marxism, and Christian Democracy.

Also in 1967, the Catholic University Student Federation (FEUC) staged a campus sit-in to demand "relevance" and "social commitment" as did their counterparts in the United States and Europe. The sit-in included Communists and Socialists to be sure; however, Christian Democrats led the FEUC and conservative nationalists were among the many students along for the ride.

When *El Mercurio* editorials painted the students with one brush—as violence-prone radicals—students retaliated by hanging a huge banner from the university for all of Santiago to see: "El Mercurio lies." *El Mercurio*'s managing editor, René Silva Espejo, took to the stage to defend his editorial column—only to dig himself deeper. It was *gremialista* Sergio de Castro who provided an eloquent defense.

El Mercurio had ceased to be a detached observer in the eyes of many readers. "[The incident] has damaged the image of *El Mercurio* as an objective news source up to the present day," said then-CEO of *El Mercurio* Fernando Léniz.[22] Everyone, it seemed, was taking up sides. "The country split in two over the conflict," wrote historian Gonzalo Vial Correa. The parties of the left and their respective youth groups as well as MAPU; Central Unitaria de Trabajadores (CUT), Chile's labor federation; and MIR were on one side. On the other, "*gremialistas* ... the Right, *El Mercurio*, business groups, etc."[23]

Chicago Boys de Castro and Miguel Kast led the effort in the economics department that gave the *gremialistas*' 1968 FEUC presidency to an economics student, Ernesto Illanes.[24] Guzmán's gifts as a charismatic speaker made him a frequent guest on the Catholic University Channel 13 talk show, "*A esta hora se improvisa*." "During the Popular Unity [period] he was one of the politicians who most contributed to the polarization," according to a current senator.[25] Resistance to campus leftists gave the *gremialistas* credibility as one of the few viable alternatives. That pleased *El Mercurio*. "*El Mercurio* was against socialism so [Edwards] joined with the *gremialistas* because they had the same ideas," said Chicago Boy Javier Vial. "It was a mutually beneficial marriage."[26]

Gremialistas founded the magazine *Portada* in 1969 with staffers Cristián Zegers and Arturo Fontaine Aldunate, both of whom would later manage *El Mercurio*. Zegers, a Chicago Boy, would become editor in chief of *El Mercurio*'s afternoon newspaper, *La Segunda*. Contributors included Guzmán, historian Gonzalo Vial Correa, Jorge Prat, and Ricardo Claro, who today owns a television network and a cable company. *Portada* emphasized nationalistic authoritarianism, Christian values, and an end to universal suffrage as the remedy for what it saw as the decadence of Western democracy, Enlightenment liberalism, and socialism. *Portada* argued that Chileans need look no farther than the authoritarianism of Diego Portales for inspiration. One of Chile's earliest leaders, Portales, introduced the censorship of foreign writings, opposed liberal democracy, and sought to impose order "under the weight of the night," as he put it. Chicago Boys Pablo Baraona and Emilio Sanfuentes were *Portada* contributors.

Zegers founded yet another magazine, *Qué Pasa*, as a showcase for neoliberal and *gremialista* ideas in 1971. Claro, before his falling out with Edwards, joined the editorial board with current *El Mercurio* editorial board member Hermógenes Pérez de Arce, Guzmán, as well as Vial Correa. *Qué Pasa* carried forward these *gremialista* ideas, with ideological modifications required by the Chicago Boy merger: Foreign ideas became acceptable as long as they were neoliberal; trade unionism was not to be encouraged.

Qué Pasa leaned quite far to the right. One 1974 article took an uncritical look at the career of Rudolf Hess, then the only surviving Nazi among those sentenced at Nuremberg. The lead says the United States, Great Britain, and France would be willing to release Hess from Spandau prison, but the lone holdout among the Allied powers was the Soviet Union:

It is she that has opposed, implacably, that Hess be released from prison, demanding compliance with the letter of the "life sentence" imposed at Nuremberg. The motive for such an attitude [from the USSR]? Officially, [they say,] Hess is guilty, as Hitler's advisor, for the German attack on the USSR....Unofficially, the Soviets suspect that his real objective was to sue for peace and a German alliance with Great Britain against the USSR.[27]

Qué Pasa was published by Publicaciones Lord Cochrane, then owned by the Edwards combine.

Shortly after the coup, a *Qué Pasa* editorial celebrated the "Wagnerian finale" of the UP and the end of "hatred and political division," pardoning in advance the bloodletting: "To open a new door, the country had to pay its quota of blood."[28] In addition, it would require the union of *gremialismo* and the Chicago Boys.

Thirty years after the coup, in an article entitled "The Economic Thought of Jaime Guzmán Errázuriz: The Soul of the Economy," *El Mercurio* credits

Guzmán with uniting *gremialismo* with Chicago thought and eventually ensconcing both in the 1980 Constitution: "He played an indubitable role in the economy by supporting and promoting the free market and private property whose legal framework he wrote into the new Constitution."[29]

The *gremialistas* and Chicago Boys set aside their spiritual differences for a greater cause. "In spite of the fact that [Guzmán] was a practicing and obedient Catholic, thanks to his friendships, he furthered his embrace of liberal economic theory albeit within certain conservative and religious traditions," said Pinochet economy minister Pablo Baraona.[30]

Guzmán's presence helped the Chicago Boys sell their ideas to Chile's conservative private sector. Radical ideas such as ending government-led development must have sounded odd as well as frightening to Chile's entrepreneurs who had grown accustomed to protective tariffs and government intervention over four decades. Some 80 percent of prices were fixed even under the conservative Alessandri government.[31] At first, only those businessmen attached to *El Mercurio* were listening.

However, *gremialistas* opened doors for the Chicago Boys, who soon overcame entrepreneurs' objections with their dynamic personalities and their ability to sell supply and demand as laws that play no favorites. That appealed to businesses tired of begging bureaucrats for raw materials, import licenses, or price hikes. The Chicago Boys spread this message through the Edwards publications, by holding classes for members of the business community, and by hiring themselves out. "All the companies in Chile were thinking of professionalizing themselves [to a greater degree] and the *gremialistas* were a group of professionals with free market ideas," said Vial.[32] Once Pinochet came to power, they would have the blessing of the business community to set their ideas into motion.

Some of the Chicago Boys began to assume the *gremialista* disdain for democracy. The concept meshed with the Chicago economists' science that was value-neutral and apolitical. Guzmán wrote that democracy had no intrinsic value as did Hayek, who told *El Mercurio* "a dictatorship can limit itself and a dictatorship that deliberately limits itself can be more liberal in its policies than a democratic assembly that has no limits."[33] An authoritarian society such as the one Guzmán proposed would make an ideal proving ground for neoliberal ideas, because a dictatorship is relatively free of political interference.

Before the coup, Chicago Boy Alvaro Bardón, who would join *El Mercurio*'s editorial board, called Chile's a "pseudo-democracy" that had been "perverted" by the ascendence of leftists. De Castro, who would become an Edwards combine executive and later Pinochet's economy point man wrote: "A person's actual freedom can only be assured through an authoritarian regime that exercises power by implementing equal rules for everyone."[34]

As Chile became more deeply polarized during the Eduardo Frei Montalva presidency (1964–1970), *El Mercurio* editorials questioned the role of political parties, including those of the traditional right and proposed a *gremialista* state:

The authority of electoral and parliamentary activity is on the way out. Fortunately, there are natural bases in Chilean society that can serve as pockets of resistance against the power of Communism in the country. The *gremios* are natural defense organizations against the anti-State power of Communism that are prepared, with the rise of social power, [to be] defenders of national liberties and values.[35]

Another editorial prescribes a *gremialista*-Chicago Boy authoritarianism in 1969—before Allende came to power. Its reference to "40 years of economic pseudo-management" is not a reaction merely to Allende or even Frei, but includes three Radical presidencies and three very conservative governments.

While the governments during these 40 years promised help to students, the landless, women, and workers, the military felt ignored. The defense budget had not grown since Ibáñez left power in 1958. Under Allende, when compared to the military, state workers prospered so that a gardener at the Congress earned twice the salary of an admiral, according to retired Commander Roberto Kelly.[36] The armed forces were taken for granted, civilians saw soldiers as rubes, and the navy fell victim to benign neglect. One of the few places men in uniform and in civvies met regularly was at the South Pacific Nautical Fraternity, founded in 1968 by Agustín Edwards and one of his executives, Hernán Cubillos, along with Kelly, who had served in the navy under Cubillos's father.

The members unanimously elected Edwards commodore of the club, although he would leave for the United States once Allende was elected. In Edwards's absence, his second-in-command as commodore was Admiral José Toribio Merino—the first man who would take charge of Chile's economy after the coup.[37]

During Allende's presidency, while the bombastic media of left and right were engaged in a shouting match, executives of one of Chile's most powerful combines had been getting some real work done. The fifth Agustín Edwards, scion of the family that founded *El Mercurio*, controlled the combine that bore his name. He left for the United States a week after Allende's inauguration and a day after Allende announced his intentions to nationalize the newspaper.

U.S. National Security Advisor Henry Kissinger had failed to prevent Allende from taking power, despite his attempt to instigate a pre-inaugural coup. General René Schneider was the military's commander who spoke against the coup and for military subordination to civilian rule. Kissinger ordered him taken out. He sent .45 caliber machine guns, tear gas canisters, and cash to General Roberto Viaux of Fatherland and Freedom, who murdered Schneider during a bungled kidnaping.[38]

Edwards met with Kissinger to amend this policy failure, which was seconded by ITT, Chase Manhattan Bank, and The Pepsi-Cola Company. Pepsi-Cola Company president Donald Kendall had earned Richard Nixon's gratitude by giving him his first international account when Nixon worked for a New York law firm.[39] Nixon ordered the destabilization of Chile by making the economy "scream." Edwards spent the first half of the dictatorship in the United States, as a vice president of The Pepsi-Cola Company and friend of Kendall.

Allende harassed *El Mercurio* with tax and weapons inspections and by withholding government advertising—all pretty much as his predecessors had done to various publications that had not seen things their way. Allende, a confirmed constitutionalist, applied laws already on the books, such as the State Internal Security Law, but with alacrity. *El Mercurio* was charged with breaching the national security for reporting that the nation was short on foreign currency reserves. Editors at *Tribuna*, founded to harry Allende, were charged on almost 50 occasions. The editor of *PEC* (short for Política, Economía y Cultura, a magazine sponsored by Edwards)[40] was jailed as well.

Allende had pulled the military close to him, by including officers in his cabinet and giving the armed forces raises. *Tribuna* taunted the soldiers, saying they would not stage a coup because Allende had bought them off. That statement irked the commander of the Santiago military command, one General Augusto Pinochet, who threatened to sue the paper for such "grave offenses to the dignity of the armed forces."[41]

In lieu of military action, Fatherland and Freedom burned fuel tanks and set off bombs in Santiago. CIA funding also fueled a trucker's strike, which further hampered delivery of consumer goods from toilet paper to toothpaste. Homemakers took to the streets, banging their empty pots. The truckers were at the core of a Gremio Command, which was composed of professional associations, shop owners led by Rafael Cumsille, the *gremialistas* led by Jaime Guzmán, and Fatherland and Freedom. Much of this was funded by foreign businessmen, according to Orlando Sáenz, then-president of the powerful manufacturers' association, Sociedad de Fomento Fabril (SOFOFA), which handled the monies.[42]

Foreign support also came to the left, as Cuba sent weapons to arm a "people's militia" that would defend the Chilean government against a takeover. This militia never materialized, but the presence of arms and the violence of leftists outside the government served as a pretext for the coup and the human rights violations that followed. The Organized Vanguard of the People (VOP), murdered Frei's interior minister, Edmundo Pérez Zujovic. Christian Democrats and Radicals pulled farther away from Allende because he had previously freed jailed members of VOP and refused to crush MIR.

Eventually, a Congressional resolution would accuse the UP of violating the Constitution and its separation of powers.

El Mercurio contributed to this air of instability. The CIA had dumped $1.6 million into *El Mercurio,* which compensated *El Mercurio* for lost government advertising revenue.[43] The paper's psychological warfare techniques played up disturbances as much as possible. Front pages would be nearly filled with such articles, on one day, cornering a lone political story headlined: "Salvador Allende's Violent Speech." The paper went out of its way to associate MIR's terrorist activities with the UP government. The front pages juxtaposed photographs of Allende with images of violence and growing food lines. The reach of *El Mercurio*'s campaign wasn't limited to subscribers, however: Sensationalism above the fold permitted pedestrians to see it as they passed the newsstands.[44] However, this campaign was the least significant of *El Mercurio*'s efforts leading up to the coup.

The lunch crowd

Despite the ultra-left violence, the nationalization of industry, and the resulting economic and political uncertainty, Chile's business community seemed unmoved through Allende's first year. Mine, land, and factory owners did not form a unified opposition immediately—in part because they were accustomed to heavy state regulation.[45]

What catalyzed the powerful, however, was Allende's attempt to nationalize Chile's paper manufacturer, Compañía Manufacturera de Papeles y Cartones. CMPC produced all Chilean newsprint, which met 60 percent of demand. CMPC is part of the powerful Matte family conglomerate that joined with *El Mercurio* in accusing the Allende government of infringing on freedom of the press by controlling the newsprint supply, despite Allende's pact not to interfere. Chile had watched dictator Juan Perón use the allocation of newsprint to control his critics just across the Andes in Argentina. The UP squeezed CMPC by dictating the price of paper. Allende's price commission included Victor Pey and PDC politician Sergio Molina.

The UP attempt at a hostile takeover of the publicly-held paper plant met a formidable opponent. Its chairman was Jorge Alessandri, the former president of Chile who was still smarting after Allende had edged him out of a second term as president. Alessandri was not at all pleased to learn that the UP government had introduced special legislation to nationalize the CMPC.[46] When the UP began to purchase CMPC shares, manufacturers formed a pool to bid up the price.[47] This tactic worked. CMPC's $30 million loss that year was the price that it paid to remain in the private sector. The greater victory for the Edwards combine was, however, that the takeover unified the business community.

No amount of publicity could occasion a coup in Chile without the approval of Chile's ruling elite. One group of elites, convened by executives of the

Edwards combine, met over lunch each Monday. René Silva Espejo, editor of *El Mercurio*, Emilio Sanfuentes of the Edwards news magazine *Qué Pasa,* and Edwards combine executives Hernán Cubillos and Jorge Ross met with such Chilean businessmen as SOFOFA president Orlando Sáenz and Javier Vial of the Banco Hipotecario de Chile (BHC) Cruzat-Larraín banking combine. They often assembled at the offices of Lord Cochrane—the Edwards combine's printing affiliate.

Those participating in the Monday luncheons were emboldened by what they perceived as weakness on the part of Allende. Jorge Ross, an Edwards combine executive, said Allende lacked the courage to close down *El Mercurio* before Castro's three-week visit to revolutionary Chile in 1971. The newspaper held up Fidel Castro's visit as proof incarnate that communism had arrived. "[The UP] should have taken over *El Mercurio* and Radio Agricultura. Why they didn't is a mystery," said Ross. "The freedom of expression [we had under Allende] was very important—restricted, but very important. If we hadn't had [some] freedom of expression when Fidel came, things could have been different."[48]

El Mercurio's then-CEO, Fernando Léniz, concurred with Ross in saying that Allende's other error was in thinking that the Banco A. Edwards was the heart of the Edwards combine instead of *El Mercurio*. "Allende fell victim to his own policy of buying up companies that were on strike," said Léniz. "But *El Mercurio* never went on strike." For Léniz, Allende's other weakness was not to have suppressed the violence of MIR and VOP.[49]

The use of violence on the left legitimized the use of violence in the eyes of the right. To head off the threat of a Cuban-style revolution, rightist military dictatorships would rule in Chile's neighborhood in the mid-1970s: Brazil, Uruguay, and Argentina. Before Chile's coup, Brazil's military government bolstered the import substitution industrialization (ISI) model by raising import and investment barriers typical of a "closed" economy and promoted growth in a declared Keynesian fashion. Later, Uruguay and Argentina imposed a *laissez-faire* approach, privatizing state-owned enterprises (SOEs), inviting foreign investment, and repressing organized labor.[50] In 1973, there was every indication that Chile would follow the Brazilian model.

However, the Monday luncheon group's navy contact was Roberto Kelly, of the sailing club and former manager of Gavisa, an Edwards combine poultry farm on the outskirts of Santiago that had been expropriated by the UP. Kelly had asked Chicago Boy Emilio Sanfuentes, of the Edwards combine, to pull together a team to draw up an economic plan, without telling Sanfuentes what it was for. The Edwards and BHC groups lent the bulk of the 10 economists who authored the economic plan known as "the brick," a revision of the economic plan sketched out in case Alessandri had won.

Of the 10 economists chosen to draft the brick, eight were "Chicago Boys." Four of the 10, Sergio Undurraga, Emilio Sanfuentes, Sergio de Castro, and Alvaro Bardón, were connected to the Edwards combine. Three others,

Manuel Cruzat, Pablo Baraona, and Juan Braun, were attached to BHC. Andrés Sanfuentes, José Luis Zabala, and Juan Villarzú had no affiliation. Only Braun and Undurraga were not graduates of the University of Chicago.

In July of 1973, *El Mercurio* demanded military intervention in an editorial. "[W]e must renounce all political parties, the masquerade of elections, the poisoned and deceitful propaganda and turn over to a few select military men the task of putting an end to political anarchy." At 5:00 P.M. the day before the coup, *El Mercurio* managing editor Arturo Fontaine was apprised of the plans and arranged to print the newspaper at the Edwards combine's Publicaciones Lord Cochrane should military action make it impossible to publish out of the downtown offices.[51] Once La Moneda had been rocketed and Allende had committed suicide, "the brick" was photocopied at Publicaciones Lord Cochrane. By noon the following day, members of the junta would find copies on their desks.[52]

We do not wish to exaggerate the impact of the Monday lunch crowd, which was far from the only group of coup plotters. This group isn't even mentioned in the most detailed account of the plot published so far. However, most other civilians limited their participation to lending their sitting rooms to military leaders and providing the cocktails.[53]

Two things distinguish the Monday lunch crowd. First, were its international connections. Its convener, Hernán Cubillos, received the CIA monies that were funneled into *El Mercurio* while his boss, Agustín Edwards, was in Washington meeting with Nixon and Kissinger who approved the funds. Orlando Sánez and SOFOFA were the conduit for international funds for the striking truckers, which likely came from the CIA. Second, while it was only one among other groups chewing the fat during the UP period, it was the only one at the all-important nexus of the navy, the business community, *El Mercurio*, the *gremialistas,* and the Chicago Boys. This group went beyond moral encouragement. What they pitched in was nothing less than the post-coup economic plan.

While there is no indication that the Monday lunches were critical to the coup, there is every indication that the Chicago Boys would not have come to control the Chilean economy had it not been for Kelly and the backing that Edwards, *El Mercurio,* and BHC gave to writing the brick. More specifically, it was the bond, created among the members of the sailing club, that united Kelly, Edwards, and Cubillos with Admiral José Toribio Merino—the member of the four-man junta who was in charge of the economy immediately after the coup.[54] In addition, *El Mercurio*'s Managing Editor, René Silva Espejo, had multiple contacts with the army and air force. "He played an important role in coordinating the coup," said Cubillos.[55] Although not crucial to the coup itself, the Monday luncheons were critical to the way that the dictatorship panned out. Thus, events following September 11, 1973 would reconfirm *El Mercurio*'s preeminence as Chile's agenda-setting publication.

While many Chileans on the right, along with many Christian Democrats and Radicals, initially applauded the tranquility brought by the coup, they did so with no reason to believe that the military regime would last so long or be so brutal. However, *El Mercurio* had put into motion an economic transformation that would take years to implement. Owner Agustín Edwards backed the military government throughout the dictatorship and defends Pinochet to this day. Edwards rooted out internal criticism of any aspect of the military dictatorship and fired *El Mercurio*'s managing editor in 1982—for criticizing human rights abuses and economic mismanagement that had become too blatant to ignore. *El Mercurio*, more than any other civilian institution, had helped to put the military in power, to supply staff to the junta, and to keep Pinochet in power for more than 16 years. *El Mercurio* would be richly rewarded.

Monday luncheon regulars

Hernán Cubillos—Edwards (President, Publicaciones Lord Cochrane)

Jorge Ross—Edwards (President, Banco A. Edwards)

René Silva Espejo—Edwards (Editor, *El Mercurio*)

Orlando Sáenz—President, SOFOFA

Emilio Sanfuentes—Edwards (*El Mercurio* writer)

Edmundo Eluchans—Edwards (*El Mercurio* lawyer)

Javier Vial— Banco Hipotecario de Chile (BHC)

Manuel Cruzat—Banco Hipotecario de Chile (BHC) [56]

Since the 1920s, Chile's aristocracy had watched from the sidelines as a succession of reformers—Communists, Socialists, Radicals, and Christian Democrats—had reduced their privilege and the influence of the Roman Catholic Church while even rightist parties increased the participation of the state in the economy. Now, it was time to dismantle the state institutions and build new ones in their stead, a process that would take nearly a generation. Only by giving Pinochet the longest tenure of any of Chile's leaders could such a far-reaching plan be set into motion to thoroughly recreate a nation so that even the vicissitudes of a decade of democratically elected governments have not been able to alter in any fundamental way.

It is here that the future of Chile begins.

The Radicals

Gremialistas Will Explain the Truth of What Happened in Chile to the World

—*El Mercurio* banner headline, September 17, 1973

Pinochet would not consolidate his power as the sole ruler of Chile for a year. At first, four members of the military junta, one from each of the branches of military service, shared the responsibilities. The economy fell to the navy, with Rear Admiral Lorenzo Gotuzzo becoming the junta's first finance minister, and Kelly heading the planning office.[57] However, that didn't seal the fate of the brick or the Chicago Boys. "It took us a year and a half to convince the military to have an open economy," said Kelly.[58]

The Chilean military initially assumed that Chile's economy would simply return to its pre-Allende model. "The military was not rightist," said the brick contributor Alvaro Bardón. "The military was more socialistic." Indeed, military coup plotters envisioned a mixed economy, with central planning right down to price structures—according to its own documents and the CIA.[59] However, none of the military plotters had a detailed economic plan except for Kelly and the Chicago Boys. The sailing partner of Kelly and Edwards, Admiral José Toribio Merino, would become number two in the military junta. Soon after the coup, Merino would make *El Mercurio* general manager Fernando Léniz minister of the economy. Léniz was a safe choice as far as the military was concerned because he was married not only to *El Mercurio* but also to the daughter of General Carlos Mezzano.

Léniz had no argument with the brick. The blueprint for a post-coup Chilean economy was neoliberal, open, and monetarist.[60] Although the brick was highly technical, it did not contain a timetable for its implementation. It was during this time that a tussle broke out between the "radicals," led by Chicago Boy Sergio de Castro and the "gradualists," led by Léniz and SOFOFA president Orlando Sáenz. The latter argued against a rapid application of the "structural adjustments"—privatization, deregulation, import tariff reduction, and an end to government subsidies and price controls—but to no avail.[61]

Meanwhile, Léniz was making a nuisance of himself by insisting to the junta that the regime's human rights record was standing in the way of obtaining foreign loans. That did not square with Pinochet's analysis that blamed Marxist infiltration into the international banking system.[62] Pinochet removed "gradualist" Léniz from the leadership of the economic team (perhaps due to the human rights issue) and eventually replaced him with de Castro—who kept his mouth shut when it came to human rights.

The final nail in the gradualist coffin was the conference that BHC held in Santiago with invited guests Milton Friedman and Arnold Harberger who, predictably, argued for the radical approach to opening the economy as well as privatization. These talks were given prominent coverage in *El Mercurio*. Friedman met with Pinochet to convince him of the need for a "shock treatment" to eliminate inflation.[63]

The ensuing structural adjustment was as painful as it was radical. The currency was devalued and the economy shrank by one-seventh. The industrial sector was damaged by import tariffs averaging 10 percent—some of the lowest in the world. The drop in industrial production by a fourth and the rise in unemployment up to 20 percent served two goals by eviscerating the labor movement: 1) Unions were a focus of leftist activity that Pinochet sought to eliminate, and 2) the economy now more closely resembled Hayek's philosophy that only the market should set labor prices.

The government's privatization policy bolstered conglomerates close to the radical Chicago Boys. The regime fulfilled the Edwards combine's wish for an accelerated privatization of the hundreds of SOEs. The sell-off favored BHC Cruzat—one of the few groups with access to investment capital in troubled times. By some estimates, firms were sold for one-half of their market values.[64]

The "sweet money"

Other government regulations favored these conglomerates. By May of 1974, in the spirit of deregulating the economy, Pinochet's newly-appointed Chicago Boy economists loosened the banking laws that favored the establishment of quasi-banks called *financieras*, which were permitted higher interest rates on deposits and short-term loans than the banks, which was a decided advantage in a capital market that was lacking liquidity. The BHC conglomerate, known as the *piranhas* for its habit of gobbling up companies, had set up Cruzat-Larraín in the *financiera* business. Between the *financieras* and the three commercial banks that it controlled, the conglomerate made 42 percent of Chile's loans. Even the Edwards combine set up its own *financiera*. All of them borrowed the cheap petrodollars on the international capital market and changed those dollars into Chilean pesos to lend.[65] The times of the "sweet money" had begun.

Year-end economic growth from 1977 through 1980 averaged 8.5 percent.[66] Many Chileans were enjoying the economic boom driven by plentiful capital. They spent heavily on luxury goods using their first credit cards. Diner's Club de Chile was the first to arrive—eventually with its own membership magazine. Chileans piled up debt purchasing the television sets, whiskey, and consumer goods that they previously had had little access to.

The owners of the Santiago daily *La Tercera* borrowed the "sweet money" to leverage a buyout of their relatives.[67] *El Mercurio* and *La Tercera* replaced their press rooms. The good economic times under Pinochet even ushered in a relaxation of political repression and the beginning of an opposition press.

The "other disappeared"

Only *El Mercurio* publications were permitted on the streets immediately in the wake of the coup. The first independent journalistic voice that the military allowed was *Ercilla*. This magazine was founded in 1933 and owed its success to having imported *Time*'s format of a weekly news magazine, pitched forward and with the added value of journalistic analysis. It owed the military leniency to its moderate Christian Democratic ownership. It owed much of its journalistic independence from the owners to editor in chief Emilio Filippi's work contract, which stipulated a strict division between the magazine's business office and the newsroom. Such a firewall was rare at the time and unthinkable in Chile today.

When the military permitted *Ercilla* to publish in late 1973, Filippi tested the military's tolerance, and the junta pushed back. They gave owner Sergio Mujica an offer that he could not refuse: Either fire Filippi, sell the magazine, or we'll shut it down. This time, the regime played the bad cop.

The *piranhas* of the BHC got to play the good cop. Once the military's ultimatum had softened the owner up, the *piranhas* moved in to purchase the magazine in 1976. The *piranhas* had good relations with the military beginning with the Monday luncheons. Once *piranha* Manuel Cruzat had taken over *Ercilla*, Filippi told his staff, "I doubt that Cruzat purchased *Ercilla* for the pleasure of watching me run it," and quit. As each successive man on *Ercilla*'s masthead was offered the managing editor's spot, he also resigned, leaving an *Ercilla* in name only.[68]

Filippi then launched *Hoy* magazine, which caught on immediately among 6,000 subscribers in Chile and 6,000 overseas. The military ordered *Hoy* shut down on June 20, 1979, for publishing interviews with two Socialist leaders. Interior Minister Sergio Fernández and Pinochet argued that *Hoy* was challenging the legitimacy of the military government to decide when and how Chile would return to democratic rule. Despite Fernández's friendship with Edwards, *El Mercurio*'s editor Arturo Fontaine took issue with the government action in an editorial. Two months later, *Hoy* was welcomed back to the newsstands by advertisers who had purchased enough ads to make the book-length issue of *Hoy* a collective act of defiance by Chilean and multinational advertisers that included General Motors, Renault, and Olivetti.

Readers saw *Hoy* as the closest thing possible, under the circumstances, to an opinion-forming, agenda-setting publication. Subscribers were from all sectors: the military, civilian government officials, and the civilian opposition. Circulation far surpassed the Edwards combine's *Qué Pasa* news magazine. Buoyed by his success, Filippi left *Hoy* in 1983 to start a daily newspaper.

THE OPPOSITION PRESS

Hoy was far from the only opposition magazine. *El Mercurio*'s editorial writer Hermógenes Pérez de Arce told the 1987 interim meeting of the Inter-American

Press Association that Chile enjoyed freedom of expression under Pinochet. Pérez de Arce, a Chicago Boy, made a compelling case. He had lugged to the San Antonio, Texas meeting some 31 periodical titles that were circulating in Santiago at the time.[69] The important among these, *Hoy, Apsi, Análisis, Cauce, Fortín Mapocho,* and *La Epoca,* harried the dictatorship, often with bold investigative reporting that sent reporters and editors to prison, into exile, and even to their deaths. And that's the good news.

The bad news is that not one of these brave publications, including *Hoy,* is with us today. Gone are magazines whose newsstand sales in the 1980s surpassed those of the pro-regime publications. The Pinochet-era journalism that used wit, sarcasm, and humor has given way to dull, bland, pack journalism that sticks to the "official story" in times of democracy. Pinochet-era corruption and human rights violations were investigated and exposed while he was in power to a degree that is not even attempted today. The daring investigative journalism of the dictatorship has simply disappeared. No nationally distributed periodical in Chile has a staffer assigned to do investigative journalism. Furthermore, none of the great investigative journalists from the opposition magazines is doing the same in a Chilean news organization today.

As a group, the opposition media did a better job of nonpartisan reporting than did the blatant partisanship of the UP years. In addition, they also did a better job of promoting diverse points of view than do the media in Chile today. The opposition media survived everything the dictatorship threw at them—from bombs to truckloads of fish. However, they proved unfit for democracy. They are Chile's "other disappeared." No one answer explains why all of them disappeared. However, they did have one thing in common: They were allied with the opposition.

Chile's vibrant journalism ended with the coup when media were seized, bombed, sold, and closed. During the dictatorship, the opposition press provided a second wave of pluralism. Once democracy returned, they disappeared. Their disappearance must be examined in order to understand how all important national print media are today held by Pinochet's *gremialista* friends and supporters.

The earliest post-coup publications were sponsored by liberal sectors of the Roman Catholic Church. In 1976, *Solidaridad* gave the Pope's writings an interpretation that was beyond the reproach of the military censors. Bishop Raúl Silva Henríquez headed the effort from his Vicaría de la Solidaridad, which also became the repository for information and testimony about those tortured, murdered, and forcibly "disappeared" by the military as well as a source of legal representation for the victims.

The Jesuit magazine *Mensaje* took a liberal Christian view of social questions. It still does but it is not a news source. However, every magazine from the dictatorship that was not backed by an institution such as the Church has disappeared. There is no tidy explanation for this occurence.

APSI

The first magazine to start from scratch was *Actualidad Política y Social Internacional*, thankfully shortened to *APSI*. Despite the awkward name, *APSI* was a writerly magazine with a wit and sarcasm that were fine and subtle. It had to be. Military censors of Dirección Nacional de Comunicaciones Sociales (DINACOS)[70] perused each number more carefully than did its readers. And the military was first to read *APSI*, under rules of prior censorship. The military stipulated that the magazine had to be printed before being scrutinized. If changes had to be made, then that was *APSI*'s tough luck.

APSI had obtained permission only to publish foreign news at first, so it had to milk this privilege for what it was worth. As with so many periodicals published under repressive conditions, *APSI* became adept at allusion and allegory. It covered military dictatorships in the rest of Latin America, the wars in Central America, and socialist politics in Europe, mostly from reprints of *Le Monde*, Agence France-Presse, and Inter Press Service. Still, such stuff was anathema to Chile's entrepreneurs. Chilean advertisers avoided *APSI* despite the fact that its circulation numbers surpassed the rightist *Qué Pasa*, which had no problem capturing ad revenue. The only display advertising *APSI* could count on was a full page from Renault each issue. An exiled Chilean engineer who worked for the company in France had finagled the ad, as well as one for *Hoy*.

In addition to its refined language, *APSI* carried film and book reviews, which increased its appeal among sophisticated readers with disposable income. Just the same, not even local vintners could be convinced to advertise, said former managing editor Andrés Braithwaite: "*APSI* could have published a magazine for alcoholics and [the wineries] wouldn't have bought space."

APSI was funded mostly by European Catholics. Staffers received a stipend of about $150 a month for their trouble, although they managed to eat well. Several local restaurants fed journalists as in-kind payment for advertisements. Other eateries simply let reporters eat for free, fearful the ads would catch the eye of the military.

American John Dinges, on his way to becoming managing editor at National Public Radio, signed on as the only staffer who knew how to operate *APSI*'s ancient hand-fed flatbed press.[71] On July 30, 1976, Dinges cranked out *APSI*'s first 12-page issue on cheap paper, with no color ink— not even on the cover. Its layout was barely recognizable from one issue to the next. The knockouts for banned halftone photographs were filled with garish polka dots.

By 1979, the military allowed *APSI* to publish national news, and by 1981 allowed it to be sold at newsstands. Circulation shot up from 500 subscriptions to 3,000 when number 102 investigated the National Information

Center (CNI), the secret police that succeeded Dirección de Inteligencia Nacional (DINA) on March 11, 2002. That scoop lost *APSI* its privilege to publish national news. In addition, it could not publish at all for nine months.

By 1982, *APSI* was back with a new look and 32 pages but still virtually no advertising, save that of a few physicians and bookstore owners. The economic crisis that year had brought on public demonstrations that were followed by a government crackdown on the media. When the military censored *APSI*'s copy, editors replaced it with portions of "Alice in Wonderland" or the image of what looked like a rubber stamp that said "PROHIBIDO."

Although the military closed *APSI* temporarily in 1984, it continued to send its subscribers its *samizdat* publication under another acronym, SIC (Servicio de Información Confidencial). Once back on the newsstands, sales rebounded, up to 25,000, and peaking at 50,000 when covers denounced the regime's torture methods and victims.

APSI suffered informal coercion, including a truckload of rotten fish dumped on its doorstep at 3:00 A.M. Editor Rafael Otano is convinced that the fish came in reprisal for the publication of some jokes about God.

By the time Pinochet had set 1990 as the year that he would step down, *APSI* began to reposition itself to play a role in the upcoming democracy. *APSI* changed its paper and logotype. The old slogan, "The right not to agree," became "What's ahead." It also added a regular department to cover the new economy. Then, it added book, video, and film supplements, added color to the photos, and toned down the color of its politics.[72] Its appearance matched the sophistication of its writing.

APSI bet that the end of the dictatorship would come to resemble Spain's perennial goodbye party when Franco died in 1975 after four decades of fascism. Spaniards called their liberalization *destape*—an action that covers everything from uncorking a wine bottle to taking off your clothes. So once Pinochet left power, *APSI* began to cover, of all things, sex. Issue number 410 was banned from newsstands in a section of Santiago despite its tame content.[73] (The concurrent issue of "Cosmopolitan" also was removed from newsstands.) Issue number 411 was entitled "Destape & Sexualidad," with articles on AIDS, the Church's sexuality, the history of underwear, as well as reviews of erotic literature and cinema. Chileans were not ready for sex or politics or anything else that *APSI* had to offer. There was no *destape* in film or literature. As television news became more reliable and when *El Mercurio* began to cover more liberal topics in its supplements, *APSI* readers got their news elsewhere.

With the coming of democracy, *APSI*'s foreign backers saw no need to keep the magazine going and the Renault ad disappeared. Issue number 411's 48 pages included just six pages of ads plus a small notice for a spray that promised to delay ejaculation. (There also was one very curious AIDS advertisement that we will return to later.)

APSI was on the skids. Its final owners were Socialist and Partido Por Democracia members Carlos Ominami, Jaime Gazmuri, and Marcelo Schilling, among others. By 1993, *APSI* was unable to pay its secretaries and still owes about $20,000 in back wages.[74]

Although it tried valiantly to adapt to the post-Pinochet years, *APSI* never found the right formula. Maybe it was the varied attempts to reinvent itself that proved fatal. Magazines need to evolve, but in a logical direction, said Braithwaite: "A dynamic magazine is something different from a publication that changes every day."

APSI, like the rest of the "other disappeared," suffered from a combination of the following factors (listed here in no particular order):

1. The end of foreign subsidies
2. Journalistic fatigue
3. The "other disappeared" did not de-politicize themselves
4. The government-in-waiting
5. Loss of readership
6. Loss of *bête noir*
7. The Concertación's conspiracy of silence
8. The Concertación's non-policy
9. Capital strike
10. No business sense
11. The market economy
12. The lopsided playing field

Such was the case with *Cauce*.

Cauce

Cauce was one of the magazines conceived as a *medio de trinchera* (trench medium) from which journalist sappers would undermine the military government. Asking questions at military press conferences proved useless, so *Cauce* took to investigating. Their reporters did an inordinate amount of jail time and even suffered the executions of their dogs and cats. The reasons are obvious: They did some breathless investigative work with all of the odds against them.

Volume 1 was published November 18, 1983, called the "year of protest," toward the end of Chile's worst economic crisis. The first issue dared to question the official version of events that led to the death of a protester, a medical student who was hit with a tear gas canister.

Cauce published several of the classic scoops of the period. Reporter Mónica González described the interior of Pinochet's opulent bunker in the Santiago neighborhood of Lo Curro. The armchair tour described every square meter of the mansion, right down to the marble in the staircase and what region of Spain it came from. The reader begins to wonder if González herself hadn't entered the mansion, but the tour was really a mosaic, assembled painstakingly from 60 interviews—some of them with members of the military who were scandalized at the extravagance of the palace being constructed during the economic downturn. By issue number 10, *Cauce*'s circulation as a biweekly had surpassed that of any other magazine. Sales rose to 25,000 with the exposé of First Lady Lucía Hiriart de Pinochet's business deals.

Cauce was inclusive enough to publish an interview with General Gustavo Leigh, a former member of the military junta and the man who ordered the Air Force to bomb La Moneda on September 11, 1973. Eleven years later, Leigh told *Cauce* "[Pinochet] only stays in power by force."[75] The fact that the military brought charges once the interview was published came as no surprise. It wasn't Leigh who was called on the carpet, however. Military police came after interviewer González. When they arrived at her home, she told them she was rushing out the door to interview one of their generals. Arresting her would be an interference in the official business of one of their superiors, she argued and concluded the syllogism: "So, you can't arrest me today!" She promised to turn herself in the following day, which she did.[76]

Cauce reporters got away with that sort of thing because the magazine did not promote a particular party and because it maintained a strict integrity that even the military could respect. To this day, González is one of the independent reporters with the best access to the military and the right. Furthermore, *Harper's Magazine* included her work in its sesquicentennial issue alongside that of Tom Wolfe and Mark Twain. However, like many "trench journalists," González's democracy-era career has not been a smooth one.

One of *Cauce*'s best covers was on March 27–April 9, 1984 with a photograph of Pinochet seated in front of a huge national seal—the rampant deer and crowned condor visible, along with part of the national motto: "By Reason or by Force." His chair had blocked the middle words, leaving only "By...Force" peeking out from either side. That cover sold more than 98,000 copies.[77]

Fortín Mapocho

That same cover of *Cauce* carried a photograph of the owner of another "trench" publication, *Fortín Mapocho*. Jorge Lavandero is pictured lying on a stretcher with the marks of a steel reinforcing rod across the side of his head. *Fortín Mapocho* had uncovered the true cost of Pinochet's "El Melocotón" mansion in the Cajón del Maipo, a vacation spot outside of Santiago. A search of deeds showed that Pinochet had acquired the property through a series of lucrative land deals.

One of Lavandero's attackers was turned in by a girlfriend whom he had gotten pregnant and abandoned. However, the judge, who moonlighted as a professor at the police academy, set him free. Meanwhile, Lavandero still faced charges under the State Security Law for having published the information.[78] Although *Fortín Mapocho* had been shut down, it distributed the pertinent information about "El Melocotón" in a free, four-page handout. It would be six months before Lavandero could walk without assistance.

Oddly enough, Lavandero was paying for the privilege of being a trench journalist out of his own pocket. Lavandero had purchased *Fortín Mapocho*, the newspaper of the produce wholesalers of La Vega, the central market.[79] Before Lavandero bought it, the bimonthly *Fortín Mapocho* was publishing two full pages of advertisements. Most of these were placed by banks eager to handle the wholesalers' checking accounts—and which were apparently not concerned that the previous owner, Hernán Pinto, made no secret of the fact that he was a leftist. Bankers included Banco A. Edwards, which was then owned by the same Edwards family that owns *El Mercurio*, along with Banco de Chile (BIC), as well as banks that are no longer around: Continental, Osorno, and La Unión. However, during the dictatorship, the weekly *Fortín Mapocho* could count on but one-quarter page of advertisements in its new tabloid format, mostly from 15 or so professionals who were friends of the paper. Lavandero says he sold two of his own properties just to keep the paper going.

Once again, the paper did better under the military than under democracy, when *Fortín Mapocho*'s only government ad was for a lottery. When private-sector ads did not come in, Lavandero asked the first elected president, Patricio Aylwin, if *Fortín Mapocho* (then a daily) could not receive just one-tenth of the advertising that the government placed in *El Mercurio*. Lavandero recalled the president's response, which were the words of his media advisor, Eugenio Tironi: "The best media policy is no media policy."[80]

Lavandero then returned to the Senate.[80]

Análisis

Many politicians kept their name recognition alive during 16 years of dictatorship by placing their by-lines in these "trench publications." Others depended on the resistance press to keep their names in the public eye by offering interviews from exile. These mastheads and by-lines are a who's who among today's public officials and intellectuals. As long as all political meetings were banned, these columns were among the few ways that the writers could communicate to the voting public that they were prepared to lead once democracy returned.[81] These columns also were testaments to their apostasy of the UP and their evolution toward the moderate Socialism of Felipe González of Spain or the Christian Democracy of Helmut Kohl. With so many politicians in exile, the trench publications never lacked for foreign correspondents.

Exiled Allende cabinet member Jorge Arrate wrote for *Cauce* but returned to government, not journalism. Other politicians such as Alejandro Foxley and Ricardo Ffrench Davis wrote columns for *Hoy*. *APSI* columnists included Juan Gabriel Valdés, who would become foreign minister, and José Miguel Insulza, who would hold various cabinet posts.

Another publication, *Análisis,* was launched in 1977 by the Christian Humanist Academy and was originally called *Revista de la Academia.* It evolved from crude black-and-white newsprint into a 64-page issue in four colors. By the time that it was sold to a group of Christian Democrats in 1991, it was selling some 20,000 copies a week with only five pages of paid advertising.[82]

After the arrival of democracy, foreign funding dropped off for *Análisis, APSI, Cauce,* and a raft of others. What had kept these magazines alive was the aid sent by Europeans who were often connected with Christian Democratic parties. Multinational corporations purchased very inexpensive and very effective advertising in magazines, many of which had high news-stand sales and which passed through the hands of many readers.

With the onset of democracy, *Análisis* went on publishing the kinds of investigations that you wonder how Chile can possibly do without. "This is how they left La Moneda" is a 1990 cover headline that leads to a photographic tour of the executive branch offices once the military mustered out, bereft of computers, fax machines, and an entire television studio.[83] Also conspicuous in its absence in today's media is the coverage of social issues: interviews with women taxi drivers, the local politics of garbage removal, or the end of a town's passenger train service—all of which were covered in *Análisis.*

Análisis, along with the rest, suffered from being over-identified with opposition to the regime. Democratic Chile was tired of feature-length articles on the murder of Allende foreign minister Orlando Letelier. For all the horror involved, it is simply difficult for readers to purchase a magazine that publishes—yet again—photographs of student Carmen Gloria Quintana's disfigured face, burned by Carabineros.

Hoy still found space for stories about exiled Chilean poets in Ottawa and the like, but it refused to be backed into a niche. Filippi's goal was to cover all the news that he could get away with. The rest of the "other disappeared" saw their role as filling in a gap in coverage left by *El Mercurio* and other pro-regime publications. *Hoy* acted as much as possible as though there were no military regime. It was nicely poised to compete without foreign subsidies, because it had a loyal readership and some of Chile's best journalists.

Hoy didn't fall into the trap of the trenches. "*Hoy* was an agenda-setting publication read by politicians, the military and exiles," said Filippi. "It was opposition in the best sense of the word: giving information in a correct style. It didn't oppose with adjectives or characterizations. Taking the opposition to heart is suicide. Other magazines made disparaging remarks that damaged [their] credibility."

So why did *Hoy* close? "I left it in the hands of my managing editor, Abraham Santibáñez, a cultured and well-prepared man," said Filippi. "He resigned and I don't know why. That's when *Hoy* lost its punch."[84]

La Epoca

Once Chile began to recover from the economic crisis, 1983 became a year of *apertura* (opening) for the press. Filippi had left *Hoy* because he was thinking ahead, toward a coming democracy. He sold his share of *Hoy* to start up a daily newspaper, *La Epoca*. Filippi petitioned the government for permission to start up *La Epoca*. By 1987, he had received no reply from the military. His lawyers argued that the right to petition the government for permission to publish implied the right of a response. Remarkably, the Supreme Court agreed. That same year *Fortín Mapocho* was relaunched as a daily. These two papers sought to break the 14-year control over the daily news media held by the Catholic University's Channel 13, *El Mercurio,* the state-owned *La Nación,* and Televisión Nacional.

Although *La Epoca* and *Fortín Mapocho* were both owned (for the most part) by Christian Democrat investors, their political programs were different and complementary. *Fortín Mapocho* was the more pluralistic of the two. It had to be, to attract readers from the working class, labor unions, and radical political parties whose newspapers were banned.[85] *Fortín* attempted to steer a course among other newspapers that were not aimed at the elite: *Las Ultimas Noticias, La Cuarta,* and *La Tercera*—all of which vied for the readership once commanded by *Clarín.* Meanwhile, *La Epoca* aimed to steal Christian Democratic readers away from *El Mercurio.*

Filippi built a following by shepherding Chile's political parties through the "Campaign for the No"—in opposition to Pinochet's 1988 referendum on another eight-year term. Filippi assumed that once the Concertación of democratic political parties was in office, *La Epoca* would have an impeccable tradition of supporting democracy. He bet that would translate into much-needed support from the incoming Concertación government. The Christian Democratic Party was the largest affiliate within the Concertación and Filippi's close ties to the party of the first post-Pinochet president should have netted him at least some of the advertising revenue and government-purchased subscriptions that *El Mercurio*'s newspapers enjoyed.

However, it was not to pass. When Filippi knocked on doors of government officials, he received the same litany as Lavandero of *Fortín Mapocho*: "The best media policy is no media policy." The State Bank, Chile's state-owned commercial bank, paid for 180 subscriptions to *El Mercurio*. But, it only purchased eight to *La Epoca*. Filippi got the same answers from the state copper company, Codelco, and the various ministries that purchased *El Mercurio*.

La Epoca sought to create a left-of-center alternative to Chile's traditional opinion-making, agenda-setting, *El Mercurio,* but that wasn't enough. If there's anything *El Mercurio* does right, it's providing politics, movie schedules, sports, classifieds, business news, culture, automobile reviews, the bestseller list, national and international news—you name it. *La Epoca* could not compete with *El Mercurio*'s staff of 300 reporters and items that its regional newspapers fed back to Santiago.

La Epoca's top press run was 32,000 copies, of which 3,500 were subscriptions. Press runs had dwindled to 14,000 by the time that it closed.

"It's paradoxical," said Filippi. "Democracy didn't favor *La Epoca*."

Who dunnit?

Isn't a democratic environment *supposed* to be more hospitable to journalism than dictatorship? How can it be that *every one* of these brave publications—plus several more that we have not mentioned—became extinct as a species? Filippi himself can only hold up his hands and say, "¿Quién sabe?"

We will deal in turn with the following 12 reasons for the disappearance of the alternative press listed at the beginning of this section:

1. The end of foreign subsidies

    Once a democratic government took over in 1990, the foreign patrons began to withdraw their backing which completely dried up by 1991. Although the stipends were meager, they made all the difference for the publication and its journalists.

2. Journalistic fatigue

    Even journalists, who were accustomed to low pay, were tired of earning $150 a month, of taking the bus, and of mooching meals at restaurants. A journalist graduated from college in 1973 would have been pushing 40 by 1990 when democracy rolled around and ready to get on with life. Many took jobs in the private sector or with the new government. Mónica González says she quintupled her salary by moving from *Análisis* to *La Nación*. Six journalists were killed by Pinochet. Five others remain among the "disappeared." Thirty more were prohibited from returning to Chile. Fifty Chilean journalists were detained, including at least 14 members of the foreign press.

3. The "other disappeared" did not de-politicize themselves

    In the time-honored Chilean "trench" tradition, the opposition publications maintained a clear editorial line that they defined as "not-*El Mercurio*." Whatever did not appear in the pro-Pinochet media deserved double the coverage. Once democracy came, the publications realized (to varying degrees) that they no longer had captive audiences and that television, radio, as well as other print media would become more inclusive with time. Despite efforts to take on a more mainstream look, the magazines simply seemed too underground within the new context. Topics such as labor, Latin American leftists, European socialism, and the debate over whether Allende committed suicide or was murdered continued to get more ink than the average Chilean cared about.

Readers were probably ready for something like the old *Hoy*, which had by now taken on the bland look and innocuous content of an in-flight magazine. Filippi tried to keep *La Epoca* in the mainstream by holding working breakfasts every Tuesday with public figures from every point on the political spectrum—his "paper parliament." Despite Filippi's efforts at pluralism, *La Epoca* looked like a party organ for Christian Democracy.

Like *Análisis*, *La Epoca* misjudged Chileans' thirst for justice in the cases of human rights violations. The fact that human rights and Roman Catholicism are closely tied to the PDC platform added to the impression that *La Epoca* was a house organ. Filippi says he does not recall incidents where he or the Church had influenced *La Epoca*'s content. But, the high-profile Christian Democrats on the board and on the op-ed page made the PDC stamp inevitable. "Advertisers told us they couldn't place ads because it was a Christian Democrat daily," said former editor-owner Aldunate.[86]

"*La Epoca* went straight for *El Mercurio*['s readership] and in 1989, was poised to be the paper of the new, incoming non-Pinochet government," said Ricardo Avello, deputy research director at the Copesa newspaper chain. "*La Epoca* was a political paper." Avello says any publication pays a price for its attachment to a political party—even *Ercilla* lost circulation by becoming too close to the *gremialistas* under ownership of the *piranhas*.[87] However, rightist publications could weather a loss in circulation because they had the advertising revenue. The trench publications could not.

4. The government-in-waiting

El Mercurio also had better access to the left than did the "trench publications." *El Mercurio* may have been "the establishment" (Chileans use the English term); however, being part of "the establishment" is what being a politician is all about. So, politicians from Christian Democrats to Communists wanted to see their faces in *El Mercurio*.

Politicians experience high unemployment during dictatorships. Several politicians created their own jobs by starting newspapers where their names regularly appeared. Once democracy came, media owners Carlos Ominami and Jaime Gazmuri left *APSI* and Juan Hamilton left *La Epoca*, as Lavandero left *Fortín Mapocho*. They became colleagues in the Senate.

Journalists working for these publications complained that the returning exiled politicians needed to appear in *El Mercurio* or they simply did not exist. That idea often deprived the trench publications of a "face" for the cover. Covers of *Análisis* were more likely to show pictures of buildings, foreign politicians, or men whose deaths were being investigated than the faces of politicians who are making things happen.

This occurred, despite the fact that in the early days of *Análisis* the editorial board included Genaro Arriagada (Frei administration ambassador to the United States), Ricardo Lagos (president until 2006), and even Tironi.

5. Loss of readership

Editors of the disappeared magazines admit that they tried to rewrite the formula and that they all got it wrong. How much could they reinvent themselves, really, without abandoning their core audiences? That is a tough question, because not one of the magazines polled its readers or held focus groups.

The one medium besides the newspaper *La Epoca* that held focus groups was Radio Cooperativa, today by far the most successful radio news network. Cooperativa found that people didn't want to hear about human rights or the Church. Even if magazine editors had been correct in deciding that those were the things Chile *needed* to hear about at the moment, those things did not sell subscriptions.

The establishment news sources eroded readership. *El Mercurio* became more inclusive, a "calculated pluralism" covering electoral politics of all parties with the return to democracy. Liberal social issues got shunted off into *El Mercurio*'s array of specialized magazines, while *La Epoca* retired its Sunday magazine. Readers were not about to pick up *La Epoca* out of political sympathies and then buy *El Mercurio* for its complete coverage.

Once it stopped being an official mouthpiece of the dictatorship, Televisión Nacional (TVN) began airing news with real content. Now, instead of paying a dollar or two for a magazine to read in the evening, readers found it cheaper to stay tuned for the television news after their favorite soap opera.

6. Loss of the *bête noir*

With Pinochet out and the "consensus politics" of the Concertación in, at whom could the trench journals fling arrows? The Concertación backed off criticism of the military out of fear that the military would "retake" the government. No one wanted the military back in power; even *El Mercurio* backed off of strident attacks of the elected government so as not to goad the armed forces into action. During the dictatorship, the military was already in power; under democracy, Chileans had something to lose from a military return to power.

7. The Concertación's conspiracy of silence

The Concertación itself buried information damaging to Pinochet on human rights violations and corruption. When *La Época* or even the state-owned *La Nación* attempted to expose military corruption, the Concertación did not stonewall; it caved in to the military. With the discouragement of the Concertación, which holds information close to the vest, the investigative magazines were deprived of the types of headlines that sell issues. However, the Concertación's shoddy treatment of the media—even of its friends—was little different from governments throughout Chilean history.

The "trench publications" missed a golden opportunity to analyze policy, especially education and the privatized pension and health systems. Their writers were great investigators and those issues were on the minds of the emerging "nervous middle class." Likewise, no one was better prepared to investigate drug trafficking, money laundering, or to do business reporting.

8. The Concertación's non-policy

Jorge Lavandero, owner of *Fortín Mapocho*, says the Concertación's policy of not helping the media of the left was meant to avoid antagonism of the right. "They bought peace with the military that way," said Lavandero.[88]

Eugenio Tironi became the Aylwin government's communications minister. He invented the "the best media policy is no media policy" in spite of the fact that he had sat on the editorial board of *Análisis*. Tironi still defends the non-policy, saying that neither the number of government-purchased subscriptions nor the total amount of government ad revenue could have kept any of the "disappeared" publications afloat.[89] However, no major news source in Chile is alive today without the help of the state, as we will see. Denial of assistance was a death sentence.

A large part of the dictatorship's subsidies to *El Mercurio* and *La Tercera* was precisely the prepaid purchase of millions of dollars in advertising. The three governments elected since Pinochet left power have not demanded restitution of the subsidies that Pinochet's men promised to the rightist media while at he same time saying "the best policy is no policy" as publications to the left withered and died.

Others claim the Concertación's role was not so passive. The former editor in chief of *Análisis*, Juan Pablo Cárdenas, said that Holland's former ambassador to Chile had offered to subsidize the magazine, but that the ambassador was dissuaded by Concertación government officials.[90]

9. Capital strike

The notoriously pro-Pinochet business community did not place ads in the opposition publications even after 1990. The "other disappeared" publications did not do a *post mortem* to establish the true extent of the capital strike. Such a scientific study is today impossible due to the lack of circulation numbers or accounting records. However, this phenomenon still exists, and it can be measured accurately by sophisticated means that did not exist during the dictatorship. (A case study appears later in the section on advertising.)

Why would Chilean businessmen punish publications that promoted democracy? "Chilean companies and businessmen aren't interested in a free press," said Filippi. "Moreover, they are not interested in democracy—nothing that could cost them money. Democracy means free unions and people demanding things."

10. No business sense

The "other disappeared" were run by journalists—with the exception of *Fortín Mapocho* and *APSI* for a time. None was managed according to business principles. The notion of a firewall between the business office and the newsroom is nonsense in offices where everyone did everything. However, all surviving publications on the right are owned by businesspeople. *La Epoca* wasted millions of dollars on printing when it could have purchased its own presses for some $600,000.[91] Instead, it used La Alborada.

La Alborada was the opposition's own press operation that went bankrupt in 1995. The print shop was donated by an Italian Christian Democratic labor movement. It consisted of two rotary offset presses—one for *Fortín Mapocho* and one for *La Epoca*—along with start-up capital.

The small shop did not control its costs, purchasing its paper and ink on the secondary market. *APSI* editor Andrés Braithwaite says La Alborada quoted prices 20 percent higher than other printers.[92] And, when *Cauce* was dumped as a client by the Edwards combine's Lord Cochrane, which cited pressure from "other clients" as the reason, the magazine was printed at Editorial Antártica, not La Alborada.[93]

Fortín Mapocho and *La Epoca* were months behind in paying their bills to La Alborada as they waited—in vain—for help from the Concertación government. That decapitalized La Alborada and then the banks proceeded with foreclosure.[94]

Other publications of lesser importance were *La Bicicleta, Chile Hoy, Hechos Mundiales, Mayoría, Onda, Paloma, Saber para Todos, Pluma y Pincel,* and lastly, *Página Abierta,* which included MIR supporters and lasted only from 1989 until 1992. *Revista de los Tiempos* was sponsored by Carlos Cardone, the Chilean weapons manufacturer who earned the wrath of the United States for selling arms to Iraq. Its journalists included Fernando Paulsen, who would move on to edit *La Tercera,* and Francisco Martorell, author of *Diplomatic Impunity,* which was banned in 1993.

11.   The market economy

The "other disappeared" were opposed to all things Pinochet, including the Chicago Boys' free market economy. Publications of the left expected the government that they had fought for the right to elect would return the favor. What they didn't expect was that even economists such as PDC Senator Alejandro Foxley and economist Ricardo Ffrench-Davis (both *Hoy* columnists) or policymakers such as Tironi would embrace the free-market model. Perhaps more to the point, these magazine owners were for the most part socialists; hustling for ads, going into debt, or "retasking the product" were not the vocabulary of trench journalists. "The right took its toll, but we made it easy for them," said González.

12.   Lopsided playing field

While the pro-democracy publications had no access to capital and little advertising revenue, pro-Pinochet publications were well-positioned, retooled, and had a loyal clientele of those whose extraordinary disposable income they owed to Pinochet and who in turn placed advertisements in the publications. Pinochet had allowed his sympathizers and collaborators to own and promote *Qué Pasa, El Mercurio, Ercilla,* and *La Tercera,* as well as the top radio networks throughout the dictatorship. In addition, they were also given some latitude to criticize. *La Tercera* was a safety valve for the voices of nationalist sympathizers with the dictatorship who criticized the Chicago Boys economy, such as corporatist Fatherland and Freedom leader Pablo Rodríguez, Ricardo Claro, and several military officers who had not been converted to neoliberal economics by Kelly.

Qué Pasa criticized the military government's foreign policy until editorial board president Hernán Cubillos became foreign minister. The magazine also departed from the government's policy of strict denial when confronted with international accusations of human rights violations. *Qué Pasa*'s take was more akin to Léniz's claim that Chile's international human rights record was hindering its domestic economic progress. An editorial said dirty laundry should be aired indoors:

Only we Chileans can detect and amend these errors, from the economy to human rights. ... The fight is *here*, not in the halls of a thousand and one useless organizations penetrated by Marxism. Let's convince ourselves, once and for all, that what we have done since the 11th of September might suffer from errors but, in the long run it is the only thing that could save Chile.[95] (Emphasis is in the original.)

Gremialista Jaime Guzmán made a personal mission out of bringing the human rights problem to light, in part because of a dispute with the head of Pinochet's DINA secret police. At the same time, he attacked the work of human rights monitors.[96] *Qué Pasa*'s human rights ideology was never adopted by Pinochet, of course, but Guzmán used Edwards's magazine as well as Cruzat's *Ercilla* to float other ideas that would become central to the regime as part of what he called the "*nueva institutionalidad.*" Guzmán penned Pinochet's 1974 speech, the junta's Declaration of Principles, which were essentially the principles of *gremialismo.*[97]

As Spanish dictator General Francisco Franco began to age, he wanted things "tied down—and well tied down"—meaning that he wanted to avoid a return to democracy after his death, which came in 1975. However, Spain's monarchy, as well as its democratic institutions, from the legislature to universal suffrage, were restored through a new constitution by 1978. Guzmán was traumatized by the rapid collapse of the fascist institutions. Even before 1975, Guzmán was at work on a *nueva institucionalidad* to avoid such a calamity once Pinochet left office. Guzmán would set up women's groups, labor unions, and a National Unity Youth Front, as a "*cívico-militar*" organization. At the groups' inauguration, Guzmán spoke of Chilean nationalism as the bulwark against the international community that was infiltrated by Marxists, especially the United Nations.[98] In honor of the military, a parade of youthful adherents carried torches in the night in the choreographed style of European fascists.

The occasion was another Pinochet speech, given in 1977 in the town of Chacarillas, which outlined what Chileans could expect from the dictatorship and beyond. Penned by Guzmán, Pinochet's chief ideologue, the speech warned that there would be no timetable for the return to democracy; instead, there would be three stages: the recuperation (of power from Marxism), the transition (to democracy), and normalcy. This last phase would not be a return to liberal democracy. Instead, under a "protected and authoritarian democracy," political parties would be replaced by "currents of opinion" under a new constitution, which Guzmán would for the most part write himself.[99]

The new constitution was intended to ensure the longevity of *gremialismo* beyond the Pinochet dictatorship, with the help of the news media. It is significant that with the return to democracy, a change in ownership and staff, *Qué Pasa* never renounced these quasi-fascist principles. Although Guzmán was murdered by extremists and the Edwards combine sold *Qué Pasa* to a group of Chicago Boys and others who supported the regime, there was editorial continuity when it came to the defense of Chile's "protected and authoritarian democracy." *Qué Pasa*'s editors announced in 1993 that the magazine would be depoliticized,[100] but the new owners' standing orders were never to question Guzmán's 1980 Constitution—one of the "Five Pillars" of the *nueva institucionalidad* of post-Pinochet Chile, which we will examine later.

By the time democracy rolled around, the pro-Pinochet publications had new offices, press rooms, computers, and trucks courtesy of the government. These media used their privileged positions during dictatorship to acquire other publications, to build business relations, and to push aside competitors. They certainly knew how to "retask the product" and how to take on debt. They never had to hustle for ads—they knew how to squeeze subsidies out of the government better than the leftists did.

Of course, the "free market" was not as free as the pro-Pinochet publications claimed. In fact, the entire *El Mercurio-La Tercera* duopoly was receiving tens of millions of dollars in state subsidies. If a group of the Chicago Boys in concert with other *El Mercurio* personnel had not masterminded these market distortions, advertisers would have had to place ads in the pro-democracy publications, because by 1985, the pro-Pinochet publications were broke.

Despite the apparent contradiction, *Las Ultimas Noticias*, of the *El Mercurio* chain, weighed in against government subsidies to the failing "trench" media: "One cannot ask the government to subsidize media that are incapable of sustaining themselves."[101]

THE GILDED CAGE

A dictatorship is like a bicycle. Once it stops, it falls over.

—Attributed to José Antonio Primo

Failed economies topple more dictators than guerrillas or foreign armies. By 1981, Chile was headed for a depression. The first domino to fall was CRAV (Sugar Refining Company of Viña), a food processor which the Chicago Boys had already subsidized to the tune of $180 million. At the helm was Jorge Ross, an Edwards combine representative at the Monday luncheons. He had used the subsidies wisely to build a small conglomerate with Edwards combine support. All went well until he bet the farm on world sugar futures, convinced that the price was about to rise. When it fell instead, the $70 million loss revealed that Chilean banks had made $250 million in loans against little collateral and they now owned a very large pile of sugar. The entire banking system began to totter under the mass of debt that simply could not be paid back by the shell companies that had no assets nor by consumers who had racked up credit card debt.

The 39 peso dollar

Pinochet had pushed aside the other members of the junta and had imposed a one-man rule by the end of 1974, ending the access of sectors of the military that opposed the Chicago Boys economy. Although the turnover of ministers was frequent, Pinochet faithfully refilled the economy posts with radical Chicago Boys. However, the economic boom that was buoyed by a pool of sweet money was coming to an end.

Until 1982, de Castro maintained a fixed exchange rate at 39 pesos to the dollar, despite the Chicago school's reverence for letting markets determine prices. This policy endured much longer than was convenient, given the sharp appreciation in the U.S. dollar. The fixed exchange rate meant that the Chilean peso rose with the dollar, making exports uncompetitive.

Why did Chicago Boy, economy minister Sergio de Castro, let the peso become so overvalued? On one hand, he was convinced that with a balanced fiscal budget, he could let the amount of foreign reserves within Chile determine the amount of liquidity so long as the exchange rate was fixed. This radical monetarist concept of the automatic adjustment of a "neutral money supply" was bound by the law of supply and demand, which would keep it in "equilibrium."[102]

On the other hand, de Castro knew that a devaluation at that moment would bring about a collapse of the banking system. In the wake of the 1973 oil shock, the *piranhas* of the BHC, Cruzat-Larraín, and Vial combines made much of their money by borrowing the abundant petrodollars internationally and lending them within Chile as pesos through their *financieras*, which were permitted to charge higher interest rates than the banks. The borrowers made monthly payments in pesos, which the bank exchanged for dollars to pay off the foreign banks.

This is the speculative scheme that in 1996 helped topple the Korean, Thai, and Indonesian economies, and for the same reason: The only way the scheme can work is with a fixed exchange rate. If the peso is devalued against the dollar, the monthly payments that the bank receives from the customer are devalued, too, and the bank cannot purchase enough dollars to pay back its dollar loans. Just as in Asia, if enough of the government's friends are doing it, the government fixes the interest rate to favor its friends.

On top of de Castro's troubles, the second set of oil shocks sent the United States into a recession. U.S. interest rates took off in 1978, with the Federal Reserve Discount Rate jumping from 6.5 to 14 percent by 1981, thus pushing the price of additional loans out of reach.

Once he saw trouble brewing, de Castro called on Jaime Guzmán's abilities as a polemicist to help script a television and radio defense of the minister's economic policies with arguments that were as political as they were economic, starting with the defeat of the UP, recapping the government's statements of principles, and reminding viewers that the Chilean economy was stable.[103] De Castro, Bardón, and other radicals would later suggest that the president could save the 39-peso dollar simply by decreeing lower salaries for workers. De Castro made a secret trip to the United States to convince banks that the Chilean economy was not on the verge of collapse, accompanied by *El Mercurio*'s lawyer, Carlos Urenda Zegers, and financier Javier Vial.

Vial, a Chicago Boy who did not join the government, had built an empire

upon the Chicago Boys' libertine banking laws. Since 1974, he had purchased 20 companies among whose holdings was enough stock to give him
control of the Banco de Chile. Vial directed the Banco de Chile, the nation's
largest bank, to lend the 20 companies that owned it 17 percent of its total
assets. Even Pinochet's threats to throw Vial out of the country did not force
him to bite the bullet and divest in time to mitigate the coming collapse.[104]
Vial, then–president of the Banking Association, was not the only *piranha* to
contribute to the banking collapse. Cruzat-Larraín's Banco de Santiago was
the second-largest bank and oversaw 12 percent of Chile's credit. It lent 44
percent of its assets to Cruzat-Larraín companies. Together, these two banks
held 32 percent of the total credit in Chile.[105]

When this house of cards began to collapse, Pinochet waited for months
beyond the obvious signs to replace de Castro. In the end, the Chilean state
intervened in 80 percent of the banking system. Instead of privatizing, the
state investment firm (Corfo) reversed itself and pumped millions into
Chilean businesses, achieving a level of socialization unknown under
Allende.[106] Wags called this "the Chicago road to socialism."

THE LEGACY

A dictatorship must justify its arrogance.

—Sidney Weintraub, referring to Pinochet, in *The Wall Street Journal*, January 3, 1984

Latin American dictators seemed always to leave behind a monument, often
a bridge or other infrastructure project, that would justify their reign in the
eyes of some. Pinochet had set his sights somewhat higher than Somoza of
Nicaragua, Trujillo of the Dominican Republic, or Stroessner of Paraguay
who treated their countries as though they were their personal *latifundios*.
Pinochet looked to Franco of Spain or the generals who ruled Brazil with
economic development on their minds. Pinochet bet heavily on justifying
his regime with the economy, which, in the wake of the 1981–1982 crisis,
made him vulnerable for the first time.

The peak organizations demanded more policy input, led by paper maker
CMPC. Pinochet even met with trade union leaders, albeit with the more
conservative of the lot. Meanwhile, the leftist unions, most notably in the
northern copper mines, fomented demonstrations while homemakers
banged their empty pots in the streets of Santiago. The regime sponsored
make-work projects in order to head off a brewing rebellion among the ranks
of the unemployed.[107] The Chicago Boys lost their berths, but only temporarily.

The principal private sector culprits behind the banking collapse, the *piranhas* of BHC Cruzat-Larraín, had their firms seized, military officers were

placed in charge of the liquidation of their assets, and Javier Vial went to jail. The Central Bank intervened in many commercial banks and propped up these and other lenders with low-interest loans, subsidies, and complex debt buy-back schemes.

These complex operations to save the banking sector took place with the oversight neither of Congress nor the press, of course. Military officers in charge of Corfo bailed out the businesses of their friends and made loans that have not been fully examined until this day. Members of Pinochet's family raked off millions. Chicago Boys who collaborated with the government and others siphoned off millions of dollars that would create an entirely new oligarchy. In addition, the privatization process made overnight millionaires out of mid-level bureaucrats who had been put in charge of the sell-offs.[108] Several of these profiteers would become owners of Chile's news media and would put a good face on the Chicago Boys economy.

But through all of these extraordinary levels of corruption and shady finance, how did the Chilean economy achieve yearly GDP growth averaging 6.4 percent during the period 1984–1989?[109]

Pinochet is remembered for—and often excused for—having permitted the Chicago Boys to perform their free market "economic miracle" in Chile. The fact is that year-on-year growth averaged just 2.9 percent during all the years of the dictatorship of 1974 to 1989.[110] By comparison, average annual growth during the first decade of democracy was 6.6 percent.[111]

The Chicago Boys did little to foment free-market capitalism. In fact, the Chilean economy is tightly controlled by the new oligarchy that replaced its landed aristocracy. These groups hoarded information and exploited their access to capital during the dictatorship in order to dominate large sectors of the economy. Although multinationals send home glowing reports about Chile's streamlined business climate, the average Chilean is arguably farther removed from access to capital, the justice system, regulators, information, and the like than he was in 1970. The dictatorship also rigidified Chile's social structure, leaving in place a "glass ceiling" against social mobility. Real wages returned to pre-Pinochet levels only during the Aylwin administration.[112]

The Chilean economy has been diversified—reducing its dependence on copper for its export earnings from 90 percent to 40 percent. However, Chile is still dependent upon copper and other primary export commodities, whose development was highly subsidized, for nearly 90 percent of export earnings. Those mineral, forestry, and fishing exports leave Chile as exposed to fluctuations in world commodity prices as most Third World exporters of cacao or sugar.

Likewise, we remember Pinochet for removing leftist parties, labor unions, and political activists from the political equation. Once again, that is not necessarily the most salient feature. In reality, he attempted to repress the entire participatory process across the political spectrum while favoring the *gremialistas*. Before 1970, this consisted of a National Front whose industrialists, politicians, and labor had entered into a power-sharing agreement behind the ISI protection of interests on the left *and* the right. The Chicago Boys broke that cozy relationship, by cutting the old-order peak organizations out of planning. Pinochet also ratified the expropriation under previous governments of land held by Chile's aristocracy by returning only a third of their properties. Because most of the land that was restored did not come from *latifundios* in the first place, Pinochet did not reinstate the old social order.[113] In the process, he forestalled the kind of influence over the economy by the land-owning aristocracy which cost Argentina its economic prowess in the first quarter of the 20th century and which slows Brazilian growth today.

Many an oligarch's fortune was lost during 1982 and 1983 when the economy contracted by 14 percent and 0.7 percent, respectively. So why would Chile's ruling class back the Chicago Boys and Pinochet? When Ronald Reagan and Margaret Thatcher thrust their nations into the neoliberal economy—albeit later, and less dramatically—they compensated losers on the right with conservative social policy. Pinochet made the same sort of compromise by subsidizing the voice of the aristocracy.

That would be *El Mercurio*. Despite owner Agustín Edwards's proximity to Pinochet's economists, his access to capital, government subsidies, the near monopoly the dictatorship granted him over newspaper circulation, and advertising revenue, he managed to drive into the ground what was once one of the largest business combines in Chile. However, Chile's aristocrats would not let Edwards or his newspaper fail after all he had done for the country. Those who had their hands on the cash inflows were friends of *El Mercurio* within the Pinochet regime. After decades of editorials trumpeting the merits of free enterprise, screeds against government intervention, and sponsorship of the Chicago Boys and of the writing of the brick, *El Mercurio* went on the dole.

Before Chile recovered from the 1981–1982 crisis, Edwards would lose control of Banco A. Edwards among other businesses. But the one business he would not give up was *El Mercurio*, his traditional power base, supporter of rightist causes, and Chile's agenda-setting publication.

SAVING THE FAMILY BUSINESS

... Nor does it correspond to the State to deploy resources to keep [the newspaper] in business, as demanded by some political sectors and communications professionals, since that would inevitably have resulted in unadvisable official intervention.

— *El Mercurio* editorial on the closing of *La Epoca*[114]

El Mercurio racked up $13 million in debt by 1980, just 30 percent of assets that year. However, the peso devaluation from 39 to 160 pesos per dollar by

1985[115] helped drive up *El Mercurio*'s dollar-denominated debt to a round $100 million in 1984.

The economic crisis affected all businesses, of course, causing a drop in advertising revenue. *El Mercurio*'s profits fell from $14.5 million in 1980 to a $22.5 million loss in 1983. *El Mercurio* cut back on supplements, laid off staff, and slashed the salaries of its remaining employees. Upper management kept on spending, even though *El Mercurio*'s debt totaled three and a half times its worth. It was time to cook the books.

El Mercurio put a good face on its balance sheet by inflating the amount of collections due from other companies in the Edwards combine. Between 1981 and 1983, *El Mercurio*'s assets under "accounts receivable from related and affiliated companies" jumped 640 percent—even while outstanding accounts from *El Mercurio*'s clients and other debtors *declined*. Edwards did this by spending $27 million on shares, largely of other companies in the Edwards conglomerate, which then paid *El Mercurio* on a regular basis.[116] Through such sleight of hand, Edwards had kept his newspaper chain alive—on paper. Although the combine and *El Mercurio,* in particular, were foundering, the state commercial bank, Banco del Estado, gave the Edwards combine fresh loans, bringing its total debt to $67 million.[117]

Such tradeoffs were simply the price that Pinochet had to pay in order to consolidate his regime. With growing unrest from labor, students, and the poor, controlling information became more critical than ever. Pinochet loosened labor laws and replaced the dreaded DINA with a National Information Center (CNI).

However, the image began to unravel when CNI was implicated in the murder of a moderate labor leader. Tucapel Jiménez was once in Pinochet's good graces because he initially approved of the coup, but he was murdered in February 1982 when his union leadership posed a possible threat to the regime. When *El Mercurio*'s managing editor Arturo Fontaine Aldunate wrote an editorial critical of the Jiménez murder and another critical of the Chicago Boys economy, Edwards fired him on the spot. Fontaine admits that either one of these editorials might have gotten him fired. But besides stating that he was ill at the time he sat down to write the columns, he refused to elaborate.[118] With Fontaine out of the picture and *El Mercurio* on the dole, some stories would stay buried as Agustín Edwards took over Fontaine's job of managing editor himself.

El Mercurio staffers who edited incoming wire copy of references to "torture," "murder," forced "disappearances," or "dictators" began to wonder why. The paper's coverage of those few human rights cases that had found a sympathetic judge were written with euphemisms that obfuscated the gravity of the case. "Undue force" (*apremios ilegítimos*) sounds more like a football penalty than what was in reality torture.[119]

If there was any doubt that *El Mercurio* might begin to publish the unvarnished truth, a $67-million-dollar debt becomes a huge insurance policy. Old-line conservatives at *El Mercurio* began to lose out to *gremialistas*. *El Mercurio*'s managing editor became Juan Pablo Illanes, a physician who had served in Pinochet's health ministry and was attached to the *gremialista* movement. Chicago Boy Joaquín Lavín, the *gremialista* presidential candidate who lost to Lagos in 2000, ran *El Mercurio*'s B section on the economy after a stint as dean of the Concepción University's economy department while it was run by the military.

Other Edwards newspapers were subject to military intervention. Pinochet was embarrassed by a cache of 3,000 Vietnam-era M-16s that was discovered in the Atacama desert—not by the Chilean military but by the CIA. *Las Ultimas Noticias* published man-on-the-street reactions, some of which questioned military competency. The military demanded that editor Héctor Olivares be fired. He was.[120]

In 1987, information continued to surface about the DINA murder of Allende's foreign minister Orlando Letelier and his U.S. assistant, Ronni Moffitt, on Sheridan Circle in Washington, D.C. When an army officer implicated in the car bombing spoke to the press, *El Mercurio*'s early-edition headline apparently fell short of exonerating the Supreme Chief of the Nation. "Pinochet Didn't Know of Letelier Assassination," was the headline on the early editions to come off the presses. Later editions were firmed up to read, "Pinochet Didn't Know of Plan to Kill Letelier," raising the question of "What did he know and when did he know it?"

The bulk of the article was a transcription of questions that *El Mercurio* asked the officer who testified about the bombing. In the early editions, *El Mercurio*'s interviewer asked if Pinochet knew about the bombing, to which Armando Fernández answered that he did not. In later editions, the question was changed: "What have you testified as to Pinochet's knowledge about this?" to which Fernández answered: "If someone suggested that president Pinochet knew about the plans, I would answer no."[121]

Mortgage payments

In 1949, *La Tercera de la Hora* was nearly abandoned by Radicals when they lost the presidency that they had held for 14 years. Former Radical cabinet minister Germán Picó Cañas bought it for a reported $200 and made it an independent newspaper. He believed that an overload of political content was what got the paper into financial trouble in the first place.[122]

The paper was called *La Tercera Edición de La Hora*, because *El Mercurio* had already founded *La Segunda*.[123] Picó and some relatives placed *La Tercera* in a holding company called Consorcio Periodístico de Chile S.A., doing business as Copesa. Picó bought out his relatives with the "sweet money" of the 1970s. At the time, advertisers were spending heavily to promote imported products that came with the Chicago Boys economy. That goaded Copesa and *El Mercurio* into a circulation war, which cost millions in promotions and new presses. When this spending was added to the buyout, Copesa's debt totaled some $8 million. The peso devaluation in the early 1980s then ballooned Copesa's debt to $19 million. Picó began layoffs and cut salaries.[124]

Manuel Cruzat, the *piranha* who had already gobbled up *Ercilla* and a majority of Radio Minería, posed an obvious threat. As owner of the Banco Santiago, Cruzat's group already held Copesa's debt. The military government offered Picó the same opportunity that it offered the previous owner of *Ercilla*: Let us control you, or Manuel Cruzat will take away your paper. Picó put 35 percent of his debt in the hands of the government-owned State Bank (Banco del Estado). The military government would protect *La Tercera* from the *piranhas*.[125]

Some protection. Pinochet's censors would from then on oversee every important decision at Copesa. Minister Francisco Javier Cuadra had veto power over the choice of *La Tercera*'s top staff. However, Gonzalo Picó Domínguez, son of Copesa's founder and at the time also a shareholder, impugned the motives neither of Pinochet nor of Cruzat. He says Cruzat was a friend of the Picó family and that they had no political disagreements. Picó says Pinochet genuinely wanted to shield *La Tercera* and *El Mercurio*: Because the government was about to intervene in Cruzat's banks (among others), Pinochet wanted to save the newspapers the awkwardness of reporting on the very banks who held their debts.

Picó denies that Pinochet used Copesa's debt to manipulate it. "The debt hung like a sword of Damocles," he said. "But you can't say there was pressure. There was self-censorship." In any case, Picó said, the military was fairer than the previous administration: Allende would not have hesitated to take over Copesa at that opportunity.

Soon *El Mercurio* and Copesa would get cash infusions—courtesy of the state.

Something was alive out there

Sportscasters were just settling into the play-by-play during a match for the Copa Libertadores de América when National Stadium went black—along with most of Santiago.

Radio Minería's news manager Hernaní Banda was at home listening in on the game when it went off the air. His neighborhood went black and stayed that way. The only way to find out the extent of the blackout was to get into his car and drive. His beige Peugeot had its own transmitter. Banda keyed the mike, reporting on the blackout block by block, pausing to warn drivers of darkened traffic lights. From La Reina, one of Santiago's overlooks, he reported that the western part of Chile's capital was without electricity. It would not be the last time guerrillas would darken Santiago.

Listeners came to count on Minería's crack news team in these emergencies. Banda's goal was to tell listeners that their world was black without causing alarm: "People used to tell us, 'You gave us the feeling that there was life out there when everything was dark.'"[126]

Radio Metro, on the air in 1940, became Radio Minería in 1941 when it was purchased by the National Mining Association (Sonami) as a way to connect the nation's mining communities through its stations in Santiago, Antofagasta, Viña del Mar, Temuco, and Punta Arenas.

During the dictatorship, television was controlled by the military or its sympathizers at Catholic University's Channel 13. The daily newspapers all supported Pinochet. The medium that had the most latitude was radio. Even networks such as Minería that were controlled by the right reported news that quelled rumors, panic, and fear with an immediacy that is unique to radio. More liberal radio networks would play an important opposition role during the dictatorship, making radio the only pluralistic medium during the periods when the opposition press was closed down.

By the time of the coup, radio was still basking in the glow of its golden era, with four nationwide networks that were good at the news business. Because many radio reporters were aggressive and some station owners were daring, radio as a whole emerged from the dictatorship as the most trusted institution in Chile. It is unusual in any country for radio to surpass television as the most credible news medium, because for humans, "seeing is believing." The fact that trust in radio should surpass trust in the Church in heavily Roman Catholic Chile is nearly a miracle (see Table 1.2).

The military closed 40 radio stations soon after the coup, and by the time the Pinochet dictatorship ended, Chile's top two news networks, including Minería, also would disappear. Some stations would be seized and never returned, while others would emerge battered but strengthened. The result was a concentration in ownership of the communications media in Chile and a narrowing of the political perspectives presented.

A new language

On the 11th of September 1973, three radio installations were bombed. Two of these were networks. Others were closed because they did not have valid licenses. The UP had simply permitted their friends to operate as they wished. Other stations were confiscated under a decree law that prohibited ownership or programming by any person or group with an ideology contrary to the institutional order of the regime or which advocated violence or attacked the fundamental values of the society or the family.

Before the coup, the Santiago AM dial was filled. That is, there was no technical way to fit in another station frequency. On a tactical level the military preferred to have all the frequencies occupied. With stations off the

Table 1.2

Do you feel the following institutions are fulfilling their missions?

Radio	83
The Church	68
Newspapers	64
Television	63
Armed Forces	63
Police	62
Your town mayor	57
Detectives	55
National government	49
Guards	45
Business community	39
The courts	37
Congress	36
Labor Unions	36
Political parties	22

Percentage of respondents answering affirmatively

Source: ADIMARK, cited in Reseña de Medios No. 35, Secretary of Communications and Culture

air, a signal could be beamed in from the mountains in Argentina. The armed forces jerry-rigged a network out of the seized stations, called it Radio National, and put it on the air in 1974. It had national reach, with 10 of its own stations. But it ranked tenth, with just one point of the audience share. More popular in Santiago was Radio Colo Colo, also made up of seized stations, which had a more working class bent and was ranked sixth.

Having the dial filled with a variety of offerings also looked better to the international community. The military had taken direct control over all television stations. *El Mercurio*'s newspapers were firmly in line. Radio became a sort of escape valve.

Radio reporters then were well paid and cocky about their duty to inform the public. Because of the immediacy of radio, journalists got away with whatever real reporting they could before the military heard about it. (Eventually, a decree would oblige stations to store tapes of newscasts for 20 days.) Unlike print reporters, whose copy colonels read before it could be distributed, radio reporters often discovered the rules when it was too late. When a military officer was driving under the influence, it quickly became a political issue, despite reporters' attempts (genuine or not) to put a good face on it. "'A tree found itself in the path of the auto the lieutenant was driving, causing the accident' was how one young reporter put it," recalls Radio Portales's Fernando Valenzuela. "The military censor called the station and that was her last broadcast."

Later attempts were not so ham-handed. Broadcasters developed a sophisticated code, especially when reporting military snafus. The military was especially sensitive about turf wars. Jurisdictional disputes between branches of the military and Carabineros, the national police, were often settled with firefights. "In a confused incident in Santiago, army lieutenant such-and-such and police captain so-and-so were wounded," was how Valenzuela reported the news. "When we didn't mention that any criminals or guerrillas were involved, people understood what was going on." Of course, the military caught on, too, and started recording broadcasts. Wayward newsrooms were telephoned and news directors were chewed out.

The military banned even particular words, like *bombazo* (bomb blast) or *apagón* (blackout), making comical reports on power outages without saying that the lights were out. So testy reporters hoisted the military on its own halyard by airing interviews with officers who used those words. Article 276 of the Military Code put an end to that, making it illegal for reporters to induce a member of the armed forces to break discipline. Also prohibited were reports that "create disgust" or "exaggerate the true dimension of occurrences." These are the kinds of vague guidelines that could be broadly interpreted. They were.

The liberal Church

Under such strict rules, straight-ahead news reporting was enough to place Radio Chilena in the opposition during military dictatorship. "We're on the side of people who suffer," said news chief Guillermo Hormazábal. "If people think that's opposition, fine, because as far as the government is concerned, we're the opposition."[127]

Furthermore, Radio Chilena can say it was around long before the dictatorship, because it was Chile's first radio station, *née* Chile Radio Company, in 1923. It was donated to the Cardinal Caro Foundation in 1955. Although it stayed among the top three Santiago stations from 1962 to 1968, the station lost advertising revenue to television. In 1978, Cardinal Silva Henríquez gave half of the archbishop's shares to the Congregación Salesiana, which runs it today.

Once the human rights violations of the dictatorship became known, Radio Chilena had a new mission. As a news station, Radio Chilena became an interlocutor on behalf of the poor and the working class, especially the PDC unions. Under the aegis of the Church, Radio Chilena enjoyed a certain protection, along with Radio Cooperativa that was owned by Christian Democrats. Pinochet deferred to only two groups: The Chicago Boys and the Roman Catholic Church.

However, the military closed Radio Chilena twice in 1984—once for covering street protests and then for scooping everyone else with General Fernando Matthei's resignation from the government—jumping the official announcement, which was the only legal source for news. For a time, Radio Chilena was prohibited from broadcasting any news at all—other than the official *bandos*. (Balmaceda, a PDC-owned station, was closed for good in 1977 after continued reporting on human rights violations.)[128]

Radio Chilena continued to innovate. It was first to connect its 14 affiliated stations through the telephone system and first to set up an AM-FM duplex operation. As the first radio news system to permanently assign a journalist the beat of covering the executive branch, it set a precedent that haunts journalists to this day. We later will see how all three of these innovations have come back to haunt radio news.

Radio Cooperativa

The dictatorship's healthiest survivor is Radio Cooperativa. Christian Democrats purchased the network from an insurance group that left Chile during the UP period. Because Cooperativa's opposition to the UP had been vociferous to the point that Allende had shut it down, the military initially saw no reason to mistrust Cooperativa. Within 12 months of the coup, when it became apparent that Pinochet was consolidating his power and human rights news could not be ignored, Cooperativa found itself once again in the opposition. Its owners of the Christian Democratic Party[129] were eager to get back to party politics, which Pinochet had sworn to rub out.

What Cooperativa had not taken into account was that 11 of the stations' licenses were coming up for renewal beginning in 1977.[130] The military refused the renewal, saying Cooperativa had missed the renewal deadline. Cooperativa protested that their applications were burned up when La Moneda was rocketed during the coup, but the military did not accept the excuse.

Cooperativa faced another blow to the wallet—from the business community which gave nearly unanimous backing to the Pinochet regime. When journalists strayed too far from the party line, often the military did not bother to chew out station owners. They let advertisers lean on the network instead—with the express or implicit threat of withholding advertising.[131]

Killing me softly

Because Radio Portales was Salvador Allende's own, his opponents seemed to have a special hatred for it. If it is possible to torture a radio network to death, they did.

Over the years, Radio Portales stayed on top through innovative public interest programming. "*Portaleando en la tarde*" is the untranslatable title of a talk show panel that tackled subjects as diverse as education, medicine, and family wills, as well as calls from listeners. "*Un Alto en el Camino*" (A Stop Along the Way) is the quaint title given a show that turned a reporter loose in residential neighborhoods, handing out armloads of the sponsors' products, and interviewing residents. Often the snapshot interviews in lower-class neighborhoods were poignant: an invalid who needed a wheelchair or a mother whose purse did not reach to the end of the month.

Over the three stations it owned in Santiago, Talca and Viña del Mar along with 21 others that rebroadcast the Santiago signal, Radio Portales reached all of Chile. The network ran just three ads every 30 minutes, while others were running 15 or more.

At the time of the coup, a majority of the network's shares were in the hands of Salvador Allende, president of Chile and godfather to the child of Alfredo Hirmas, the textile magnate who gave Allende the shares. Besides holding the Firestone tire franchise in Chile, Hirmas kept 31 percent of Radio Portales, and general manager Raúl Tarud held 18 percent.

Tarud found out about this deal from Allende, who dialed him up to say: "We're partners!" Tarud did not trust Allende's Marxist leanings or his business sense and left for Panama. Tarud said that a month after the coup he received another phone call, this time from Orlando Sáenz, the president of SOFOFA who joined the Monday luncheons. Sáenz and Enzo Bolocco (father of Cecilia, a future Miss Universe and future wife of former Argentine President Carlos Menem) invited Tarud to return to Chile and Radio Portales. The goal was to raise money and get back its pre-coup rating.

Allende did not appear as the nominal owner of Radio Portales, of course. The shares were in the name of Jorge Venegas of the town of Talca, where the network was born. With Allende dead and with Chile under military control, SOFOFA convinced Venegas to sell out for a mere $41,000.[132] (When contacted, Venegas would only say he did not want to relive those "bad moments."[133])

When Tarud returned, his family needed cash. He cut a deal to sell his 18 percent to the Luksic family. But he was stopped by representatives of SOFOFA, who had not forgotten the Luksic family's appeasement of Allende to protect their interests in the mining sector. Tarud said he was threatened with firing if he sold out to Luksic. Tarud was forced to sell his 18 percent to Javier Vial at a lower price.[134]

When Vial and the other *piranhas* went broke, a majority of Radio Portales was auctioned off to other Pinochet supporters headed by the Matte group.

Tarud continued to work with them and purchased Radio Carolina on the FM dial in order to position Radio Portales for duplex operation. Despite having made all the right moves, Tarud says he was fired because he was not part of the pro-Pinochet club.

By 1984, Vasco Costa (former Pinochet labor minister), Juan Eduardo Ibáñez, Herman Chadwick (now a *gremialista*), and Ignacio Astete (a self-declared "*pinochetista*") were firmly in control of Radio Portales,[135] but the network's new owners could not make the newsroom veer to the right. Journalists were tenacious about maintaining their jobs as well as journalistic integrity. The owners let the network slowly starve for lack of advertising revenue.

Decades after his adventures as a cub reporter, Fernando Valenzuela became news manager at Radio Portales and was the last newsman to pick up his check in June 1999. The nationwide news and information network with the number one rating from 1965 to 1985[136] wound up in the hands of an Evangelical church that ran the station on listener donations.

Radio Minería hits bottom

These days, Javier Vial shares a dingy office with some other businessmen and may receive visitors in his stocking feet. One end table of his sofa holds a photograph of himself with Henry Kissinger. Vial chuckles as he thinks back to the moment that the fate of Radio Minería lay literally in the flip of a coin.

In 1971, Vial and nine of his friends, including Patricio Prieto, Manuel Cruzat, and Sergio Cardone, purchased Radio Minería from one of Allende's ambassadors, a former mining region senator named Hernán Videla Lira. They wanted to gain control so it could join the opposition to Allende. By September 11, 1973, Minería was part of the network that served as the mouthpiece for the military. The general manager was Joaquín Villarino, now at *El Mercurio*. Vial, Cruzat, and Fernando Larraín owned Minería outright by 1975, but the *piranhas* had found better ways to make money through their *financieras*. They all wanted out of Minería simultaneously, but someone had to hold the bag. The partnership agreement included a simple dispute resolution mechanism: the flip of a coin. Vial won, giving him the right to name his price. The loser got the right of first rejection and Vial sold out to Larraín and Cruzat.

The *piranhas* group of BCH Cruzat-Larraín collapsed in 1981 and the government intervened in its holdings. The Comisión Liquidadora y Administradora del Conglomerado Forestal held 91.5 percent of Minería, with General Sergio Onofre Jarpa in charge. Minería was strapped for cash by the time it was returned to the *piranhas*. Because the *piranhas'* credit rating was now national news, loans were hard to come by. Cruzat suspended publication of *Ercilla* and *Vea* to improve cash flow, but he was still obligated to make severance pay to the journalists.

To raise that money, Cruzat sold off Minería's FM station, Galaxia. Selling off a station to save a network may have looked like the right move to a financier, but radio in the 1980s was soon to be ruled from the FM dial. When import barriers were lowered, Chile was flooded with the sounds of album rock and millions of new home and car radios—nearly all with FM receivers. No national network has survived without having had an AM-FM duplex operation to phase in FM and to completely switch over by the 1990s. By the time Minería realized this, the other networks had already scrambled to buy up every FM frequency on the dial and Minería could not rectify its error.

The network was reportedly bleeding half a million dollars a month by the time it was sold in 1999.[137] In 1985, Radio Minería had held 12.4 percent of the AM audience in Santiago. Minería's former news director, Hernaní Banda, is now dean of a small journalism school in Temuco, 10 hours south of Santiago. The Universidad Mayor is housed in what used to be a newsroom. Outside the dean's office hangs a sign on rusty cables that no one ever bothered to take down. It says: "Radio Cooperativa" and is a testament to Cooperativa's closure of 14 local newsrooms (see Table 1.2):

EL MERCURIO'S *DEBT TO SOCIETY*

[W]e are in the presence of a grave danger: That this important [agricultural and manufacturing] sector opt for economic freedom when it is convenient but opt for a socialist policy when its interests are affected.

— *El Mercurio* editorial "The socialist heritage," March 23, 1974

In 1985, *El Mercurio* moved to a bucolic campus in the style of an American multinational headquarters. *El Mercurio*'s buildings at Avenida Santa María No. 5542 are today separated by vast expanses of manicured grass. The hissing sprinklers and the drone of riding mowers are the sound of money.

When the campus was built, owner Agustín Edwards had planned a short drive to work, but his $5 million mansion in nearby Lo Curro—the same neighborhood where Pinochet built his personal bunker—had been repossessed by creditors. However, in climbing out of debt, *El Mercurio* did not have to sell of any of its assets. In fact, during the dictatorship, it went on a buying spree of regional newspapers, growing from 8 to 14. *El Mercurio*'s aggressive marketing pushed competing newspapers out of business in three markets, helping the chain to double the proportion of all Chilean newspapers that it owned from 22–45 percent between 1973 and 1999.

The government's strict control of the opposition press permitted *El Mercurio*'s newspapers to conquer 46 percent of circulation in Santiago, up from 22 percent in 1973,[138] while advertising sales nearly doubled between

1979 and 1981.[139] Still, by 1985, the year *El Mercurio* moved to its new digs, the devalued peso and a drop in advertising revenue had ballooned *El Mercurio*'s total debt load to $100 million. It was time for a bailout.

Incestuous deals

Pinochet's refusal to receive business leaders during the early days of the dictatorship[140] did not apply to *El Mercurio*. Its executives had access to the government that ranged between excellent and revolving-door. Pinochet and his communications minister, Francisco Javier Cuadra, had held regular meetings with Edwards over breakfast on Thursday mornings in search of a solution to *El Mercurio*'s debt problem.[141] As further insurance, Edwards had in his employ outgoing finance minister and Chicago Boy Sergio de Castro, as well as former minister of the Interior Enrique Montero Marx (who was promoted to the rank of Air Force general in 1982).[142] Montero is today legal counsel for *El Mercurio* and for others of Edwards's businesses.

To rescue *El Mercurio,* Montero and de Castro cobbled together a deal with three commercial banks that were controlled by the dictatorship. Two of these had been intervened by the government and the third was the state-owned State Bank. Negotiating on behalf of the State Bank was its vice president Andrés Passicot. Passicot was a business partner in the consulting group Gémines with once and future *El Mercurio* editorial writer Alvaro Bardón, who also was Passicot's immediate successor at the State Bank. Both Bardón and Passicot currently sit on *El Mercurio*'s editorial board.

With such incestuous interests, it is no wonder *El Mercurio* got a sweetheart deal. Not only would *El Mercurio* keep functioning normally, but it would not have to sell off any of the assets that it had acquired in the times of the "sweet money." (See Table 1.3.) Edwards went ahead with the move to the new plant, which boasted of computerized composition and a new pressroom. Most important, *El Mercurio* did not have to give up any part of the chain of newspapers that it had acquired in the south: *El Diario Austral de Temuco, El Diario Austral de Valdivia, El Diario Austral de Osrono,* and *El Llanquihue. El Mercurio*'s printing and publishing affiliate, Publications Lo Castillo, installed an offset plant in a new building at a cost of $20 million.[143] On the company's articles of incorporation appears a small, nearly illegible amendment in the margin: The name of Sergio de Castro was added to the list of Publicaciones Lo Castillo's directors in 1989.[144]

Under the deal, *El Mercurio* would not be permitted to make any purchases outside of its core newspaper business. It *could* have purchased more newspapers, but it would not be permitted to invest in, say, the Banco A. Edwards. *El Mercurio* would have to pay off 30 percent of its loans in the next 10 years. Shareholders would not receive any dividends during the duration of the loan. However, because shareholders were members of the board as well, they did not miss a paycheck or expenses, which averaged

Table 1.3

El Mercurio's chain before and after the dictatorship

	73	circulation	99
La Defensa de Arica		500	
La Estrella de Arica		10800	E
La Estrella de Iquique	E	10800	E
La Estrella del Norte	E	6000	E
El Mercurio de Antofagasta	E	9000	E
La Prensa de Tocopilla	E	3000	E
La Estrella del Loa		6800	E
El Mercurio de Calama	E	5000	E
Atacama de Copiapó		500	
El Día de La Serena		1000	
La Provincia de Ovalle		500	
La Estrella de Valparaíso	E	24000	E
La Estrella de San Antonio		3000	
La Estrella de Quillota		3000	
La Estrella de Aconcagua		3000	
El Trabajo de San Felipe		500	†
El Andino de Los Andes		500	
El Mercurio de Valparaíso	E	20000	E
El Mercurio de Santiago	E	100000	E
El Rancagüino		1000	*
La Region de San Fernando		500	
La Prensa de Curicó		2500	
El Heraldo de Linares		500	
La Mañana de Talca		3000	
La Discusión de Chillán		3000	
El Sur de Concepción		10000	*
La Tribuna de Los Angeles		1000	
El Diario Austral de Valdivia		4800	E
El Diario Austral de Temuco		10000	E
Las Noticias de Victoria		500	†
El Diario Austral de Osorno		4000	E
24 Horas de Valdivia		5000	†
24 Horas de Osorno		5000	†
24 Horas de Temuco		5000	†
El Llanquihe de Puerto Montt		1000	E
La Prensa Austral de Punta Arenas		4000	*
TOTAL	36		31
TOTAL - EDWARDS	8		14
PERCENT - EDWARDS	22		45

* = Part of *El Mercurio* advertising network.

† = Out of business

E = Part of *El Mercurio* chain

$70,000 per board member per year. Interestingly, the deal specifically guaranteed Edwards complete control of editorial policy,[145] meaning that Edwards was at least mindful—and possibly fearful—that Pinochet sought to control his newspaper.

Edwards got a four-year grace period before making payments on the loans. He enjoyed fixed interest rates, while market rates over those four years have averaged 4.59 percentage points higher. The State Bank absorbed the difference, of course. The total cost of carrying charges for the 13 years of the contract depend upon *El Mercurio's* ability to pay. If carried to term, the subsidy would reach into the hundreds of millions of dollars—all defrayed by the Chilean government.

In the end, how much was the state dumping into Chile's newspapers? The Finance Ministry was not talking. When minister Luis Escobar Cerda agreed to answer 20 questions put to him at a forum of Christian Democratic politicians, he sidestepped question number 20, which asked how much the state had gifted *El Mercurio* and Copesa. He said: "As to the data on the indebtedness of the large Chilean news conglomerates, the information that the Superintendency of Banks and Financial Institutions has on the matter is confidential and cannot be divulged to the public."[146]

What we do know is that El Mercurio Sociedad Anónima Periodística (EMSAP), which is the newspaper itself, did not shoulder the bulk of the loans. Edwards instead used his other businesses as conduits so that in the case of another bankruptcy, EMSAP would be protected. "These were shell corporations whose only purpose was to take on debt. Everyone did it back then," said Alvaro Bardón, *El Mercurio* editorial writer. "In those days, the government only kept track of the banks' accounting procedure, not their business practices."[147] From the presidency of the State Bank in 1989, Bardón would engineer a series of debt swaps to save *El Mercurio* from control by the incoming democratically-elected government.

One of Edwards' shell companies is Comercial Canelo S.A., an investment and real estate company that held 91.66 percent of EMSAP as well as controlling shares in two of Edwards's insurance companies. Canelo's total worth

Table 1.4

State Bank's *El Mercurio*-related loans

3,002,000 pesos – Empresa El Mercurio S.A.P. =	$ 38.0 million
784,000,000 pesos – Mobiliaria Tierra Amarilla =	9.9 million
1,005,000,000 pesos – Agustín Edwards =	12.7 million
4,792,000,000 pesos[149] – TOTAL =	60.6 million

1983 average exchange rate: 79 pesos = $1.00.[150]

was $9.51 million in 1989, at the same moment it owed the State Bank $15.3 million.[148] See Table 1.4.

Copesa

Copesa was in even worse shape than *El Mercurio*. By 1987, it could not service its debts whose market value had shrunk to 50 percent of face.[151] Instead of taking possession of *La Tercera* and the three-year-old *La Cuarta*, State Bank lent one of Copesa's parent corporations, Chillán, $1 million. Then, the State Bank governing board voted to capitalize Copesa's other shareholder, Mallán, by purchasing 70 percent of its shares for $2.3 million. Current *El Mercurio* editorial board member Andrés Passicot signed off on the deal as then-president of the State Bank.

Among friends

El Mercurio and Copesa were not the only well-treated media; they were simply the best-treated of the lot. In all cases, preferential treatment was a reward for the behavior of the media owners. A 1984 memo signed by the State Bank's general manager, Jorge Casenave, listed 22 debtors whose obligations were valued at 3 percent or more of the bank's assets—followed by instructions to destroy the list (see Table 1.5). The State Bank was not making loans only to friendly media, but also to other businesses that belonged to the same combines.

Table 1.5 shows the state-owned commercial bank carrying the debts of the armed forces, of SOEs, or debts of important friendly combines or labor organizations. Nearly all of the friendly combines included in the list owned some medium or another, representing all of the newspapers then circulating in Santiago and most other parts of Chile. Loans also were made to combines with investments in the officially-sanctioned magazines: *Paula* and *Qué Pasa* (Edwards), *Ercilla* and *Vea* (*piranhas*) and *Cosas* (of the Comandari family, perennial Pinochet supporters). Loans also were made to the owners of the two highest-rated radio networks, Radio Portales and Radio Minería.

Whether these combines were important because they held news media or whether they were allowed to hold media because they were important hardly matters. What is significant, however, is the fact that nearly all of the combines that held media got loans from the State Bank. The only exceptions are those owned by the Roman Catholic Church (Catholic University's Channel 13 and Radio Chilena (which then included Aurora FM) and those attached to the Christian Democratic Party (Radio Cooperativa). The radio networks were owned by liberal elements within the Church or by Christian Democrats, which may have helped them avoid being shut down completely, although their recalcitrance did not qualify them for loans. Catholic University needed no loans because it received state subsidies and because its

Table 1.5

Debtor	Owner	Media also owned by combine
Central Bank	State	
General Treasury of the Republic	State	
Commander in Chief Navy	State	Televisión Nacional
Carabineros Pension Fund	State	Radio Nacional†
Army Logistics Command	State	Radio Colo Colo
Army Intelligence Command	State	Radio Novísima
LANChile	State	University of Chile Television
Banco O'Higgins	State	
Compañía de Acero del Pacífico CAP	State	
Industria Azucarera Nacional[152]	State	
Ferrocarriles del Estado	State	
Confederación Nacional Sindicatos Trabajadores Independientes de Taxis	Labor union friendly to regime	None
Banco de Chile	Intervened (Cruzat-Larraín Vial)	Ercilla, Vea Radioemisoras Unidas S.A. Radiodifusora Latinoamericana S.A.
Compañía Cervecerías Unidas	Edwards and Cruzat	Radio Minería, Radio Portales,
CRAV*	Intervened (Cruzat-Larraín Vial)	Radio Galaxia
Banco Sud Americano	Luksic, de Molineros Schiess, Vial, Matte	Sociedad Periodistica del Sur
Banco A. Edwards	Edwards	El Mercurio, La Segunda
Empresa El Mercurio S.A.P.	Edwards	Las Ultimas Noticias, 10 regional newspapers
Compañía Nacional Fuerza Eléctrica	Edwards (8%)	Qué Pasa, Paula
Malán Inversiones S.A.	Shareholder in Copesa	La Tercera, La Cuarta
Comandari S.A. Hilados y paños de lana	Comandari family	Revista Cosas
Vidrios Cristales Lirquén	Alcalde family	(none)

* CRAV was the *piranhas'* sugar concern whose 1981 led the combine's collapse.

† Radio Nacional was the nationwide network that was composed of seized stations.

Channel 13 earned top rating by being the only national television network not directly run by the military.

Two of the banks on the list, Banco O'Higgins and Banco Sud Americano, have something else in common with the Banco de Chile. They were to be used as conduits for a series of debt swaps that placed the surviving news media in the hands of Pinochet's friends.

The return

When democratic governance returned in 1990, it had been 17 years since *Clarín's* owner, Victor Pey, escaped on a plane headed for Caracas. Once in his native Spain, he got news that Spain and Chile had reached a bilateral investment agreement under which each country would guarantee investments by citizens of the other in cases of, among other things, expropriation. The accord was retroactive, giving Pey, a Spanish citizen, the right to enter a claim against Chile for the expropriation of *Clarín*.

Pey returned to Chile in 1990. The newly-elected Congress did not take up the restitution of seized properties until 1993. Individuals and political parties on the left and right had lost homes, cars, radio stations, and newspapers. The original draft of the bill had based compensation upon the full value of the confiscated goods, including reparation for their deterioration and lost profits. However, the eight non-elected senators provided under Pinochet's 1980 Constitution blocked such compensation. A watered-down version was passed in 1998, which provided only for the return of the goods—in their current condition, whatever it may be. In addition, the government also could make reparations if it wished to keep the property or if the property could no longer be found.

Pey did not file for restitution under the law, because he felt that it would not make him whole for the newspaper's goodwill, its deteriorated property, or the lost profits. Besides, he said, Congress need not write a law in order to return his property: "The state took my property with a decree and they can return it with a decree," he said.

Pey, now pushing 90, is living in Santiago's bohemian Ñuñoa neighborhood. His one-bedroom apartment is lined with family photos and a reproduction of Picasso's "Guernica," which depicts the fascist bombing of that town. The apartment, which is filled with boxes of yellowing files, is Pey's war room from which he has filed a claim that could yield hundreds of millions of dollars. His claim includes two downtown Santiago buildings and two printing presses—state of the art when they were seized and still in their shipping crates. They are now being used by the *El Mercurio* chain to print *El Diario Austral de Valdivia*.[153]

Because the Concertación has not returned his property, Pey has filed his case under the dispute resolution procedure in the bilateral agreement, which is a hearing conducted by the World Bank's dispute resolution board, Ciadi. The Concertación government has hired a law firm to fight his claim.

When *Clarín* was on the streets in the 1970s, Pey was courted by leftist politicians. He still rubs elbows with many of those who are today members of the Concertación governments. He says that he has asked them repeatedly why they don't simply give back his newspaper. He says he has not received adequate responses either to his casual questions over dinner or to formal letters to government officials.

Why does the Concertación oppose a return of *Clarín*? The likely managing editor is one of Chile's finest journalists, Patricia Verdugo, a winner of Columbia University's Maria Moors Cabot award. It's difficult to imagine she would steer the paper down the questionable paths it blazed 30 years ago. In any case, the formula of "page two girls" and street slang had already been adopted by *La Cuarta* as of 1984. Even the name has been appropriated by *El Mercurio*, which used the trademark "Clarín" as collateral for a bank loan.

Verdugo is a Christian Democrat and a highly respected investigative reporter. The Concertación has no fear of Verdugo, but it does fear investigative journalism, as Verdugo demonstrates in the following chapter. The Concertación also fears that journalists who do their jobs could upset its hold on power through a deal it cut with the dictatorship in order to return to democracy. As for Pey, he may be a friend to the Concertación, "but he is not *of* the Concertación," according to a Concertación minister. This implication is sobering: It is not enough for a medium to be neutral or even pro-Concertación to have its property returned. Pey would need to have an actual stake in the Concertación.

As of 2000, only a handful of properties had been restored. Every one of them belonged to Christian Democrats—the largest party of the Concertación coalition and the party of the first two post-Pinochet presidents.[154] At the same time, the Concertación complains that there are no media in its camp, except Radio Cooperativa and Radio Chilena. The Concertación even coined a phrase to describe the demise of the *pluralism among the media* and the rise of the media on the right: "the concentration of the media."

The Concertación does not favor a free-flowing debate to ameliorate "the concentration of the media," as the next chapter shows. Politicians of the Concertación have made unabashed use of some of the most restrictive press laws in the hemisphere as a way to insulate themselves even from friendly media. This dynamic is examined in the following chapter.

Chapter 2

Journalism and the State

A DICTATOR MAKES DEMOCRACY

The period of transition that His Excellency announced is above all a call to consciousness since it pertains to the need for a significant change in the personal conduct of individuals as well as that of the authorities. It is the step between a typical military setting and a system of civil participation under the protection of the Armed Forces.

—*El Mercurio*, on Pinochet's announced return to democracy, September 17, 1978.
(Emphasis added.)

Soon after the banking collapse forced the military government to include a broader segment of the business community in its planning, angry street demonstrations and strikes did the same for the political class. Tough economic times spurred strikes in the copper mines in the north, while homemakers banged their empty pots in Santiago. The "trench" media and Radio Cooperativa promoted the 1983 "Days of Protest," while *El Mercurio* honored government requests to refrain from publishing the announcements.[155] In 1984, a National Alliance of pro-democracy parties approached interior minister Sergio Onofre Jarpa to request Pinochet's resignation and a constitutional convention. Jarpa said Pinochet would allow neither.

Politicians huddled and former Senator Patricio Aylwin conceded that a democratic government would contain an element of continuity with the military regime when it came to the Constitution of 1980. "That Constitution—whether I like it or not—is the one that's in force. It is a fact that is part of [our political] reality and that I abide by."[156]

While politicians mulled that over, Pinochet tightened his grip. Protesters, politicians, and even part of the business community wanted change. Pinochet replaced Jarpa with a newcomer, Francisco Javier Cuadra, who changed the course of any future dialogue: There would not be any. Neither would there be any public debate nor street demonstrations. The regime would dictate the terms and timetable of the transition.

Cuadra announced a state of siege, which meant prior censorship for the resistance press. Curiously, he called a press conference to relate this decision.

Pinochet's shaky position was bolstered from unlikely quarters. The Manuel Rodríguez Patriotic Front ambushed Pinochet's motorcade, killing five bodyguards. Pinochet received a cut hand and so much more: a grand television appearance. Standing before the wreckage of his motorcade, he told a Televisión Nacional reporter all about the attack, pointing to the debris, as cool as Jackie Kennedy touring the White House. Suddenly, he had an air of invincibility. Four unarmed leftists were apparently murdered in reprisal, including José Carrasco Tapia, international editor of *Análisis*.

Then, Pope John Paul II visited, saying Pinochet's dictatorship was not something really awful like the dictatorship in Poland. The Pope granted Pinochet a photo-op on the balcony of the presidential palace—just the two of them, side by side.[157]

The 1980 Constitution called for the people to vote in 1988 if they wanted to extend the dictatorship another eight years. Pinochet's junta unanimously nominated him their candidate despite waning popularity. The nomination was engineered by then-Interior Minister Enrique Montero Marx, now corporate counsel at *El Mercurio*.[158]

Pinochet's campaign spots reprised *El Mercurio*'s anti-Allende campaign, linking democracy with images of chaos. The spots' tag line was: "You decide. We continue moving ahead or we return to the UP." State-owned TVN and Catholic University's Channel 13 newscasts virtually ignored the existence of an opposition campaign.

The referendum

Seventeen center-left parties formed the *Concertación* (Concert of Pro-democracy Parties) and lobbied for access to public spaces and air time. The Concertación waged a masterful media campaign, airing upbeat segments that thematically captured Coca-Cola's™ "We Are the World"™ slogan, using videos of "just folks" from every walk of life, with the slogan, "Joy is on the way!" Each 15-minute segment was introduced like a news program and tackled an issue such as human rights or poverty without portraying tragedy or suffering. They used humor, not hatred, to skewer Pinochet's air of invincibility.[159] These segments, dovetailed with grass-roots organizing, helped carry the day while raising the bar for communications strategies in the post-Pinochet years.

On election night, October 5, 1988, radio reporters were up to their usual tricks. They dared not declare a winner before the official announcement, but they did give results from individual polling stations. Listeners with a pad and paper handy could tally up the results themselves, as did the 1,076 accredited foreign journalists.

The Concertación rigged up a computerized system to avoid the stuffing of ballot boxes that plagued ratification of the 1980 Constitution. The computers outpaced Pinochet's counting system, allowing the Concertación to claim victory at 10:00 P.M. Editors at *Fortín Mapocho* wrote the next day's headline: "He ran alone and came in second." At 2:38 A.M., the regime admitted defeat.

Pinochet's loss brought more questions than answers. Could he leave office voluntarily? Would he demand conditions? Although 54.7 percent had voted "No" to a continued dictatorship, 43 percent had voted "Yes," so many simply believed power would not change hands at all, including many within the regime. Although the military would have a year and a half to break camp, some of Pinochet's men waited before covering up and destroying evidence.

Keeping Chile safe from democracy would take some effort at the government-owned Banco del Estado de Chile. The "State Bank" in 1988 still held tens of millions of dollars of debts owed by *El Mercurio*'s chain of newspapers and by Copesa—along with 700,000 shares of one of Copesa's parent companies. The State Bank had taken on the debts as a favor to the regime's friends in times of need. However, the favor came with strings attached: With the power to call the debt at any time in his hands, Pinochet could be sure that the newspapers never strayed far from the government line—which was fine until the government was poised to change.

By 1989, the Concertación behind the "No" campaign melded into a political coalition that gave every indication of sweeping the upcoming elections. Once the coalition controlled the government, it would control the State Bank. Once it controlled the State Bank, it would control Chile's two newspaper conglomerates, the thought of which traumatized Pinochet's men. "They acted as though the Communists were coming," said the incoming State Bank president, Andrés Sanfuentes.[160]

The job of keeping these media out of the hands of the elected center-left government fell to Chicago Boy Alvaro Bardón. He had taken a break from writing editorials for *El Mercurio* during the dictatorship because he was busy—first as a vice president and then as president of the Central Bank. By 1989, he was president of the State Bank. If Bardón had not intervened, the Concertación government could have come to control the two top-circulation newspapers, a chain of 17 regional newspapers, the top weekly news magazine, and the lion's share of readership and advertising revenue, as well as Chile's agenda-setting newspaper, *El Mercurio*. To avoid such a catastrophe for the right, Bardón devised a series of debt swaps. The State Bank would trade the newspapers' debts for other portfolios of debt held by private-sector banks, thus placing the debt beyond the reach of the incoming government. "Otherwise, the left would have a monopoly over the press," said Bardón a decade after the fact.[161] That is not what he told the judge, however.

Once the Concertación was in power and had named its own president of the State Bank, Bardón was charged with aggravated fraud and was jailed for a month. The accusations involved several bankers and army officers. Some were arrested, but none of them was ever sentenced, despite a stack of evidence 15 inches high.

Bad apples

Concertación candidate Patricio Aylwin won the election and would be inaugurated as president on March 11, 1990. It wasn't until December 27, 1989, that Bardón made his gambit. He would close his last deal on March 9, 1990—just two days before Pinochet would hand over power to Aylwin. In the rush, Bardón even accepted boxes of apples as collateral.

Although the State Bank had given Copesa and *El Mercurio* fresh loans in the mid-1980s, the duopoly was nowhere near being in the black. University of Chile business professor Erick Haindl analyzed El Mercurio, Inc. (EMSAP) and found that its cash flow would permit its debt to be retired after 10 to 20 good years[162]—which was about 10 to 20 years more than Bardón had. It was crunch time. Bardón managed a series of swaps between State Bank and two private banks: Banco de Chile and Banco Sud Americano (BSA) and, through back-door deals, included Banco Osorno (BO) and the U.S.-based CFI.

But, what was in it for the private banks? Bardón may have been on a mission, but the banks had to show something for the work involved. For example, it was the lawyers of the private banks who drafted the hundreds of pages of legal documents that were signed by the parties. (This came to light when the Concertación-appointed inspector general pointed out that letting the competitors draft their own contracts for the State Bank to sign violated bank policy.) The private banks came out ahead in three ways:

1. *State Bank consultant Juan Germain overestimated the value of the debts that the State Bank received.* Banks classify debt risk according to two factors: the quality of the collateral it holds and the likelihood the debtors will make the payments. A collateralized loan whose debtor is solvent and who makes timely payments is placed in category "A," meaning that debt's commercial value is 96–100 percent of its face value. A nonperforming loan may be classified "D" and be discounted by 40–79 percent of its nominal value.

2. *Germain underestimated the value of the debts traded away.* By systematically lowballing the commercial value of *El Mercurio* and Copesa debts, the

State Bank balance sheet gave the appearance that the incoming and outgoing portfolios of debts swapped were of equal value. A loan to one of EMSAP's parent companies, El Canelo, was classified as "A," but it was nonetheless swapped at 31 percent of its face value—as a Class "C" debt.

The State Bank's Concertación-era inspector general complained that these values were estimated without the benefit of the standard analysis, according to the bank's established procedure: "The Banco de Chile and the State Bank permitted the trade of credits with identical face values but with very different commercial value. This operation meant an economic ... loss to the State Bank of between $6.3 million and $8.1 million."[163] Price Waterhouse assessed the swaps and concluded Germain consistently calculated in the private banks' favor.

3. A number of back-door deals allowed the commercial banks to dump nonperforming loans onto State Bank. Some $10 million of the debt that BSA swapped with State Bank had been acquired the same day of the swap from the Banco Osorno, with most of it worth less than what it was swapped for.

In one deal, a private commercial bank, Banco de Chile, allowed EMSAP to withdraw its new campus it had put up as collateral on a $4 million loan and to substitute 180 trademarks. Included were the names of its regional newspapers and its name in foreign languages—"Mercury," "Merkur," and "Le Mercure." These names were unused and their value had not been assessed. Among the 180 names on *El Mercurio*'s list was that of *Clarín*.[164]

Nonetheless, State Bank gave the Banco de Chile $4 million of sound debt. Banco de Chile operations constituted a "fraud," according to Concertación-appointed State Bank President Andrés Sanfuentes, because the assessments of the worth of the debts were "unreal" and "without precedent at State Bank."[165]

Banco de Chile's director Sergio de la Cuadra Fabrés later became a shareholder in the Edwards family's *Paula* magazine.[166] He served briefly as Pinochet's finance minister and sits on the board of Editorial Lord Cochrane, of which the Edwards combine owns 20 percent and of which Editorial Tiempo Presente Ltda. (of the Comandari family, which owns *Cosas*), holds a nominal 0.02 percent.[167]

Another commercial bank, Banco del Pacífico, swapped overvalued loans for Copesa's and *El Mercurio*'s holding companies' loan packages whose values were "totally false," costing the State Bank $2.7 million.[168] Banco del Pacífico director Danilo Rivas Zlatar was the commercial representative in Chile for a New York State corporation named CFI International Corp., whose only business was to play an intermediary role in such debt swaps.

On the eve of the swaps, Banco de Chile purchased $33.4 million of failing loans for $11.2 million—a Class "D" discount. Then, Banco de Chile sold the loan to CFI International Corp., thus establishing a market price for the discounted loans. That same day, CFI swapped the debt with the State

Bank, which in return gave CFI $33.4 million of debt belonging to the *El Mercurio* holding company, Comercial El Canelo. CFI forgave $21.2 million of Comercial El Canelo's debt. That left CFI with $11.2 million of El Canelo-*El Mercurio* debt, which it sold to Banco de Chile, nearly covering the $11.4 million it had originally paid for the undervalued debt.[169] Edwards could then pay Banco de Chile $11.2 million for what three days before had been $33.4 million debt.

State Bank made one more unusual loan on December 31, 1989, of $1 million to the Universidad Finis Terrae. Bardón sat on the university's board and would become dean of the business school, a post that he held until September of 2000.[170] The university's investors included the brick authors de Castro and Baraona. Later, backers would include the Legionnaires of Christ, CMPC's Matte family, and Edwards. Alvaro Saieh, who dismembered the University of Chile, also chipped in. He would become part owner of Copesa about the time the debt swaps were completed.

State Bank's inspector general questioned a whole portfolio of debt that was swapped from BSA to the Banco Osorno on the same day that they were swapped to the State Bank. Not only were the contract documents drafted by BO lawyers, he protested, but the debtors were, for the most part, going broke. The swaps, which the inspector general testified were not approved during a normal session of the board, cost the bank $12 million.[171]

Private bank owners benefitted in one additional way: Loans that Banco Osorno received from State Bank were for Malán, one of Copesa's parent companies. BO's principal owners in 1989 were Carlos Abumohor and Saieh, who purchased Copesa. The result of the three-way swap was that Copesa's owners managed to buy much of its debt at a 50 percent discount.

One more debt swap was not considered remarkable for its size—at $117,000—but for its collateral. State Bank had become owner of IOU #7529, which the Apple Suppliers' Association backed with boxes of apples.

The whole bunch of loans was spoiled. "What caused so much damage—and what made it such a crime—... is to be found in the economic assessment of the loans that were described in the swap agreements as though they were of equal value to loans that were completely bogus," said Andrés Sanfuentes, who in 1991, estimated the swaps cost State Bank $26 million.[172] A decade later, Sanfuentes said the loss was much higher because many of the debtors had since gone under.[173]

The regime's generosity did not end there: State Bank purchased in advance all the advertising space that it would need for the next decade. On December 1, 1989, State Bank bought 87,916 column/inches of advertising space in *El Mercurio* and immediately credited $1.8 million against the paper's debts. Copesa cut an even better deal on 32,480 column/inches—with a miserly 30 percent discount on volume—for $1.6 million in debt relief. The incoming State Bank bookkeepers questioned the propriety of writing off loans in anticipation of received services. However, the incoming

State Bank public relations director said it appeared as though the advertising space had been put to proper use.[174]

The advertising purchase had one additional benefit: qualifying *El Mercurio* for a Citibank loan of $6.8 million.

In response to growing criticism, *El Mercurio* published an interview with its general manager, Johnny Kulka, in which he said the swaps were not meant to help *El Mercurio* avoid its obligations with State Bank. "What was swapped were credits that the State Bank held for companies associated with El Mercurio S.A.P.'s owners, but [EMSAP] continues to be a State Bank debtor under practically the original conditions."[175]

Kulka said that State Bank was *obligated* to swap the debt, because the combined loans to EMSAP, Tierra Amarilla (the combine's ink factory), El Canelo, and to Agustín Edwards had risen to 14.5 percent of State Bank's total capital and reserves, thus surpassing the legal limit for loans to a single debtor.

There is an inherent contradiction: On the one hand, Kulka says that the debts of *El Mercurio*'s holding companies are not really *El Mercurio*'s debts. However, he also said that it was the total debts of Canelo, Tierra Amarilla, EMSAP, and Agustín Edwards that had surpassed the legal limit for combined loans to a *single debtor*. The argument is spurious in any case: The lending limits went into effect after the loans were made and the regulation was not retroactive.[176] Small wonder this article was rewritten and appears in two different versions in early and late editions of *El Mercurio*.

The cover-up

None of this activity showed up on the State Bank's 1989 year-end report. Bardón apparently edited it out of an early draft, which happened to fall into the hands of investigators. All mention of the debt swaps had been crossed out with a large "X." In the margin, a handwritten note said: "There's no reason for this. It has to be removed. This has been discussed with the banking superintendent."

To discover the notes' author, the tribunal ordered Bardón to give a handwriting sample, which came out looking pretty much the same. Bardón's affidavit on the notes covered all the bases: "I'm almost sure of having spoken about that by telephone with the [banking] superintendency, but that handwriting is not mine although it looks like mine but lighter. It must be someone from Accounting and Finance."[177]

It was Clintonesque, but it worked. On December 11, 1991, Bardón was released from jail and warrants were dropped for the other State Bank officers. State Bank appealed, but the superior court refused even to hear it. Bardón later picked up with his former job as *El Mercurio*'s editorial writer and now has a job as a professor at the Universidad Finis Terrae for which he approved the million-dollar loan.

While Pinochet's men tied things down, the Chilean electoral system sprang to life. It was time to meet the candidates.

The thawing of democracy

I believe that society has the right to ask you to regulate yourselves, something which, for reasons of a higher order, you must establish as a norm.

—Transitional President Patricio Aylwin addressing the Chilean College of Journalists[178]

One of the early opportunities for politicians to meet the press came during the Televisión Nacional (TVN) series of fora for presidential primary candidates. On May 15, 1989, the guest invited to sit under the television lights was Alejandro Hales, a candidate with support on the left who had served as minister of agriculture and of mining during the Ibáñez presidency. Hales was president of the Chilean bar association toward the end of the dictatorship, which entitled him a seat on the Appeals Tribunal of the Cinema Classification Council (CCC).

The CCC, a creation of Pinochet's 1980 Constitution, had banned the showing of Scorsese's "The Last Temptation of Christ" in Chile. Hales, from his seat on the CCC Appeals Tribunal, voted to confirm the decision, saying that such a film was unacceptable in a profoundly Roman Catholic country such as Chile.

One of the four invited questioners on TVN that evening was the 27-year-old political editor of *APSI*, Nibaldo Mosciatti. He asked Hales why he voted to ban a movie in what was soon to be a democracy. Hales answered that the film was a sore spot for the Church, having incited Catholic protests around the globe. However, Mosciatti was a tenacious questioner and didn't let up until the unprepared candidate was shaken. Hales said 11 years later that he didn't like to recall the incident.[179]

Neither does Mosciatti. He was criticized from all sides for placing the incipient democracy at risk. In a communiqué, *APSI*'s owners left Mosciatti twisting in the wind by saying that he didn't speak for the magazine. *APSI* journalists backed Mosciatti with a work slow-down, handing in their stories days past their deadlines. Writers were already angered about the magazine owners' attempt to promote Concertación candidates, while refusing to interview politicians on the right—leaving that job to *El Mercurio*. The Hales incident "was the straw that broke the camel's back" at *APSI*, said Mosciatti.[180]

Many other resistance publications—most of which also were largely controlled by once and future politicians—concurred with *APSI*: Pro-democracy candidates were not to be questioned. The intrepid publications that helped pressure the end of a dictatorship largely became the courtiers of the re-emerging political parties. Many of the publications' owners themselves sought elected or appointed office and would not risk offending the Concertación.

The Concertación defended its attitudes toward the press in the name of democracy. That was only possible due to: 1) the particular nature of the negotiated transition, 2) the assumption of deference to those in power, and

3) the legal impediments to freedom of expression that were, until 2001, "restricted in Chile to an extent possibly unmatched by any other democratic society in the Western hemisphere."[181] After a decade in government, the Concertación had left in place not only the 1980 Constitution but also onerous laws that inhibit public debate. How did this come about?

The Concertación's negotiations with the dictatorship were aimed at achieving a nominal democracy as quickly as possible, while accepting certain compromises along the way: The Constitution of 1980 would remain in force, Pinochet would continue to head the armed forces and then would become a non-elected "senator-for-life," one among a sufficient number of non-elected senators to prevent the 1980 Constitution from being amended. The transition would be, as *El Mercurio* said, "under the protection of the Armed Forces." Pinochet defined this: "I don't threaten. That's not my way. I have never made threats in my life. I only warn once: 'No one touches anyone.' The day that one of my men is touched is the day the rule of law ends. I have said this once and I will not repeat it again, but know that it is the way it is going to be. The thing [is] quite clear."[182]

Author Felipe Portales makes the case that the Concertación granted Pinochet a list of concessions in order to make the transition happen. Others claim that there was no agreement, only Pinochet's non-threat. In any case, the effects were the same. There would be no substantive changes to the *gremialista* Constitution. The Concertación would begin to "administer the truth," in Portales's words: making excuses for the military excesses especially when it came to human rights. The Concertación would dismantle the very grass-roots organizations that, along with the opposition press, eroded Pinochet's power and led to his loss in the plebiscite: labor unions, professional associations, student federations, and neighborhood groups.[183] These are the same groups that the *gremialistas* had sought to usurp as their intermediary organizations.[184]

Several of the items that the Concertación got in return were of interest to journalism: the elimination of the Radio Council and the elimination of presidential powers to restrict news during states of emergency or to impose censorship during a state of siege.[185]

The Concertación banded together the parties of the center and left (with the exception of the Communists) into a united front against a return to dictatorship. The parties would not risk internal fissures in the face of periodic saber-rattling from the military, so the Concertación demanded that the news media not create bumps along the road to democracy. Even *El Mercurio*'s editors warned their reporters not to provoke a return to military rule. At the same time, Chileans had not forgotten the acrimonious news media of the Allende years and wanted to avoid a repeat performance. Politicians were eager to enjoy their honeymoon with the press—which sometimes insisted upon doing its job, nonetheless.

The black berets

The closest that democratic Chile came to being "retaken" by the military was in response to a newspaper headline. Pinochet was commander of the armed forces under the terms of the transition when an investigation discovered that the army had made out checks to the general's son. Some $3 million went for the purchase of a small munitions supplier that somehow never appeared in the military's inventory. Pinochet sought a meeting with Aylwin, and Congress quietly dropped its investigation. However, when the Fifth Criminal Court picked up the investigation, that news item was reported discretely on the inside pages of most newspapers—except for state-owned *La Nación*'s banner headline: "Case of Pinochet son's checks reopened."

The timing of the headline was as offensive to Pinochet as its point size. Mounting human rights revelations were behind a movement to retire Pinochet as head of the armed forces. The military commander mustered a squad of special forces near La Moneda, wearing their distinctive black berets and armed with rocket launchers. Inside the presidential palace, the heads of Chile's political parties huddled and decided to accede to the military's demand to dictate the following day's headline in *La Nación*.

General Manuel Concha communicated the deal to the newspaper's publisher who then told the managing editor to make the general happy. Gen. Concha then asked managing editor Alberto Luengo to publish a Comptroller's report absolving Pinochet's son—one that *La Nación* had published a year earlier. When the general began to dictate the headline, Luengo balked and called Communications Minister Enrique Correa to say that he would quit rather than take dictation from the military. The rest of the staff stated the same, with the exception of editor in chief Abraham Santibáñez. Bolstered by the solidarity, minister Correa threatened to quit, as well. In the end, the journalists did run the military's headline, "Army acted within the law in checks case"—albeit over a dramatic photo of the fierce black berets deployed in the streets of downtown Santiago.[186]

In this case, Chilean politicians traded away the right of the people to be informed without government intervention. By viewing this right as fungible, they debased journalistic independence by using it as Hales had used human rights: as a bargaining chip. In both cases, the chip rendered was not theirs to give. Both rights belong to the citizens. However, Chilean politicians often don't see it that way—independent of their political ideology.

Whacked by phone

When in May of 2000, a reporter requested a copy of the Senate's committee attendance records, the President of the Senate, Adolfo Zaldívar, retorted: "This is not high school!" Such a comment did not come from a legislator of the right; Zaldívar is a Christian Democrat. The rightists in Congress seconded him, however, when he added, "That sort of thing is playing with the prestige of the Senate!"[187]

Just as politicians threw the man who would become Chile's first journalist, Father Camilo Henríquez, out of the country at the request of the Roman Catholic Church for reading Rousseau's *The Social Contract*, Chile's politicians still have not warmed up to the idea that they serve at the pleasure of the people. They reduce democratic expression to electoral politics, shut the public out of the debate, and call in the press to report on what was decided. This relationship with press exists independently of the politicians' position on the political spectrum. From Portales to Pinochet, from Alessandri to Allende, governments have sought to restrict citizen access by controlling and dominating the press. The Concertación has not changed this fact.

Members of the coalition resort to economic or political power or the denial of press access and credentials. And then there is the loathsome *telefonazo*. It is the politician's follow-up call to an unfavorable story and translates literally as a whack with a telephone. There is no strict definition of *telefonazo*—and surely every politician has his personal style—but the volume is usually full and the large bore vocabulary is aimed at the reporter's boss. The *telefonazo* is effective because of personal pressure. "It works in Chile because we all know one another," said *El Mercurio* editorial writer Hermógenes Pérez de Arce. He said *telefonazos* are nearly as old as Santiago's telephone system, naming administrations going back to 1958: "Alessandri, Frei, Pinochet, the Concertación—all have used *telefonazos*."[188]

Media control

Once elected, Concertación politicians reverted to their common political heritage, sometimes in niggling ways. When Aylwin suffered a spontaneous nose bleed at a business forum, the executive branch at La Moneda tried to quash the photographs. The government of Eduardo Frei (1995–2000) harangued *El Metropolitano* for writing the word "president" without a capital "P."[189] Such silliness would hardly be worth mentioning were it not for the messianism, *realpolitik*, and good old political expediency behind it.

When international human rights groups reported that police continued to use torture in democracic Chile, former TVN reporter Patricia Verdugo found victims who spoke on camera, as well as the police commander who promised to get to the bottom of the abuse and indeed punished the offending officer. Nonetheless, Verdugo received a round of *telefonazos* from government officials after the story aired. "The press was free to denounce torture before 1973, but not now," she said. Even *during the dictatorship*, some of *APSI*'s best-selling issues were number 136, "How Chile Tortures;" number 137, "Who Was 'Disappeared' and Why;" and number 139, "Those Executed by the Regime."

Verdugo says several issues that challenge the *status quo*—including campaign financing, the continued presence of non-elected Senators, the "binomial" election system, and the 1980 Constitution—are not covered on TVN or anywhere else. The largest scandal of the Concertación's first decade, Copevea, received low-key treatment. The construction company built leaky homes for 25,000 families with public subsidies. About the time the leaks were discovered, Housing Minister Edmundo Hermosilla received a show horse as a gift from Copeva and felt compelled to resign. Even *El Mercurio* resisted the temptation to put the Concertación through the wringer.[190] Paradoxically, the medium that gave it the most coverage was the state-owned TVN.

The kid gloves can be understood to some degree in such a highly-polarized society as Chile's. You don't criticize either side for fear of being tagged a "communist" or a "*pinochetista*," respectively. Verdugo, author of books chronicling human rights abuses of the dictatorship, said: "Not only were people of the left victims of Pinochet. The entire Chilean society is a victim. Everyone panics at the thought of being in disagreement." Any Fourth Estate journalism is viewed as an attack on someone or on democracy itself.

Politicians who negotiated the deal between the Concertación and Pinochet don't talk about this agreement, so its exact terms—if they existed—are not known. So, journalists and politicians must guess as to what will be allowed, thus it becomes self-censorship and just as dangerous for the same reason: If one knows exactly what the rules are, it is easier to toe the line. If the rules are vague, there is a greater tendency toward caution. The Concertación has clearly opted for the margin of safety.

The Concertación is of necessity the enforcer of this accord because it is the administration in charge. That has meant finding some sort of unknowable balance between the threat of a return to military rule on one hand, moving toward true democracy on the other, and just plain political expediency. To what degree you may be a leftist, a rightist, or a cynic will color your interpretation of the following events:

• The military celebrated Pinochet's return from London as that of a conquering hero, with bands and flag waving. Much of the ceremony was not caught on tape because the military information officers kicked the journalists out of the standing room that had been reserved for them. Even Pinochet's lawyers Miguel Alex Schweitzer and Hernán Felipe Errázuriz—both of whom currently work for *El Mercurio*—admitted to *La Tercera*: "The reception could have been more prudent."[191] However, the government did not demand military subordination to civilian rule when it came to allowing cameras to capture the ceremony. The reason is simple: Because the military celebration was an embarrassment to the administration, the governement would just as soon not have had it videotaped.

• Twice in as many weeks, state-owned Channel 7 nearly pulled a special on prisoners "disappeared" by the military and another on recently-released U.S. documents showing the amount of clandestine involvement in Chile going as far back as 1942. Out of apparent fear of the military's reaction, the chapters of "*El Mirador*" and "*Informe Especial*," respectively, were delayed. They were eventually shown—with no martial backlash.[192]

• During Aylwin's presidency, Televisión Nacional was set to broadcast its exclusive interview with Michael Townley. He was a former DINA agent serving time for the 1976 murder of Allende's defense minister Orlando Letelier and his American assistant, who were blown up in a car on Sheridan Circle in Washington, D.C. The Aylwin administration apparently feared that Townley would name military officers in active duty and asked that the segment be pulled.

In response, TVN's anchor read on the air a petition signed by the network's journalists arguing for TVN's independence from the administration. The interview was shown two weeks later—without provoking a reaction from the armed forces.[193]

These informal incursions on press freedoms cannot match the force of laws, as we shall see in the next section.

The revenge of democracy

Francisco Javier Cuadra was Pinochet's communications minister who clamped down on the news media and put the teeth in the 1984 state of siege. However, once democracy was restored, the tables were turned and Cuadra found out what it was like to be censored. Cuadra wore an incredulous look as he told the story of how he had denounced drug use in the halls of Congress with the aim of protecting the institution. It is odd enough that he was dragged through the courts for making such a statement. But what exasperates Cuadra was having been tried and sentenced for making a statement that was factually true about drugs that were indeed being taken, as later proven in a court of law.

Experience in government gave Cuadra connections to enough clients so that he could set up a media consulting firm in a wood-paneled office in Santiago's tony Vitacura section. Cuadra is a lawyer, which didn't keep him out of trouble. But it does contribute to the depth of his incredulousness.

In January of 1995, Cuadra told *Qué Pasa* magazine that drugs were circulating in the legislature. Interviewer Cristián Bofill asked if legislators were involved. Cuadra said that there were reports of that. He quickly added that the problem was with a few individuals, not with Congress as a body, or with political parties.[194] Cuadra had not named names, so individuals could not bring charges for slander. Instead, Congress itself brought charges based on Article 6 (b) of the State Internal Security Law (LSE) that made it a breech of national security to libel, defame, or calumniate the nation's top officials and public institutions.

Cuadra's guilty verdict was overturned by a unanimous appeals court decision, which was worded broadly to serve as jurisprudence that might limit the LSE, and so encourage citizens to denounce wrongdoing. However, the Congress hired lawyers who convinced the Supreme Court to overturn the appeal. Cuadra was not off the hook, although eight congressional workers confessed to drug violations and eight others faced charges. Cuadra's conviction was nullified only when the pertinent section of the LSE was repealed in 2001.

In the end, Cuadra spent 20 days in jail, shelled out $12,000 in lawyers' fees, and lost clients who didn't want to work with someone on the wrong side of the law. Cuadra said democracy is often unpredictable. "A dictatorship has the logic of a dictatorship and you suppose a democracy has the logic of a democracy," said Cuadra. "The problem is when democracy does not define its legal framework. You don't know what might happen."[195] Such charges have been brought 18 times against reporters. Ten non-journalists also have been charged, including Cuadra.

Cuadra's first accuser was then-President of the Senate, Gabriel Valdés, a Christian Democrat who would become foreign minister. Taking a potshot at Pinochet's chief enforcer of press curbs during the 1984 state of siege may be poetic justice, but proponents of free speech question the wisdom of using authoritarian methods as a political tool during times of democracy.

The LSE has the ring of a Pinochet-era decree, but it is not. The law dates back to 1958 when it was known as the Defense of Democracy Law, a descendant of a family of laws dating back to 1931. These laws made it illegal to disseminate any news that is false or tendentious. A 1932 law proscribed apologies for violence, subversion, or terrorism.[196] The fact that these laws predate Pinochet and that they are replicated in other bodies of Chilean law indicates that they are not a fluke. Instead, their existence speaks volumes about Chile, its laws, the relationship of its citizens to the state, the state's attitude toward journalists, and Chileans' attitudes toward authoritarian rule.

The question of honor is yet another Chilean tradition.

A question of honor

A Chilean professor asked my help in translating his biography of a photographer from Ohio. The article traced the photographer's adventures to Santiago and ended abruptly with his death in Buenos Aires. I suggested that the *gringos* would be curious as to the cause of his death at a relatively young age. The professor winced and said: "Well, he died of cirrhosis [of the liver] and it wouldn't be right for them to think he was an alcoholic."

Chileans shy away from disparaging even a man who died generations ago. And, because Chile's legal tradition descends not from the radical English model of free speech but from the moderate Continental tradition, a person's honor may take precedence over the public interest.[197]

The Black Book

Until recently, Chilean journalists faced criminal, not civil, penalties for wounding someone's "honor." The chilling effect is patent and it should come as no surprise that investigative journalism is a dead art in Chile.

The most recent Chilean to hold a job as an investigative journalist was having breakfast in April of 1999 when she got word the police were on the way. Alejandra Matus left her boyfriend seated at the breakfast table when she hightailed it for the airport. She accepted exile in Miami rather than face charges under the LSE.

Matus had been laid off the year before, when *La Epoca* went under for the third and final time. Because no newspaper in Chile at the time published investigative work, she, like many investigative journalists before her, wrote a book, *El libro negro de la justicia chilena. The Black Book of Chilean Justice* covered judicial abuses of power.[198] The courts responded by impounding copies of her book.

The Free Speech Forum petitioned for the free circulation of the book, arguing that an examination of the justice system is a matter of public interest. The Supreme Court rejected the petition on the grounds that the association was not a party to the dispute, implying that the public has no standing when it comes to free speech.[199] What happened next could not have been scripted better as an argument for free speech.

Investigate this

Appeals Court Judge Gloria Olivares was removed from the bench in 2000 after an ethics board inquiry into a parole that she had granted a drug trafficker. During the hearings, Olivares criticized news reports about her case as "an illegitimate abuse of press freedoms." Yet, once removed, she herself began to denounce judicial abuses of power—not only through the ethics board, it should be noted, but also through statements to the press.[200] Her accusations sparked a congressional inquiry.

Because *The Black Book* is about abuses of justice, members of Congress used it to bolster ethics charges against members of the judiciary. Matus points out that some of the same congressmen who defended the LSE, which had kept her book off the shelves, made use of the evidence the book provides when it was politically expedient to do so. "It's part of the surrealism of Chile's social and political life," said Matus.[201]

After eight years of debate, Congress repealed the most restrictive sections of the LSE as well as the "Abuse of Publicity Law" as part of the so-called Press Law of 2001. Now, politicians who want to muzzle the press must use Chile's criminal code like everyone else. The criminal code restricts free speech in much the same way as the LSE , but without being tailored specifically to the needs of top officials and without making criticism a matter of national security.

Journalists are still hampered by the Constitution of 1980, which makes it a crime to spread falsehoods about others. The Constitution specifically enjoins *communications media* from disparaging the honor of persons or their families and establishes criminal penalties. The accused may present the truth as a defense— "unless such would itself constitute a further offence to the individuals."[202]

A "permanent state of exception"

After Compte and Marx, after sociology, after the long historiography of the last 150 years, there is no room for the ingenuousness that places faith in the magic power of constitutions.

— *El Mercurio,* September 9, 1978

Once the Press Law was passed in 2001, the 1980 Constitution remained the great legal stumbling block to free expression in Chile. Not only does it contain some curious features for a nominal democracy, but it also ensconces impediments to change: *enclaves authoritarios.* The "authoritarian enclaves" seated Pinochet as a "senator–for–life," along with enough non-elected senators to block any constitutional amendment requiring the super-majorities specified by the Constitution.

Although it has been amended to some measure, the Constitution of 1980 still condemns Chileans to a permanent state of exception. Typical among constitutions of repressive governments, the Rights of Man are set up and then knocked down. Chile's Constitution starts off well, echoing other consititutions' protection of free speech. However, it is immediately followed by the fine print, which is a killer: "The freedom to express opinion and information— without prior censorship—in any form and by any means, *notwithstanding crimes or abuses committed in the exercise of these freedoms* according to law, which shall be [approved] by special quorum."[203] (Emphasis added.)

Whereas the U.S. Constitution *limits* the role of government in infringing on personal freedom, Chile's Constitution *invites* the government to abridge those rights, converting them into mere privileges. Several of these rights may be exercised only when they meet the test of what is considered to be "moral" or "good customs" (*buenas costumbres*), which is an overly-broad test—especially since the Constitution does not define them.

Chile's 1980 Constitution lists eight freedoms and 17 rights. Of these, the Constitution invites Congress to modify 13, including all of the freedoms. Others are subjected to vague tests, for example: "Freedom of conscience, the practice of all beliefs and the free exercise of all sects not contrary to morals, good customs or public order." From the Constitution's rights and freedoms, we have extracted Table 2.1.

The Constitution of 1980 was written by a committee appointed by Pinochet, which included then-Justice Minister Mónica Madariaga (who went on to the Finis Terrae law faculty), former president of Chile and of

Table 2.1

The 1980 Constitution guarantees:

freedoms	morals	good customs	public order	law
	\-*—except when limited by:*			
of conscience	✓	✓	✓	✓
of choice in business activity	✓	✓	✓	✓
of movement/travel				✓
in establishment of learning institutions	✓	✓	✓	✓
of expression	✓	✓	✓	✓
of assembly				✓
of association	✓		✓	✓
in choice of work and collective bargaining	✓		✓	✓
rights -				
to life				✓
to equality before the law				
to equal protection				
to honor				
to privacy				✓
to a clean environment				
to protection of health				
to education				
to petition				
to equal employment in government				
to social security				✓
to labor union affiliation				✓
to fair taxation				
to fair business with the state				
to private ownership				✓
to be indemnified for expropriation				✓
to intellectual property ownership				

CMPC Jorge Alessandri, as well as Pinochet minister Carlos Cáceres (who argued for a constitutional restriction of suffrage to property owners).[204] However, the Constitution was the brainchild of *gremialista* Jaime Guzmán,[205] who tailored it to the needs of the neoliberal Chicago Boys. He gave it the moniker "Constitution of Liberty"—the title of the book by Freidrich von Hayek.

The 1980 Constitution also is remarkable because it expressly mentions news organizations among the three groups having additional and particular obligations under the Constitution. The other two are politicians and labor unions—the three groups Pinochet most sought to crush or control. Journalists actually have heavier constitutional burdens than any other group: 1) You may not practice journalism or manage or own a medium if you have been convicted of a terrorist act in the last 15 years. 2) You must be "responsible" in your reporting. 3) Journalists must respect Chileans' right to privacy and to personal "honor." Although the state, politicians, the military, or ordinary citizens have no express constitutional obligation to respect the honor of persons, journalists do.

Things could have been worse: Former president Alessandri argued for a constitutional ban on the protection of journalists' sources, which was guaranteed by the 2001 Press Law.

Journalists as watchdogs

There is no groundswell among Chileans to modify the Constitution. Because the news media have historically been activist promoters of the ideologies of their owners rather than a Fourth Estate, journalists are not seen as the protectors of the citizenry. Journalists are often seen as gadflies who could threaten the social order if left to their own devices.

On a broader scale, Chileans generally do not view freedom of expression as a proper organizing principle for society. Freedoms, which in the United States are hallowed rights, are to many Chileans more akin to a privilege granted when the state can afford it, like a tax cut or a hot lunch for the poor. Even Chilean proponents of free speech may say: "Such freedom is fine in the U.S., but we are not yet a mature country." (As though Americans were mature about their self-expression.)

In Chile, freedom of expression is a "good idea" and something to strive for, but not a fundamental principle: It is the icing, not the cake. For Americans, it is the eggs, the flour, and the pan. For example, whistle blower laws in the United States protect the individual's right to free expression. However, that is only as a by-product of the law's intent. That is, protecting the individual's right to speak out is the *mechanism* by which citizens fight corruption. It is a self-regulating enforcement mechanism that rectifies wrongs without a standing army of investigators. Protecting free speech helps organize the society by letting vigilant citizens police their own government. There are some specialists within this mechanism of vigilant citizens.

Journalists in the United States are merely citizens with enough time on their hands to go snooping around the court house. Our right to do that is derived from the First Amendment, just like that of any other citizen. Chilean journalists defend the right to practice journalism as a group—a group separate from the citizenry. Journalists are not seen as representing the interests of the people.

In fact, reporters are seen more as a nuisance than as a part of society. "The public doesn't understand the role of the press and neither do the newsmakers understand why a reporter has stuck a microphone in his face," said Verdugo.

"Politicians believe that the media should be at their service," said Mosciatti, ten years after his grilling of Hales. When *APSI* folded, writers sought backers to start up another independent publication, said Mosciatti, "But they were all political sponsors."

Chileans largely believe that it is up to government to police itself. Citizens think that they should stay out of it and that goes double for journalists. Because of that sort of thinking, journalists' freedoms are not embraced by citizens as being their freedoms, too. While Chileans have high expectations when it comes to the rule of law, they are skeptical about allowing the exercise of unfettered expression. Thus, journalists are left pretty much alone to strive for increased freedoms. Few populations really like their journalists (imagine U.S. journalists arguing for exclusive rights that citizens don't have), therefore Chilean journalists are left to go it alone when they are up against Congress. Because Chileans don't embrace journalists' freedoms as their own, legislators pay no political price for restricting press freedoms. And, they are quick to do so if it means pre-empting stories that could get them in trouble.

Another way for politicians to keep the dirty linens indoors is to inhibit public access to information.

HOBBLING INVESTIGATIVE JOURNALISM

It is no longer sufficient to know how to work or the best way to work in a particular field; one needs instead to be abreast of what will be most advantageous to produce. Business planning and decisions about credit or risks today demand more accurate and detailed information than before.

—*El Mercurio*, September 27, 1977

Once President Ricardo Lagos took office in 2000, he propped open the iron gates to the courtyard of the presidential palace at La Moneda. Now citizens may enter through the huge archway built for carriages, view the guards and the fountain and, before exiting the other side, maybe get a glimpse of their government at work. The allegory was obvious: The government will now be more open.

Right behind La Moneda is the *El Diario Oficial*. There, I asked for a copy of a law because I knew it had to be published in the daily before it could take effect. Copies were sold out, so the man at the window sent me to the National Library, which didn't have it, either. I returned to the newspaper office and I was told to try the Library of Congress, whose staff was out to lunch. Four hours after I began, I obtained a copy of the Ley de Probidad.

What is the purpose of this "Integrity Law"? To make it easier to obtain government documents. Really.[206]

The "Integrity Law" is Chile's attempt at a "sunshine law." Of course, in the absence of improved procedures, such laws are mere gestures—like opening the doors of La Moneda. Lagos, it turns out, has an intimate knowledge of the importance of information divulged by the government; he wrote a book based on it, which we will return to later.

State secrets

The real disappointment came once I had the Integrity Law in hand. The law begins by making all government documents public. As with the Constitution, a terrific preamble is subsequently undermined. The law says that before disclosing a government contract to an interested citizen or journalist, a government official must seek the approval of the private-sector party. The contractor may refuse if he feels the disclosure could harm his business. (Of course, corruption investigations are *intended* to harm his "business.")

Moreover, the law does not define clearly which types of information or contracts must be divulged. In lieu of clarity, the law defines several levels of appeal, first, to the section chief who has 48 hours to respond. Then, the citizen may appeal to the section chief's boss, and so forth, all the way to the Supreme Court, which then defines what the legislators would not. By that time, the citizen, journalist, or investigator has spent a lot of time and money, and whatever the matter was about is probably moot. And, because Chile's Napoleonic legal code means that the courts are not bound by precedent, the crusading citizen-journalist has no idea based on past decisions whether or not the game will be worth the candle.

It could be argued that access to information is more critical than the right to publish it. Imagine a journalist uncovering information critical to the public debate. She can publish it—even if it lands her in jail—if she feels it is crucial to saving the republic. Without access to the information, she does not have that decision to make. The genesis of this problem is tradition and the law.

Statistical secrecy

As a student, Paulo Ramírez set out to catalog all the sources of government information that journalists could use. "It was difficult to convince officials that we didn't want access to the information. We just wanted to know what they had and how that information is managed," said Ramírez, who became *El Mercurio*'s on-line editor before becoming programming advisor at Channel 13. "But we just couldn't make them understand what we were talking about. We couldn't finish the job." In many cases, said Ramírez, he could not even get access to the public information officers in these bureaucracies to ask them these basic questions.[207]

Ramírez's first stop was Chile's National Statistics Institute (INE), which centralizes statistics from state bureaucracies. INE employees are obliged to secrecy about the numbers in their care under threat of punishment for breach of "statistical secrecy." INE publishes an annual one-volume "Statistical Compendium," which contains a paucity of information. Economic information is limited to two pages and does not include exchange rates, interest rates, government budget figures, or similarly rudimentary information. Journalists often resort to unauthorized wandering in INE hallways to find the person who has these statistics.

The INE also offers a series of publications. However, Ramírez was told that he could not obtain a price list because it is considered "privileged information." INE set out to change its corporate image at the end of the 20th century by posting subway billboards boasting of its service to the nation. These billboards listed neither fax nor telephone numbers, neither street nor Internet addresses.

Central Bank

The 1980 Constitution made the Central Bank independent of the government (and politics) as is the Federal Reserve. That independence came at a cost, because the Central Bank alone may determine what information is divulged and under what rules. The Central Bank studies everything from the Latin American economy to free trade pacts to the local and regional economies within Chile. The public's interest in these studies is obvious, but access to the Central Bank library is limited and often denied to journalists. It is impossible to determine what information is available without access to the catalog. In the course of his research, Ramírez was unable to discover even the Central Bank's criteria for divulging information or its internal regulations. "That's privileged [information]," said the public relations officer.[208]

Greenpeace's repeated requests for information about fishing stocks were ignored by the Central Bank. However, *La Nación* published a leaked report of the findings: Spanish sardines had been depleted by 96 percent in eight years, Southern hake was down 85 percent, and conger and clams were down 74 percent.[209] Clearly, the public interest was taking a back seat to the fishing industry. *La Nación* may publish as many as three articles a day on environmental issues, however, it has the lowest circulaton of any nationally distributed daily. The Central Bank was keeping the public in the dark. Nothing that could be construed as a pro-environmental report on the fishing industry was published in *El Mercurio* or *La Tercera* during the study period August 10, 1999–March 10, 2000.

Former Central Bank president Alvaro Bardón justified such secrecy, saying the free market should be left to regulate everything from the environment to illicit drugs. However, he does take exception to the marketplace of ideas. "People don't know," said Bardón, "And when the people don't know, they can't criticize."[210] Pinochet's Chicago Boys did their best to prevent the people from knowing much of anything by drying up information on the private sector. In 1982, they made what used to be a relatively open system of corporate registry nearly inaccessible. Lagos's 1958 cross-section of corporations in Chile was based on hard data that enabled him to quantitatively measure the concentration of economic power in his book by that name, *La concentración del poder económico*.[211] However, such a measurement is nearly impossible today. We will explain why later on.

Corporate information[212]

The Superintendency of Securities and Insurance (SVS) is similar to the U.S. Securities and Exchange Commission (SEC). They share the purpose of inspiring investor confidence in the purchase of company shares through management transparency. In Chile, a corporation with more than 500 shareholders, or which offers its stock publicly, is called an "open" corporation because it must provide SVS with the following:

1. A yearly Uniform Codified Statistical Sheet (FECU), not unlike the SEC's 10-K

2. A quarterly balance sheet that conforms to standard accounting procedures

3. A copy of the annual report to company shareholders

4. Any changes in the business that could affect its worth in a "truthful, complete and opportune" manner

5. Articles of incorporation and board minutes along with other information

An SVS office will instantly supply you with the first three documents on any public corporation for the price of photocopying. You must go to the office and present positive identification to obtain them; don't look on the Web page or ask for the information by fax.

Further information is more difficult to obtain. The SVS mandate is to divulge, in a manner that is "truthful, sufficient and opportune, all information essential to the securities traded." The salaries of corporate directors are not considered "essential" and SVS does not divulge them. Furthermore, if three-fourths of a corporate board decide that certain information is proprietary, only through an attenuated appeals procedure may the SVS wrangle the information out of a recalcitrant board. SVS keeps the information secret while determining its essential nature. How long this determination takes or what criteria are considered is not openly known.

SVS regulations require corporate officers to keep mum about information that could affect a corporation's worth. Ramírez says this requirement reflects a peculiarly Chilean attitude that afflicts even journalists. "Reporters in Chile tend not to give bad news that would make the value of a share drop," said Ramírez who was once an *El Mercurio* business reporter. "In the U.S., reporters feel it is their *obligation* to publish this information." In a three-month attempt to discover SVS criteria for divulging information, Ramírez was unable even to get the public relations person to the telephone.[213]

The "closed" corporation

Privately-held corporations may declare themselves "closed corporations." This is the creation of Pinochet's Chicago Boys. Before 1981, all corporations were "open" and their financial information was public. Lagos based his book on those disclosures. He concluded that, in 1958, when the thesis was written, the Edwards combine had effective control of corporations whose total worth equaled one-fifth of all the corporate investment in the country.[214] However, the 1981 Decree Law, written under Finance Minister (and future Copesa stockholder) Sergio de Castro and signed into law by Pinochet, ended that openness.

Privately-held media corporations immediately opted to be "closed"—unanimously. (TVN's government charter requires it to be "open.") *El Mercurio* closed its books, making it nearly impossible to follow the millions in government bailouts. The corporate structure of the Edwards combine and Copesa was traced through the following onerous process.

Corporate research

Closed corporations must file their articles of incorporation with a notary who then sends a copy to the Recorder of Deeds along with any changes in its statutes, directors, or investment. Minutes of yearly board and shareholder meetings are filed with the Judicial Archive in addition to the articles of incorporation.

To obtain this information you must do the following:

1. Obtain the company's tax number (Rol Unico Tributario [RUT]).

2. Take the tax number to a credit agency (Dicom) or the name of the company in question to *El Diario Oficial*, which, besides publishing laws, must also publish corporate news. Either search will yield the dates of changes in corporate structures and will cost you about $10.

3. Take the dates to the Recorder of Deeds, where the scene is a cross between Kafka and Dante: a room full of messengers who are elbowing their way to tables piled high with leather-bound ledgers. Once you find the book that corresponds to the year and month of the publication of the abstract you seek, find the exact day and go down the handwritten entries line by line until you find the name of the corporation. To the right, you will see two four-digit numbers. Write them down. You then fill out a form, pay $9, and wait three days. Then, you may stand in another line to pick up a sometimes illegible photocopy of the articles of incorporation.

(The recorder of deeds also will provide you with information on deeds, of course, provided you know the date of the sale. Then, you are free to look down the lists of all properties that changed hands on that day until you find the one you seek.)

4. Or, you may take the date the company was incorporated to the Judicial Archive where you can obtain the minutes of board meetings and the articles of incorporation. Photocopies cost $4 per page and you must copy the entire document, which may be 20 pages long.

You have invested about a day's labor and at least $19 plus car fare. Keep in mind that the owners of a "closed corporation" are nearly always other corporations—so you get to start this whole process over again. Compare this to Colombia, where the same information is computerized and is provided instantaneously and free of charge by the Chamber of Commerce.

A Chilean business journalist complained: "It's this way because they want it to be this way." "They," of course, are connected to Chile's communications media.

Presidential investigation

Annual reports were the raw material for Lagos's book, and we may assume that he simply examined them for free at the SVS. However, today's closed corporations do not submit annual reports. Using the above method to trace only the holdings of the Copesa combine described in the following chapter required several thousand hours of work and the outlay of several thousand dollars. This information can be obtained by journalism fellows with the help of student volunteers. However, it is well beyond the resources of Chileans wishing to know who controls the media in their country.

This is often the only way to obtain any information at all, given the air of secrecy surrounding the workings of corporations and peak organizations—including the communications media. The executive director of the broadcasters' association, for instance, refused to provide a membership roster or copies of the membership magazine.[215] The National Press Association membership list is entitled "Internal Guide 2000," meaning the names of officers and members are not to be divulged. And, one could question whether *El Mercurio* deserves to be called Chile's "newspaper of record," because it does not maintain a "morgue" of published articles listed by subject available to the public—just back issues and microfilm at libraries. An electronically stored, searchable data base is not available on the World Wide Web; it is only available to certain employees.

Private sector reticence means a dearth of the salesman's guides, business listings, media guides, criss-cross directories, city directories, and a million other sources of names, dates, and places that journalists use elsewhere. This way of doing business has rubbed off onto SOEs—to such a degree that the head of the national copper company refused to reveal the terms of a contract when called before a congressional committee.[216]

Chileans are so conditioned to this way of doing business that they don't seek or demand more openness. "In Chile, people have the sense that everything goes on in secret and it's alright that it be this way," said Ramírez. One student in my investigative journalism class asked if the use of information on "closed" companies was not illegal.

Making book

Because no newspaper is serious about investigative journalism, Chile's best journalists have taken to writing books. Obviously, not every investigation deserves to be book length. In addition, books only reach an elite group. The tiny potential market of 16 million Chileans makes books prohibitively expensive, because the economy of scale is critical to the printing and manufacture of books. Books get an 18 percent value-added tax in Chile, so that even an imported book with universal appeal and a long press run, such as the official dictionary prepared by Spain's Royal Language Academy, costs 20 to 25 percent more in Santiago than it does in Buenos Aires.[217] Most Chileans would have to spend a day's salary to buy a book—assuming it is available. Such high prices and low demand mean bookstores are poorly stocked.

In addition, Chilean libraries are poor. The National Library does not list Lagos's book among its holdings. The notoriety of the author aside, the book merited a mention in *Time* magazine when it was published in 1961.[218] However, when I asked librarians for the book and described its importance, the librarians appeared not to be impressed—neither by the book nor by its absence. I had to pay a rare book searcher the presidential price of $30 for the yellowed paperback because I could not find it in the library—even though the gates of La Moneda had already been swung wide open.

With so little information and so many laws holding journalists at bay, it would seem undesirable for journalists to further limit themselves, but that is the subject of the next section.

Ethics panels

Chile has three main ethics panels that oversee the business of communications. Curiously, although these panels are made up of journalists and media representatives, *not one decision of any of the panels calls for increased freedom of expression for journalists or the news media, or for more liberal government disclosure.* Instead, the ethics panels become one more encumbrance for journalists.

Two of the four panels are government-mandated controls on expression. One of these is the cinematic censorship board, which is of journalistic interest since films are cultural artifacts and because journalists sit on the council. Although the Communications Media Ethics Council and the College of Journalists ethics panel are private-sector bodies, we will deal with all the boards in this chapter.

The Communications Media Ethics Council was founded after the return to democracy by the associations of the radio, television, and print media: the Radio Broadcasters' Association of Chile (ARCHI), the National Television Association (ANATEL) and the National Press Association (ANP), respectively. The Council is made up of seven members, plus the secretary (*fiscal*). Five of the members serving in 2000 identified themselves as journalists, six as lawyers. (Three of these claimed both titles.) The Council hears complaints brought before it by any person or entity and has only the power of moral sanction.

The Council seeks member news organization compliance with the Constitution, which, as we have seen, protects privacy at the expense of the public interest. The Council most frequently sustains complaints about journalistic violations of these constitutional protections: personal honor, a person's right to privacy, and the rectification of incorrect information.[219]

On the other hand, the findings based on non-constitutional concepts (accuracy, fair means of obtaining information, relations among news organizations) tend to favor free expression. In one such case, a medium accused a competitor of violating a government news embargo. In another, a medium accused a competitor of incorrectly reporting the imminent closure of the complainant's medium. In each case, the council backed the right to be wrong.

However, in the wake of its decisions favoring free expression, the Council has the unfortunate habit of emitting "doctrines" that are exhaustive lists of recommendations. For example, Council Doctrine Number 13 says investigative journalists must consult the greatest number of sources possible and must conduct the investigation without preconceived notions. Under such rules, the "60 Minutes" investigation depicted in the film "The Insider" could not have been made: The "60 Minutes" crew had a preconceived notion that cigarette maker Brown & Williamson lied when it said it didn't know nicotine was addictive—because every investigation begins with a hypothesis. Former B&W vice president Jeffrey Wigand was the only source consulted because his stature as a former vice president of B&W and as holder of a doctorate in chemistry made his comments newsworthy and worthy of a film.

While the Council circumscribes journalists' behavior, it has not proscribed the spiking of stories by management for business reasons or under duress of advertisers.[220] Nor does the Council emit doctrines against self-censorship. Although the Council prescribes appropriate methods for journalists to collect information, it does not advocate increased access to public or private-sector information. Journalism would be better served by lobbying for a larger pie instead of figuring how to slice it into ever-smaller pieces.

In its 77 findings (1993–1999), the Council has not considered the following: self-censorship; conflicts of interest between a medium and its owner's other businesses; or the interference by the medium's commercial side. More succinctly, the Council has not challenged the restrictions placed on reporting by the state or the private sector. Although the medium is the party named in the complaint and it is the medium that is reprimanded, only the journalists' behavior is considered, never the behavior of management.

Asked why this is so, the Council chairman, Arturo Fontaine Aldunate, a former managing editor of *El Mercurio*, said the Council is "as 'establishment' as you can imagine." "It is a group of journalists and lawyers trying to improve the news [business] within the existing system. We can't be the media's moral oversight board," Fontaine said. "What right do we have when we are appointed by the media themselves?" When reminded that the World Soccer Federation has the power to fine not only players but owners as well, Fontaine responded: "You ask some very controversial questions."[221]

The Council has taken up complaints defending the honor of two dead men (one sustained, one denied) and the complaint of a magician against a journalist who revealed the secrets of his trade. (The Council found in favor of the journalist.)

The second ethics board is under the auspices of the College of Journalists. College membership was obligatory for working journalists through the 1960s under a law that was rescinded during the dictatorship. The 2001 Press Law reinstated obligatory membership only for public sector journalists. So, in the private sector, the College may impose its standards only upon those choosing to be members. It does so through regional ethics boards whose findings may be appealed to the national Ethics Tribunal. The Tribunal issues findings on any case brought before it, whether or not a member is involved, giving the College a forum in which to opine on the practice of journalism. The College has only once sanctioned a government official between 1998 and 2000—a member of the College serving as a presidential press officer. Her six-month suspension from College membership in no way affected her employment status.[222]

Unlike the Ethics Council, College tribunal findings in general sought to defend and expand the exercise of journalism rather than further restrict freedom of expression by encumbering journalists with additional rules. However, the jurisdiction of the College means that its rulings have little or no bearing on management decisions.

One more oversight body controls the news media from the public sector. The 1980 Constitution originally called for a National Television and Radio

Council, but its oversight was restricted to television in 1989. That's the good news.

The bad news is that the Supreme Court expanded Consejo Nacional de Televisión's (CNTV) regulatory mandate to include cable transmissions in 1995. This, despite the fact that the legal basis for government regulation of television and radio is the use of a public asset, the electromagnetic spectrum. However, the Supreme Court ignored this legal theory to shoehorn cable transmissions into CNTV's oversight.

Chile's president appoints CNTV's chair and nominates others for approval as a slate by the Senate. The president must name a slate that represents an acceptable compromise to all political parties. Such a process politicizes the appointments, converting CNTV into a forum for political posturing. The meetings can be rancorous.[223]

CNTV must penalize stations for violating any of 14 standards, including: the family, honor, cultural values, peace, democracy, pluralism, and protection of the environment as well as the spiritual and intellectual development of young people. Television is one of the few institutions where pluralism, democracy, or environmental protection are mandated. Likewise, CNTV is one of the few state institutions that invites public participation, here, in the form of viewer comments on programming. However, public oversight has the effect of *restricting* freedom of expression rather than expanding it: Because the public is not as likely to complain about images that are not shown, they will complain about things that are. For example, viewers are not likely to lodge a complaint because a banned film was *not* shown.

Film censorship

A year after the 1973 coup, the military began vetting films until the Cinema Classification Council (CCC) was established in 1975. The 1980 Constitution granted the CCC the power to censor films. In all, some 600 films were banned in Chile. However, because all of the films and videos entering the country needed to be viewed and classified at the owners' expense, it is impossible to say how many films were not evaluated by CCC because distributors had not found this cost effective for a country of 15 million. Naturally, many of the films not shown are of journalistic significance, such as "La batalla de Chile," "La tierra prometida," or any documentary presented to the censors that mentions "the disappeared." CCC banned "Day of the Jackal" and "Fiddler on the Roof," while allowing broadsides against authoritarianism such as "The Conformist" or "One Flew over the Cuckoo's Nest."

The CCC's days of censorship were numbered once the Organization of American States (OAS) Human Rights Court found in 2001 that Chile violated the charter by banning "The Last Temptation of Christ." Early that year, when former presidential candidate Alejandro Hales was asked why he voted as he did a decade earlier, he answered: "Because the Church asked me for it and I did it because of the work they had done for human rights."[224]

Hales presided over the bar association during the dictatorship and beat the drum for the publication of the "Truth and Reconciliation Commission" human rights report. Yet, Hales viewed human rights as bargaining chips. Hales's deal with the Church can be read thusly: Because the Church spoke out against repression during the dictatorship, we will compensate it by directing the state to violate the human rights of other Chileans who would like to participate in a free exchange of ideas with which the Church disagrees.

Therefore, a note of caution is in order before we begin the final section of this chapter: While Chile's legal and ethical frameworks are indeed written down, they are not written in stone. In Chile, one gets away with what one can, by circumventing the desire of the Church and state to set boundaries laid down not along any universally-applied principles, but which are set by political expediency and a tendency among the people in power to take it upon themselves to tell other Chileans what is good for them. One of the primary victims is the press. This tendency means that Chile's state-owned media are politicized. However, the structure of Televisión Nacional makes it the most pluralistic medium—and the most watched.

State-owned media

I disapprove of what you say, but I will defend to the death your right to say it.

— Voltaire[225]

The University of Chile, home of Chile's first journalism school, was a shadow of its former self when the military turned it over. Budget cuts and the spinoff of its regional campuses had reduced its weight within the university system. However, the return to democracy did not mean a return of the Universidad de Chile's former status. Apparently, the Concertación decided that demanding restoration of university property would have caused waves within what was to be a government of consensus.[226] The new rector sold off the university's Channel 11 to defray the cost of repairing 16 years of abuse.

Finance Minister Sergio de Castro had slashed fiscal expenditures from 1.2 percent of gross domestic product to 0.5 percent (a 68 percent drop), and university spending dropped from the 1974 level of 6.3 percent of the national budget to 2.2 percent—a 65 percent drop. However, those numbers do not describe the total impact. Cuts came by firing 130 public university professors, many of these leaders of their professional association. Much of the budget was redirected toward research centers and away from students. One military rector spent scarce resources on a car for his secretary and for office decorations.[227]

The university's Channel 11 had a $23 million debt by 1983. "[I]n spite of financial problems, the corporation proceeded to raise salaries of executives and talent, to give away goods swapped for advertising for personal benefit of its staff, and to direct funds to the payment of activities different from its mission," according to the General Comptroller's office.[228] With a negative cash flow, Channel 11 could not produce or purchase the top shows. Ratings fell.

The Chicago Boys cut subsidies for their *alma mater*, Catholic University, by only by three percent. Catholic University kept its television station and rating. While generals ran Chile's other networks, Channel 13 was trusted to run its own affairs under the Opus Dei management of Eliodoro Rodríguez. This modicum of independence gave it the lion's share of rating over Televisión Nacional Channel 7 (TVN).

TVN was deeply in debt by 1990, the result of martial pilfering and princely salaries paid to intelligence agents who posed as reporters. Rightist congressmen wanted to sell TVN, an SOE that the Concertación would control once democracy was restored. The Concertación wanted TVN to remain an SOE. The right agreed to a one-time debt-relief package in exchange for promises that the military's accounting procedures would not be questioned and that TVN would become self-sufficient. The latter meant that content would be dictated by viewers and ratings, not the Concertación. In addition, the CNTV board's Senate approval assured that it would not favor the Concertación.

TVN had an enormous challenge. First, it had to rationalize its bloated structure. Then, it had to find an audience among viewers whose tastes were virtually unknown and untested, because television was in its infancy in 1973. Advertisers of Chile's oligarchy balked at having their products associated with the incoming government. The news operation had to contend not only with Chile's hypersensitive and litigious politicians but also with a television advisory board that took up the partisan battles internally. TVN director Jorge Navarrete applied the Concertación's idea of "government by consensus" to board decisions rather than submit matters to a vote. TVN's coverage, then, tended toward that which would least offend the greatest number of politicians.

The result was one that neither the right nor the left expected. TVN unsullied its reputation as the talking head of the dictatorship. And, because TVN was balanced in its reporting and inclusive in its entertainment, by the century's end it had surpassed dominant Channel 13's ratings during the evening news and prime time entertainment, and soon thereafter trounced it in advertising revenue.[229]

Some were disappointed that the Concertación had failed to claim a medium as its own. However, the complex deal likely saved the Concertación from itself. Without the discipline imposed by the right, parties associated with labor might not have found the courage to slash salaries. And, in the rush to promote the ideas of the left so as to counterbalance the rightist message in private-sector television, TVN would not have shaken its image as the voice of the government in power. Instead, the imposed dedication to balance through the board structure made possible what no other medium had the discipline to put on the air: a truly balanced offering. TVN's corporate advertising campaign became: "The Medium for All Chileans."

Because Chilean tradition made the media the mouthpieces for their owners, it took an SOE to create a pluralistic medium. Left to its own devices, neither the state nor the private sector—free market or no—had shown itself capable of achieving a balanced or pluralistic news medium due to a flawed social and professional understanding of what constitutes journalism in a democratic society. The state-owned newspaper is a sad example of what could have happened to TVN.

See Figures 2.1 and 2.2.

Figure 2.1
Profits and Losses

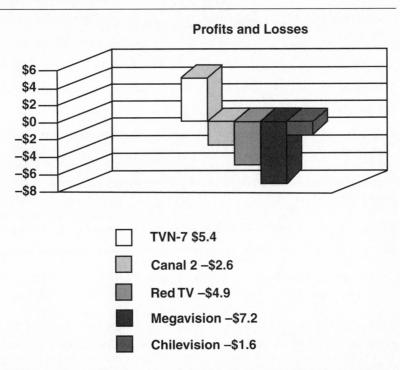

Source: Televisión Nacional 1999

Figure 2.2
Q3 1999 Network Rating

Ratings of News Shows

points

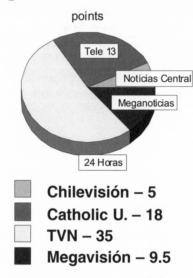

Tele 13

Noticias Central

Meganoticias

24 Horas

▨ **Chilevisión – 5**
■ **Catholic U. – 18**
☐ **TVN – 35**
■ **Megavisión – 9.5**

La Nación

La Nación faced the challenge of democracy from the same starting point as TVN—as an SOE with a pro-Pinochet reputation—but with the benefit of not having to make ends meet. It is subsidized by *El Diario Oficial*, with its monopoly over the publication of laws, regulations, and certain private-sector announcements.

The government's 70 percent stake gives the incumbent administration effective power to name the paper's managers. True to Chile's history of politicians who rush to control media, the Concertación appointed editors whom they could trust to promote their interests.

That became an obvious problem during the 1999 presidential election campaign, which began to look like the first one that the Concertación might lose. The promotion of candidate Lagos became an occupational imperative for the editors of *La Nación*, who soon made it the most biased among the Santiago dailies. That didn't escape the watchful eye of the opposition, which argued that the government had no business supporting one candidate over another.

La Nación responded in an editorial run under a familiar epigraph: "I disapprove of what you say, but I will defend to the death your right to say it." The column defended the editorial decision to "inform an audience ... that is not being adequately served by other communications media."[230] That statement alludes to the *concentration of the media*: Because the right owned most of the other media, *La Nación* felt justified doing what it could to tip public opinion toward the boss's favorite candidate. That is what the Chilean media do, that is what *La Nación* has always done, and, in fact, that is what *La Nación* was founded to do.

The editorial continued: "[The press] should not merely inform but should also attempt to subject such information to an editorial policy that seeks a balance between its own interests as an enterprise and those of the reader." This statement is unusual even when compared with dictatorship-era propaganda, which typically justified state policies as being "good for you." *La Nación* said that its interests were *different* from yours and it would try to find a balance between the two. It quoted Voltaire to justify its right to say what *it* wants to say in its corporate interest, not the readers'.

However, the editorial does not explain why Journalistic Enterprise La Nación Inc. has an interest in one candidate over another. Because neither candidate promised to privatize *La Nación* or cut its subsidy, the only entity threatened by the outcome of the election is the apparatchik who wrote the editorial. (Readers would not be affected, because a mere 20,000 bother to purchase the newspaper.) In light of the success at TVN, *La Nación* failed to get the message that its interest "as an enterprise" rested in *rejecting* partisanship. It could have raised its credibility (and maybe its circulation) by remaining nonpartisan.

In Europe and Canada, SOEs such as Radio France, the BBC, and the Canadian Broadcasting Corporation maintain balance because of the existence of a set of industry-wide journalistic standards combined with structures that insulate journalists from their employers. Furthermore, their publics' expectations are such that if this independence did not exist, the SOEs would lose audience share. These media often enjoy *more* independence, especially from their government/owners, and are frequently tougher on politicians than are the commercial media. One Radio France journalist deals with whining politicians in the following manner: "I tell the politicians: 'I will be here four years from now. *You* will not be here four years from now.'"

La Nación editors lack such independence because they are political appointees. If the Concertación wanted to save *La Nación*, it should have let citizens nominate an independent board or at least copy the TVN formula. The other missing piece is the public's expectations. Chilean audiences judge news reporting as to whether it promotes some combination of their own politics, religious philosophy, and economic interests. Chileans consume the news product that most closely matches their tastes. The European or Canadian media mentioned previously retain their listeners because the media and their audiences have closely matching expectations when it comes to balance, fairness, and pluralism. Chileans are not motivated to watch TVN because it meets their expectations of a more balanced news source. Chilean news consumers largely do not demand balance (fairness, "objectivity," and so forth) because they do not understand its value.

So, why, then, have Chileans made TVN the most-watched channel? The answer is not that it is more balanced from a politician's point of view, although it is. The answer is that it is more pluralistic from a citizen's point of view. If you tally up all the Chileans who feel that they and their ideas are excluded from the private sector media (as we see in the following chapter, this is a large proportion), you have a large potential audience. Viewers choose TVN for the same reason that wealthy readers of the right choose *El Mercurio* or Catholic University's Channel 13: They see themselves and their values represented there.

In the absence of a societal consensus of pluralism and tolerance ("I disapprove of what you say, but I will defend to the death your right to say it"), what fills that vacuum is the promotion of the owners' own interests. If the editors of the state-owned newspaper have such a mistaken understanding of the principles that make journalism work, reporters, citizens, or politicians cannot be expected to internalize the rules of pluralistic free speech. Balanced expression is a principle that everyone must value—all of the time, whether it suits you at the moment or not. That is the only guarantee that it will be there when *you* need it. That is what Voltaire meant.

This chapter has shown that the Chilean business community has been successful at promoting the private sector as the alternative to the increasing power of Christian Democracy, Communism, and Socialism in the second half of the 20th century. The military, the *gremialistas,* the Chicago Boys, and the Edwards combine spearheaded this reconstruction that took 16 years. Once and future Edwards executives filled more ministerial appointments in Pinochet's cabinets than either the Carabineros or the Air Force. While the number of once and future Edwards combine executives was surpassed by the Army, Navy, *gremialistas,* and Chicago Boys, the combine provided even more cabinet personnel than did Chile's business associations.[231] See Table 2.2.

Not only does the notion of private-sector predominance meld with the economic philosophy of the Chicago Boys and the "subsidiarity" of the *gremialistas,* but it also gives the private sector the opportunity to control the news media and ethics boards to pursue its own goals much to the exclusion of others'. While the state is the entity that we would least want to monopolize the news, a private-sector monopoly does not guarantee pluralism, as illustrated in the next chapter.

The Concertación hurriedly accepted a return to a protected, authoritarian democracy under which it tamed the press, smoothed Pinochet's feathers,

Table 2.2
The Men of the Edwards combine who served the Pinochet government

	Edwards link	Military Government Position	Post-Military
Sergio de Castro CB	The Brick author, Banco A. Edwards board, *Qué Pasa* economy writer	Economy Minister, Finance Minister	A. Edwards assistant, D: Banco A. Edwards, D: Lo Castillo, Copesa, Finis Terrae University
Fernando Léniz	*El Mercurio* General Manager	Economy Minister, University of Chile	Angelini executive, Fundación Siglo XXI (Büchi), P: Corma
Alvaro Bardón CB	The Brick author, *EM* economy writer, *EM* editorial writer	P: Central Bank, P: State Bank	*EM* editorial writer, Universidad Finis Terrae
Emilio Sanfuentes Vergara CB	The Brick author, *Qué Pasa* founder, *EM* economics page writer	Monday luncheons, Minister Foreign Relations	Deceased
Hermán Cubillos Salato	P: Lord Cochrane	Monday luncheons, Minister Foreign Relations	Consulting, Deceased
Jorge Ross Ossa	VP: Banco A. Edwards	Monday luncheons, President CRAV	Business
Orlando Sáenz	CCU board, P: SOFOFA	Monday luncheons, Foreign Relations Minister	Consulting
Enrique Montero Marx	Private law practice	Sub-Secretary Interior, Interior Minister, Auditor General Air Force	*EM* editorial board, Lawyer EMSAP, Lawyer Edwards companies
Roberto Kelly	Edwards poultry farm	Minister of Planning	P: Banco de Trabajo
Miguel Alex Schweitzer Walters	*EM* lawyer	Ambassador to Great Britain, Foreign Minister, Consejero del Estado	*EM* lawyer, Pinochet lawyer, UDI
Miguel Schweitzer Speisky	*EM* lawyer	Minister Justice	Deceased
Cristián Zegers CB	Editor in Chief *El Sur, Portada, Qué Pasa*, Editor *EM* Sunday magazine	Managing Editor *EM*	Editor in Chief *La Segunda*
Juan Villarzú Rhode CB	The Brick author	Central Bank, Budget Director, VP: Inversiones Sud Americano	Banco de Concepción board, Codelco

Table 2.2
(continued)

	Edwards link	Military Government Position	Post-Military
Arturo Fontaine Aldunante	Editor in Chief *EM*	Ambassador to Argentina	Universidad Santo Tomás, Ethics council
Hernán Felipe Errázuriz		P: Central Bank, Ambassador to United States, Minister of Mining, Communications Minister	*EM* editorial board, Pinochet attorney
Alvaro Puga Cappa	*Las Ultimas Noticias*, Radio Agricultura, *La Segunda* columnist "Alexis"	Civilian advisor to junta	
Andrés Passicot	*EM* economics writer	VP: Banco del Estado (fired '88), Instituto National Estadística, Economy Minister	*EM* editorial board, *EM* economics writer
Hernán Büchi Buc		Minister Odeplan, Finance Minister	Copesa
Miguel Angel Poduje Sapiaian		Housing Minister	Copesa, Ecsa
Gonzálo Vial	*Portada, QP*	Education Minister, Finance Minister	*Ercilla* editorial board, U. Finis Terrae
Jaime Guzmán	*QP* editorial board	Constitution 1980	Deceased
Sergio de la Cuadra Fabrés		Finance Minister, P: Central Bank, D: Banco de Chile	Paula (Editora de Publicaciones)
René Silva Espejo	*EM* editorial writer		Deceased
Hermógenes Pérez de Arce CB	Editorial page editor *EM*	SNA, Radio Mineria commentary, Editor *La Segunda*	*EM* editorial columnist
Alvaro Saieh Bendeck CB	United Nations	Head Economics Division, Central Bank	Banco Osomo, Copesa
Carlos Cáceres		P: Central Bank, Finance Minister, Constitutional committee	Paz Ciudadana
José Eduardo Folch			Edwards private secretary, *EM* editorial writer
Alfonso Márquez de la Plata	Ex-director SNA	Agriculture Minister	*EM* agro magazine
Carlos Urenda Zegers	Edwards corporate lawyer, also CRAV	"Comisión Urenda"	Headed *EM* team to renegotiate debt

96

Joaquín Lavín CB	Economy editor, *EM*	Odeplan, dean Universidad de Concepción	Economy and business section editor, *EM*
Juan Pablo Illanes		Health Ministry	*EM* science editor, *EM* managing editor
Mauricio Poisson Eastman		Navy Chief of Staff	*EM* editorial board
Juan Carlos Dörr	*EM* lawyer	"Bustamante" University reform commission	Finis Terrae
Jovino Novoa	*EM* Asst. Managing Editor, "The Week In Politics" writer	Communications undersecretary	UDI Senator
Francisco José Folch		"Bustamante" University reform commission	*El Mercurio* editorial board, Paz Ciudadana
Ricardo Claro	Metropolis-Intercom	Special Envoy to China, OAS meeting in Santiago (offered ambassadorship to United States)	Megavisión, Metropolis-Intercom

P: President

VP: Vice President

D: Board of Directors

CB = Chicago Boy

EM = El Mercurio

QP = Qué Pasa

A. Edwards = Agustín Edwards

B. Edwards = Banco A. Edwards

Communications Minister = Ministro Secretario General de Gobierno

downplayed the cause of human rights, and disbanded the grass-roots organizations that impelled the heady participatory democracy of the 1960s,
which challenged Chile's elite. The following chapter shows how this power
shift to the private sector has affected the press.

Chapter 3

The News Media and the Private Sector

[I]n fact, Christ was not the son of a poor carpenter; Joseph was a *tekon* (which means architect as well as builder-investor) and the Wise Men praised the Christ child not in a stable but in Joseph's house ... For the Jews, Jesus was essentially a prince of royal blood.

— *El Mercurio,* July 19, 1980

In *El Mercurio's* gritty downtown offices, receptionists take walk-in orders for subscriptions and classifieds on the first floor. A few reporters who cover the government, such as Mario Parada, work out of the editorial offices on the second floor of the building, which is near the presidential palace. Parada is handsome in a way that goes with a starched white shirt, and he greets me like a young man who is going places.

I had requested an interview with him because he had reported on a labor reform bill that had been killed in the Senate. The bill's main provisions would have extended the initial period during which a striker could not be fired, from 15 to 30 days; it would have required companies to provide bargaining information to their unions; and it would have permitted pattern bargaining across an entire industry, as auto workers do in the United States.

That *El Mercurio* had opposed the bill was not surprising. What I wanted to know was how, in 41 articles published, *El Mercurio* quoted union officials just four times in more than 1,000 inches of copy and quoted working people not at all.

Parada slid a copy of an *El Mercurio* editorial across the table and said: "Perhaps you will find the reason here." *El Mercurio* gave the following four reasons for opposing the legislation:

• Reason #1: It was a ploy for garnering votes. The Concertación's presidential candidate, Socialist Ricardo Lagos, was losing his comfortable margin over rightist Joaquín Lavín. Concertación President Eduardo Frei had left the bill to languish in committee for nearly his entire term. However, just a month before election time, he dusted it off and marked it for immediate action by Congress (as he is allowed to do by the Constitution). Putting the right in the position of voting the bill down would throw votes Lagos's way.

• Reason #2, says *El Mercurio*: "Chile hasn't had any important labor problems in the private sector since the previous modification [of the labor law]."

• Reason #3: "The world is evolving toward more self-employment, out-sourcing, and a more direct, personal relationship between those seeking work and individuals endowed with more human capital."

• Reason #4. "The classic business of socialism's peak era is disappearing and the large unions of uneducated workers [*obreros sin educación*] are declining in numbers and militancy."[232]

I asked Parada why he felt this editorial should govern his coverage. Doesn't *El Mercurio*'s policy require that the news pages be independent from editorial opinion? "There is an editorial line that you can't ignore," he said.

Doesn't the editor ask you to be objective? "'Objectivity' is the word that's least used around here," said Parada. "The idea is to be as balanced as possible, but news should agree with the medium's editorial line. The radical difference between opinion and news gets narrower all the time."[233]

El Mercurio sticks to the shopworn formula of placing reporters on the street who collect information for inside news writers. I asked if this system creates an ideological filter between what is reported and what is printed. "It could be that the person who puts the final thing together gets instructions," he said.

Had he, perhaps, included a quote with a union official or a worker that was edited out? "No," he said, "You get to know what's most important to the paper. I can figure that the opinion of the CUT is not what's important; it's the president of the manufacturers' association [whose opinion is important]." Anyway, he said, *El Mercurio* had published the opinions of the Central Unica de Trabajadores (CUT, Chile's AFL-CIO) on similar matters some weeks before the legislation was returned to the floor of Congress.

Parada said that when he went to union headquarters, the CUT directors were not forthcoming, did not have clear positions on the labor reform bill, and repeated themselves so he gave up. (Former CUT public relations people confirmed this, saying the confederation's famous reticence had been exacerbated by the fact that the current CUT directors were sitting on a lame duck board.)

Why, then, had he not hit the streets to ask individual workers what they thought of the bill? "That's a good question," he said. "It's difficult for us, perhaps because of the type of newspaper we are, to talk to regular people." Parada recalled that the paper *had* spoken to regular people about the use of child labor at a supermarket chain. (*El Mercurio* and the people it interviewed supported it.) And, they had asked regular people about mass transit problems. (Indeed, only regular people ride the bus.) He could not recall other times he had interviewed working-class people.

Had journalists proposed any stories about working people in news meetings? He thought so, but that the editors had lost interest. He repeated that it is hard to talk to workers. (Remember: His beat is labor.) The other difficulty is that readers are accustomed to stories that quote known sources, so he tries to interview someone with a high profile.

I commented that other journalists complain about editors who dictate the sources that a journalist is to consult and that these sources frequently share the newspaper's point of view. "I think that happens in all the media. You do what's assigned. If you are assigned to talk with so-and-so, you talk with so-and-so. That's the owner's privilege," said Parada, although he believes it should not be that way. "If I were an editor, the last thing I'd want is for the reporter to do what I asked."[234]

This interchange illustrates two sets of problems. First, *El Mercurio's* editorial line perpetuates the class cleavages that have been the source of much strife historically in Chile. Second, the prevalence of those same class cleavages within *El Mercurio's* newsrooms results in a rigid management style that undermines journalistic initiative, diversity, and quality. Both of these problems may be subdivided into several problems, which we will deal with in turn later.

The perpetuation of class cleavages

The Chilean elite's disdain for manual labor and its opinions of working people are well-documented.[235] The landed aristocracy reacted, sometimes violently, against land reform and the growing union movement as far back as 1920. During the 1960s, the Chicago Boys heard their professor Friedrich von Hayek advocate the abolition of labor unions. Allende's revolution was met with 16 years of vengeful repression against workers, to the applause of Chile's elite.

In an attempt to be as objective as possible, I will avoid saying that Chile's newspapers should be more balanced. Maybe the business leaders really do have better-articulated opinions and maybe *El Mercurio's* readers don't care what the workers have to say. But, there is no denying that class divisions are the fault lines along which Chile's historical earthquakes have occurred. The news media could bring the sides toward understanding, rather than driving them apart.

However, Chile's polarization—exacerbated by *El Mercurio*—leaves no middle ground for a discussion of labor issues, just as there is no middle ground on, say, abortion. One of the few objective statements one can make about abortion is that if the pregnancy is avoided, there will be no abortion. In the same way, we can say that without the deep class cleavages in Chilean society, there would not have been a UP or a coup.

But there was. The dictatorship deepened these class divisions and made the hierarchical social structure more rigid.[236] These class differences are underscored by the increasing concentration of wealth resulting from the Chicago Boys policies.[237] Yet, the news media propagate the class tensions by excluding the majority of economic actors.

El Mercurio and other newspapers of the duopoly gave front page play to the leader of the business community who called the labor reform "worse than the Popular Unity" period, meaning that passage of the labor reform bill would return Chile to the conditions that led to the coup. No newspaper of the duopoly challenged the idea that extending the protection of strikers from 15 to 30 days was "worse" than the wholesale expropriation of industry and banking, and random violence on the left and right along the road to a dictatorship of the proletariat.

Compare this anti-labor bias with media in the United States, which are more conservative than the media in Europe. Even periodicals considered "conservative" (*The New York Times*) or "probusiness" (*Business Week*) track labor and social issues such as the concentration of wealth, quality of health care, public education, and social welfare in general. As of this writing, *The New York Times Magazine* is concerned about workers displaced by globalization. *Business Week* is on a campaign against sweatshops. How do Chile's newspapers stack up? During a year-long study period, August 1999–August 2000, Chile's newspapers of the duopoly ignored completely the topics of displaced workers, sweatshops, health, retirement, public education, the concentration of wealth, and social welfare systems as they affect working people.

However, the "peak" business associations received ample opportunity to put forth their arguments. *El Mercurio* telephoned Wall Street investors who expressed fears that passage of the labor reform bill would dissuade foreign investment. However, *El Mercurio* found it difficult to speak with the working people who crowded the streets in front of its downtown offices.

The labor reform bill

The following study compares Chile's three top-circulation newspapers plus the more pluralistic *El Metropolitano* in terms of the relative amount of importance each granted to various actors in the debate around the labor reform bill. The quantities represent the number of times any person was mentioned by name in a news article about the bill. Because each actor's name also is identified with some institution, we get an indication of the relative importance that the medium gives to the institution's opinion. This method avoids assessments as to whether the medium is publishing "positive" or "negative" stories. What is measured is whose opinions are included and whose opinions are left out. The period covered begins November 19, 1999, the day the bill was introduced, and ends after the bill was killed and newspaper commentary trailed off on December 12th. See Table 3.1.

Table 3.1

Coverage of Labor Reform Bill

		El Mercuio	La Tercera	La Cuarta	El Metropolitano
Number of mentions of:	Business leaders	55	48	12	23
	Labor leaders and workers	3	1	7	0
	Politicians	377	260	83	56
	Wall Street analysts	2	3	0	0
	Professors and economists	52	43	0	6
Op-eds written by:	Business	2	1	0	0
	Labor	0	0	0	0
Interviews with:	Business leaders	3	1	0	0
	Labor leaders	0	0	0	0
Total column/inches:		1069	1538	381	530
Total number of articles, sidebars, etc.		41	46	19	13

Study conducted by the author and Marcela Nagel.

The purloined letter

The newspapers did not use photographs of working people during the labor reform story with one exception. Leaders of Chile's major unions were on their way to a meeting with Labor Minister Hermán Molina, most with sport coats, neckties, and briefcases. One of them carried a letter for the minister. As they walked toward the ministry, television footage showed no aggression on the part of the labor leaders before police turned them back with water canons and night sticks. The interior minister publicly called the Carabineros on the carpet for this treatment, facts that were not mentioned in the newspapers.

Lost in the *mêlée* was the content of the letter. *El Mercurio* did not disclose it nor did any other major print medium. The public may never know what labor wanted to say to the minister. *El Mercurio*'s editorial policy is that whatever labor leaders have to say is not important. However, associating them with violence is a worthwhile criterion for inclusion.

La Tercera also published a photo of the shoving match on December 1, 1999, with a Carabinero on the ground looking for all the world like the victim. The only mention of a worker or labor leader's name in *La Tercera* during the entire labor reform debate was the photo caption of this shoving match, which named the president of the CUT.

El Mercurio and *La Tercera* refuse to include common people in their coverage unless violence is involved. This phenomenon is common to Chile's news media, occasioning Chilevisión news anchor Alejandro Guillier to comment that a regular person does not have much of a chance of appearing in the news unless he is either the victim or perpetrator of a violent act.[238] Expressed another way: The newspapers denied working people any verbal expression of their choosing during the entire labor reform debate. The expressions that were communicated were limited to photographic representations of working people in circumstances that they neither chose nor controlled. Although the communication at the heart of the matter (the letter) was committed to writing, was a message the workers desired to communicate, and whose message could have been communicated whether or not the workers were "available," the newspapers chose to associate working people with violence.

Workers with class

After the study period ended on December 12th, *El Mercurio* published a travel section with three feature-length articles accompanied by large color photographs of working people performing interesting jobs in remote parts of Chile. The "*Visión Nacional*" section appeared each Wednesday and sold advertising space primarily to the travel industry. The December 29, 1999 section featured a story on a man who holds a record for shearing sheep in the south. On page 3 is the story of the mechanic who maintains the public elevators that climb the steep urban cliffs in Valparaíso. A third article checks up on how people laid off 30 years ago in the phosphate mines have made a go at tourism. These sound like the high-carbohydrate filler for most newspapers, but they are rare stuff in *El Mercurio*.

I called *El Mercurio*'s editor of the section and asked why in one day his section had carried more stories about working people than the rest of *El Mercurio* had in a year. He answered that the section is written by freelancers in various cities in Chile. This editor simply commissioned the articles without the writer having to propose them at a news meeting.[239] This squares with Parada's observation that while writers may have story ideas that feature working people, they are simply afraid to suggest them. Because freelancers don't participate in the morning news meetings where such ideas may be shot down, they don't know any better.

El Mercurio editorial board member Tomás Mac Hale admitted that having no specialized labor writers is a shortcoming of the newspaper. But how can *El Mercurio* justify its exclusion of labor and the working class? "We don't have many working-class readers," said Mac Hale.[240]

The paper's managing editor until 1982 confirmed Mac Hale's understanding: "*El Mercurio* has never had contact with regular people [*gente popular*], [or] the homemaker," said Arturo Fontaine Aldunate. "*El Mercurio* has stuck with the traditional sources [of information]: the president, [military] commanders, the president of the association of engineers, the economy and finance ministers."[241]

Steering clear of the working class meant that *El Mercurio* could claim ignorance about human rights violations during the dictatorship. "We had little information—from any part of the country. It really was a surprise [to learn about the repression]. Everyone knew there was violence but people were so up in arms after Allende that the well-off didn't want to hear about it," said Fontaine.

Mac Hale says Fontaine is being disingenuous: "My office was right next to his. He can't say he didn't know. He was the best-informed person in Chile."[242] Editorial writer Alvaro Bardón adds: "*El Mercurio* didn't divulge what it knew about the violations of human rights."[243]

El Metropolitano *and labor*

Hardly a leftist publication, *El Metropolitano* is the only daily that published "public service" articles of concern to working people during the period of August 1999 to August 2000. *El Metropolitano* prints regular features on industrial health and safety. Moreover, *El Metropolitano* exposed the continued use of asbestos in cement despite a March 1999 ban. The article quotes an environmentalist and labor leaders.[244]

El Metropolitano gave the 1999 labor reform bill a more balanced treatment, publishing side-by-side pro-and-con analyses from labor and business perspectives. However, *El Metropolitano* quoted even fewer actual labor leaders or working people than *El Mercurio* or *La Tercera*. Any prolabor messages carried by *El Metropolitano* were delivered by politicians, economists, or other experts.

La Tercera *and labor*

Long before the end of 1999, labor leaders had given up on having their voices heard in *La Tercera*, which was once more open to varying opinions. Former CUT leader Diego Olivares published a labor column in *La Tercera* when it was owned by Radicals. Labor reporters on staff also had free rein.[245]

After the Chicago Boys-*gremialistas* purchase of *La Tercera*, Olivares's labor column became sporadic before being dropped entirely,[246] as were reporters specialized in labor coverage in both *La Tercera* and the working-class *La Cuarta,* which also is owned by the former Pinochet advisors.[247] The newspapers' coverage of the labor reform bill was so lopsided that it moved a former top-level editor to say, "It would have forced my resignation if I had still been there." The editor says those attitudes toward working people carry over into the newsroom, which he called "autocratic" and "antiquated" in their labor-management relations, which the following section is about.[248]

The school of hard knocks

Bárbara Patarrieu was an entertainment reporter at *La Tercera*, which is located in an industrial section of Santiago. We sat down for lunch at a working-class restaurant where she waved to a group of pressmen who were seated at the bar.

"I don't work for a news organization. I have that clear. I work for a business," she said as she pulled out a cigarette. "That's *not* what they teach you in journalism school." She still looks the part of a student, in jeans and a T-shirt. It was then I discovered Patarrieu had graduated from the Diego Portales University, the private school where I taught, but I had cold-called her because I had not interviewed a working entertainment writer.

Patarrieu complained that students at UDP and other journalism schools are trained to use their own judgement but are not warned about the real-world necessity of writing around possible conflicts with the owners' other investments or the dictates of advertisers. "It's not *La Tercera* and it's not the editors [that are the problem]. It's the system." Patarrieu squashed out her cigarette and said: "Hey, I'm resigned to this." Patarrieu was all of 26 years old. I asked her why she continued to practice journalism. "I'm getting experience— because one day there has to be a new medium in Chile," she said.[249]

Across the street, at the offices of *La Tercera*'s owner, Copesa, the sub-director of corporate research confirmed Patarrieu's version of how the conglomerate runs its newspapers. Ricardo Avello said that it is a constant battle because reporters are forever attempting to exercise independent judgement in the newsroom: "The journalists can't seem to understand that they are the suppliers [*fabricantes*]. Management tells them 'what' and they supply the 'how'." Failure to understand who's boss comes from poor training, said Avello. "I have the feeling that in Chile's journalism schools, they don't think this way; [They think] it's not the editor who makes the decisions."[250]

Avello is correct that students are not taught Copesa's standards. Perhaps if they were, they could better refute them. Journalism graduates I met—including past and current employees of *El Mercurio* and of Copesa's *La Tercera, La Cuarta,* and *Qué Pasa*—said their universities taught idealized versions of "how things should be."

Avello said what is newsworthy is not a newsroom decision. "A newspaper is a product that has to satisfy the public, but the people who know what the people want are management, not the journalists." Copesa is in business to make money, Avello said. That requires a more fluid relationship than the "firewall" between newsroom and management. As one example, he said advertising managers have the leeway to inform advertisers about upcoming negative stories so that they can pull their ads.

To avoid conflicts of interest, Avello said Copesa publications do not cover businesses that their owners are invested in. That sounds like a proper way to avoid beating their breasts, I said, but what if an owner's business is caught polluting? "You have to use common sense," he said. So, in lieu of a clear official policy, journalists engage in self-censorship.

The goal, said Avello, is to replace editors who think like journalists with editors who are administrators. "A traditional editor judges if the scoop is picked up in other media. But that's an intra-journalistic standard. It may not be what the people want to know about. That's the difference between the old style editor and administrative editors,"[251] said Avello. "Copesa is the height of the administrative editors." Although Avello and Patarrieu disagree about the merits of newsroom labor relations, they do not disagree on the facts.

The latifundio

Newsrooms are no different from other workplaces in Chile. They are authoritarian and plagued by the same class cleavages. Chilean journalists describe the newsroom as a *fundo*—short for *latifundio*—in which workers are expected to address the boss with the honorific *don*, meaning "sir." Hierarchical relations between landowners and hired hands or a disdain for industrial workers do not disappear when the actors are called "editors" and "reporters."

The result is a command and control model better suited for the factory floor than for the newsroom, preventing the reporter from using all her faculties. Said the former high-level manager at *La Tercera*: "The reporter gets firm direction, right down to indicating what sources to quote."

This assessment is seconded in a study of newsroom dynamics conducted by University of Chile journalism professors Rafael Otano and Guillermo

Sunkel, who conclude that reporters do not work well under those conditions: "[T]he frustration that has accumulated during the decade [of democracy] for lack of a pluralistic and free[ly practiced] journalism, is found to be associated with a weakening of the professional culture among journalists." The study shows that the hierarchical management style, the oversupply of graduating journalists in the labor market, and the lack of union representation or protective labor laws gives practicing journalists little job security, which promotes obedience.

Otano was a former managing editor of *APSI* and Sunkel sat on the National Television Council at the time the study was written, giving them both access to working journalists from various media. Reporters said: The journalist is treated as a professional neither in the way work is assigned nor in the way the work is treated; there is little of the give-and-take that could eventually increase the reporters' professionalism; reporters avoid trouble and risks through "pack journalism," avoiding controversial story proposals, hewing to the "official story," and by quoting the sources the boss prefers.[252]

The result is a cautious journalism that is not dynamic, engaging, interesting, or that supplies information a bourgeoning democracy needs for an informed public debate. The *fundo* newsroom is instrumental to the promotion of the media owners' interests and agenda, which we address later in this chapter.

Otano and Sunkel recommend that journalists press to include differing points of view and different stories than the news outlet is accustomed to carrying—in short, to go against the grain. Cast in these terms, the defense of journalistic standards becomes a labor *versus* management issue, placing journalism on the same court as any other labor-management relationship. The professors may be correct in that the only way journalists can improve standards is by flexing their muscles. But, first we must ask: What do journalists want the freedom to do? What are the criteria they wish to exercise?

The university system

Chilean journalists graduate without a clear concept of the role of the news media, making it difficult to defend their ideals. They are introduced to "objectivity" and given lessons in ethics. But most of them cannot cite Jefferson, Locke, or Rousseau to defend their points of view and ultimately, their independent judgement. If they cannot draw parallels or comparisons with the media outside Chile, the editor (who, as we have seen, may not understand Voltaire) is left with the impression that the reporter wants it her way "just because."

Journalism graduates do not have the technical skills to defend their independence, either. In brute terms, a good reporter can get away with a lot more than a poor one. Graduates who are not confident in their writing abilities or who have not internalized a set of journalistic standards are more easily intimidated—if for no other reason than they cannot count on finding another job. Students who cannot justify their use of background material can be more easily convinced that the inclusion of such material is an attempt to editorialize or falls outside the realm of "objectivity."

Lessons learned

Universities fall down on the job of preparing students for the following reasons:

Journalism teachers don't understand the standards. To their credit, Chilean journalism schools often hire journalists as professors. Some of those in their 50s were left unemployed by the closure of the "trench" periodicals. However, many of the generation of retired journalists now teaching began their trade before the first journalism school was established in 1953. Only two schools taught journalism from 1973 to 1982. Many professors lack the theoretical framework to teach effectively.

Professors don't distinguish between standards and ethics. Standards set the bar for quality journalism. Ethics proscribe behavior in the practice of journalism. If you will, standards are the positive form of promoting better journalism, while ethics is a limitation on getting too enthusiastic about it. In the previous chapter, we reviewed the dampening effect of the various ethics boards. Like the ethics boards, the universities' academic journals are more stick than carrot. Instead of goosing writers to higher levels, professors, editors, and the Constitution promote ethics and "responsibility."

Students face a bleak job market. A thousand students register in a score of journalism schools every year in Chile. Some 800 of these graduate. For them await between 50 and 100 job openings in journalism, depending upon who is doing the counting. In the past, most of these students wound up in public relations jobs.

Pay and benefits are poor. Bárbara Patarrieu started at $12,000, puts in 11-hour days and works one weekend out of every three. At that rate, she works 294 days a year, 3,240 hours per year, which when divided into the yearly salary is $3.70 an hour (minus 10 percent for retirement and 7 percent for health care leaves $3.07 take-home pay). If she reaches the top scale as a reporter ($16,000 a year) she will earn $5.19 an hour. *La Tercera* is a nationally-distributed, top-circulation newspaper.

Private universities have owners and patrons. Chile's top journalism schools are Catholic University and the University of Chile. Top private J-schools include the Diego Portales University, Finis Terrae University, and Andrés Bello University. Diego Portales is a nonprofit school funded by a secretive group of Masons. Finis Terrae and Andrés Bello include among their donors and shareholders the owners of Chile's media duopoly.

Private universities seldom consider media ownership as a factor in the practice of journalism in Chile. An examination of academic journals of the Diego Portales University, Catholic University, Los Andes University, and Finis Terrae University revealed no articles that examine media ownership as a factor in determining the news produced, although individual professors may take up the matter in the classroom. To the best of my knowledge, no private university has even done the research to determine just who are the owners of the news media and what their other holdings might be. The exception is the state-run University of Chile, which is independent of the financial and societal interconnections that influence private education in Chile.

University takeover

By some accounts, half of the public university professors and students were arrested or in hiding by the end of September 1973. Some of them were killed. Once in power, the military sought to control the universities that they felt posed a threat to the regime. The rectors were replaced by generals. This dovetailed with the *gremialista* call for depoliticizing universities. Guzmán saw to it that the ban on political meetings did not prevent *gremialistas* from building officially-sanctioned organizations of students during the dictatorship.[253]

While future Copesa investor Sergio de Castro was minister of finance, he slashed the public higher education budget by 43.3 percent and it would fall 33 percent more by 1983.[254] Public universities were forced to find alternative sources of funding beginning in 1981. Tuitions at the public universities were raised by a fourth, cutting out many of the poorer students.

Chicago Boy Alvaro Saieh was appointed vice-rector of the University of Chile in 1980. From that post, Saieh hived off the regional campuses from the main campus in Santiago with the help of Jorge Selume, Saieh's future business partner at the Banco Osorno. They were stopped in the attempt to subdivide the main campus into independent institutions by the university's rector, General Alejandro Medina Lois.[255] Former economy minister and former *El Mercurio* general manager Fernando Léniz joined the university governing board and contacted Selume about the possibility of carving the engineering department out of the university, "But that's as far as it went," said Léniz.[256] The journalism school was set up at a distance from the main campus.

Once Saieh's work was done, Pinochet appointed a university reform committee that included then-interior sub-minister Francisco José Folch (now on *El Mercurio*'s editorial board) and Banco A. Edwards director Juan Carlos Dörr. Pinochet used the committee recommendations as the basis for decreeing his 1981 Law of Universities, which allowed for the first time the establishment of private universities. Before the year's end, former Central Bank president, former economy minister, and the brick coauthor, Pablo Baraona, announced the founding of Finis Terrae University "in a Chilean, Christian,

Western tradition"—and with the direct influence of the Chicago Boys, including former *El Mercurio* economics page editor Adelio Pipino. Baraona announced that de Castro, Interior Minister Sergio Fernández, and then-undersecretary of justice, Francisco José Folch, would participate in the project, along with Justice Minister Mónica Madariaga[257] who redacted many of Pinochet's repressive laws as well as the decree naming him "Supreme Chief of the Nation"—ending the four-man *junta* and creating one-man rule in Chile.[258]

Finis Terrae opened several years later and today offers degrees in law, business, and journalism. It received capital from Chicago Boy and *piranha* Manuel Cruzat, and 50 percent of its shares are in the hands of the Legionnaires of Christ, a Catholic fundamentalist group similar to the Opus Dei. Board members include Agustín Edwards (*El Mercurio*) and Sergio Cardone (part owner of Radio Minería during the dictatorship). The Matte family of CMPC chipped in a plot of land.[259]

De Castro and Saieh went on to invest in Copesa together. *El Mercurio* operatives Alvaro Bardón, de Castro, and Léniz pitched in to teach at Finis Terrae University. *El Mercurio* editorial board member Bardón approved a $1 million loan to Finis Terrae while serving as president of the State Bank, the SOE that wrote the loan.[260]

Once Saieh had weakened the University of Chile, he founded a second competing private school, Andrés Bello University. It is now the largest of the private universities, with 11,000 students, of which a thousand are journalism students. Andrés Bello recently purchased Channel 22 Gran Santiago Televisión, putting it a step ahead of the University of Chile, which sold its television station to meet the obligations forced upon it under the dictatorship. "[Saieh] is one of the backers of the idea of building a great private university [system] in our country," said *Capital*.[261]

Andrés Bello's other owners include Miguel Angel Poduje, a *gremialista* and business partner of de Castro, along with Andrés Navarro and Jorge Selume, both fellow investors in the Banco Osorno when it was controlled by Saieh and Carlos Abumohor.[262] Poduje was a Pinochet minister of housing and of communications. He is today a shareholder in Copesa.

Where to look for answers

Chilean journalists agree that the state of their press is inadequate considering the demands of democracy. It also is out of line with other indicators of social development in which Chile usually tops the list of Latin American countries. However, there is great disagreement as to how it got that way, which is divided largely according to whether you are part of the journalistic establishment or not. With nearly all of the news media and a growing number of J-schools in the hands of the right, ownership is discarded as a factor contributing to the poor state of journalism. So, for those of the establishment, the whipping boys become the legal restrictions, or the journalists themselves.

Otano and Sunkel take the non-establishment point of view, blaming owners more than lazy journalists. The work culture, which should ideally be a supportive training experience for young journalists, has become instead a negative learning experience of downward-spiraling expectations. They say that journalists are *encouraged* to take the easy way out. If that means giving a press release a light edit and sending it to the composing room, that is what often happens. Editors permit reporters to rely on one-source stories, most frequently with a government official. Journalists do not get opposing opinions. Reporters rely far too heavily on anonymous sources.

Eduardo Arriagada, who runs the extension service of the mass communications department at Catholic University, agrees with Sunkel and Otano that news operations in Chile are run like a *fundo* and that the law may not be the most important pressure journalists face. "It's hard not to agree with nearly any criticism of our news media," said Arriagada.[263]

However, Arriagada takes the establishment's view of blame. "The responsibility for the weakness in the press falls fundamentally on the journalists themselves and their professional practices," Arriagada said, pointing especially to the practice of *coleguismo*. This term might be translated as "colleague-ism" were such practices permitted in English-language news operations. *Coleguismo* often happens when reporters form an informal pool and send one of their fellows to record an interview and share the tape afterwards. Or, one reporter with a scoop may share it with a friend at a competing paper, so no one has an exclusive.

When newspapers don't have scoops, they don't sell, argues Arriagada, which is why so many newspapers must throw prizes such as dictionaries and compact disks in with their subscriptions. "*Coleguismo* is … responsible for the fact that Chile's journalism is less developed than that of its neighbors."

For Arriagada, newsroom dynamics cannot be explained by the ownership of the news media. It is not the owners who encourage *coleguismo*, after all. If the owners had their way, journalists would produce more scoops. Instead, the problem stems from journalists' attempts to exercise independent judgement when they should be working toward the same objective. That objective may be a perceptible editorial line (*líneas de interés*), "which in many cases are reasonable and necessary decisions," said Arriagada. "If a medium defines its editorial policy, what we are faced with is not self-censorship but an exercise of freedom of expression."[264]

Arriagada says that journalists don't take the opportunity to develop story ideas with their editors in news meetings. Reporters simply mention what they plan to cover and then the meeting breaks a few minutes later without having further developed the story idea.

The next section provides a close-up of how the *fundo* newsroom works.

Life on the fundo

The editor in chief of *El Diario Austral de Temuco* invited me to do some consulting in order to assess why his reporters lacked aggressiveness. Iván Cienfuegos wanted greater depth and more investigative pieces, but he could not inspire his writers to go the extra mile. This flagship of *El Mercurio's* chain of four southern newspapers is in the city of Temuco, 10 hours' drive south of Santiago. It publishes a local issue for the city of Temuco as well as the national and international content it shares with its sister papers farther south, in Valdivia, Puerto Montt, and Osorno.

At the morning news meeting, reporters did not bounce ideas off of the managing editor, nor did the managing editor challenge them with ways to look for tension or controversy in their stories, to find an interesting angle, or to dig just a little deeper. The managing editor noted story ideas and reminded the writers to use the spell checker.

I caught reporters after the meeting to ask them why they didn't investigate or find other ways to inject tension into their stories. They said they assumed that *El Diario Austral de Temuco's* editorial policy was that of *El Mercurio* in Santiago. I assured them that the boss didn't want what was "safe." Instead, he wanted to give them their own heads, to take risks. The reporters were pleased to know that, but each said in a different way that if they published a controversial article that came to the attention of *El Mercurio* in Santiago, that would be the end of their young careers.

Improvisation

On another consulting task, this time at *El Diario Austral de Valdivia*, I learned how difficult it was to convince writers to stray outside their narrow version of "objectivity." During a week of workshops, I could not convince young journalists to include background material that put their articles in the context of recent events. Neither could I talk older, practiced journalists into including background information that tells the reader why a particular article is important. I argued that a writer has to answer the reader's perennial question: What does this article mean to *me*? However, the writers feared that anything beyond a recounting of the most immediate details was liable to be criticized by the public, the news maker—and even the editor. The journalists were cowed by legal restrictions over their work as well as informal pressures, not the least of which was the abominable *telefonazo*.

The journalists' salaries are poor and their equipment is poorer. They do not have Internet access. The photographers' film quota is one frame per interviewee. The managing editor feels that if he could improve quality, he could increase circulation. But as long as *El Diario Austral de Valdivia* holds a monopoly on display and classified advertising in the area, *El Mercurio's* chain will profit and will not need to attract more readers with better journalism.

I also suggested sending the journalists to conferences or classes as a way to improve quality, but there isn't a budget line for that. The managing editor says the journalists themselves should foot the bill. So, there is a standoff: *El Mercurio* doesn't want to invest in quality because it is content with its circulation and ad revenue. The journalists are frustrated with the newspaper because they don't have the infrastructure to get the job done, so they are not motivated to take money out of their pockets to invest in improving quality.

Stuck to the source

Another common problem is the assignment of beats. The division of labor is based on the structure of the government: A journalist assigned to cover economic matters covers the ministry of the economy, the court reporter deals with the justice ministry, and the armed forces reporter deals with the defense ministry. *El Mercurio* on-line editor Paulo Ramírez says this system is a vestige of the dictatorship. Then, Pinochet and his ministers were the *only* sources of news. When reporting was limited to picking up and publishing government decrees, consulting other opinions was out of the question. These beats made perfect sense.

Unfortunately, democracy did not alter the thinking of reporters or editors. "Chile has changed, but journalism has not," said Ramírez. "Journalists believe that the important thing is authority in general." Reporters' contact lists comprise government and party officials. This tendency to be *pegado a la fuente*, or "stuck to the source"—along with a fear of stepping outside the realm of "objectivity"—means that reporters seldom answer the hypothetical reader's question: What does this mean to *me*?

"What is important to regular people is much less developed," said Ramírez. Reporters simply repeat that there will be a 2 percent rise in the cost of health care, "But we [journalists] don't mediate a discussion of what a 2 percent rise in health care really means," said Ramírez. "We think our role is just to let each side have an equal say in the matter rather than to bring out its significance." He continued, "Chile could be a country where it's very easy or very difficult to do journalism. It's very easy if you just want to go through the motions. If you want to get to the bottom of things, it's difficult."[265]

While journalists may be guilty of laziness and *coleguismo*, it is hard to ignore structural obstacles to optimal newsroom performance if one has to explain why today's crop of journalists falls so far behind the gutsy journalists of the dictatorship. Media owners use Chile's hierarchical social structure within the newsroom to direct the flow of information in a way that suits the conservative upper classes. By way of comparison, a branch of journalism that is not so strictly vetted for economic, moral, or political content is sports. A quick look reveals greater depth, analysis, and commentary where appropriate, making the case that Chilean journalists can do the job if permitted.

The next section illustrates the difficulties of presenting what is important to "regular people" when there are economic interests at stake.

THE MAPUCHE QUESTION

El Mercurio must be a tribunal open to the national debate.

— *El Mercurio* editorial, January 6, 1970

The Mapuche Indians in the south of Chile harried the Spanish *Conquistadores* and helped turn Chile into the only crown colony that actually lost money. The Mapuche took heavy losses only initially from the Spanish muskets. Soon, they learned to attack during rainstorms when it was impossible to light the guns' fuses.

In 400 years of struggle, the Mapuche never actually surrendered to the Spanish. They still fight the Chilean and multinational forestry companies occupying the land that the Mapuche say is theirs. Some of this land was signed away by Mapuches under the influence of alcohol. Other land was traded for television sets under questionable circumstances.[266] Four centuries ago, Mapuche warriors attacked Spanish war horses. Today, they block the foresters' bulldozers. And, they hold press conferences.

In early 2000, they called a press conference at the Mapuche Center, an old house in the regional capital of Temuco in the midst of a particularly destructive campaign against forestry company property. Mapuche leader José Huenchuanao ignored the klieg lights and cameras, speaking directly to reporters. His voice was firm and level, like a student reciting a lesson he was tired of repeating: The Mapuche have always struggled to defend their lands, so don't expect us to give up now.

Huenchuanao faced the press flanked by a couple dozen Mapuche elders. They, too, told reporters to expect more of the same in the forests around Temuco. The trees, planted in oddly perfect rows, stretch over hilltops and valleys, covering two percent of Chile's available land. Every once in a while, you may see a black hole burned in the straight rows, some of it the work of the Mapuche. Huenchuanao says such destruction is the only way that the Mapuche get attention. Indeed, coverage of supposed Mapuche attacks give news programs ratings of 20 points and higher.[267]

El Mercurio did not give any coverage to this particular press conference, even though a correspondent from its regional newspaper, *El Diario Austral de Temuco*, published a story that was available at no additional cost to *El Mercurio* in Santiago. Instead, *El Mercurio* published a stringer's story that day from Temuco and gave it the headline, "200 Hectares of Forests Burn in Midst of Mapuche Area." Although paragraph six says "there is no certainty as to the causes of the fire," the Mapuche are at fault as far as *El Mercurio* is concerned. If the Mapuche were called for comment, the story does not say.[268]

The Mapuche press conference got the attention of the state-run National Television and Chilevisión, who sent their Temuco correspondents. Absent was Megavisión, whose owner, Ricardo Claro, has investments in the forestry industry. National newspapers did not pick up the story, either, because they have an interest in the newsprint that is produced in Chile.

Indian territory

If you get on the wrong side of the news conglomerates, you do not get any sympathetic press in Chile (see Table 3.2). In fact, during a six-month study, Chile's most serious newspaper printed only three articles that did not link the Mapuche to some act of violence. In 91 percent of its articles, *El Mercurio* had nothing to say about a million Mapuches except that they are a nuisance.

A typical *El Mercurio* article under the headline, "Unknown Suspects Burn Mininco Forestry House," ran on September 26, 1999 with the kicker: "It Is Assumed They Were Mapuches." In the copy, police say they won't accuse anyone because there were no witnesses. The spokesman for the forestry company that owns the property is quoted in the article as saying: "We don't know who burned the house." The only people who could have "assumed they were Mapuches" are the reporter, the editor, and the headline writer.

Only one article came to the defense of the Mapuche during the six-month study of the nationally-distributed newspapers, and it was published in *La Tercera* of January 28, 1999: *La Tercera* does not fully identify Ms. Quintremán (she is a Mapuche leader), but quotes her lawyer instead.[269] He levels charges of genocide at the builder of the Ralco hydroelectric dam—Endesa, a Spanish electric company—that will flood out Mapuche communities.

Things Spanish are targeted in the Chilean press for two reasons: Some Chileans are angry because the the Spanish invested heavily in the electrical supply and telephone systems. Also, because a Spanish judge, Baltasar Garzón, tried to extradite Pinochet to Spain to face human rights charges.

Table 3.2

Mapuche in the Chilean press
Articles August 25, 1999 to February 25, 2000

	El Mercurio		*La Tercera*	
	#	%	#	%
Articles associating Mapuche with illegal acts	7	20	14	58
Articles that judge or accuse Mapuche	24	70	10	42
Articles on Mapuche not associated with crime	3	9	0	0
TOTAL articles mentioning Mapuche	34		24	

Percentages do not total 100 due to rounding.

During the study period, the Mapuche did not get to air their grievances in the press unless they (or their lawyers) pointed an accusing finger at foreigners. The U.S. State Department's 1999 human rights round-up contained "harsh criticisms," said an article in *La Tercera*, which quoted the Chilean human rights advisor to the foreign ministry as saying that the accusations had not been "sufficiently investigated" by State, which failed "to recognize that there have been advances" in Chile. The advisor, Alejandro Salinas, is quoted as saying the State Department "left the impression that the situation was out of control." Even Mapuche leaders criticized the U.S. report, said *La Tercera*, because it left things out. Nowhere, however, does the paper mention whatever it was that the report actually said.[270]

While *El Mercurio* complained that Pinochet was being tried in the European press, there was nothing wrong with trying Mapuches in the press. On January 12, 2000, *La Tercera* condemned the Mapuche for killing one of their own under the headline "Mapuches kill Indian employee of Mininco." *El Mercurio* said that the killing was out of spite for the worker's "not having left his job despite warnings received over the last few months." Neither article makes use of the word "alleged," "accused," nor any similar disclaimer such as "police say." This is not simply a matter of *El Mercurio*'s style, because it only recently stopped referring to "supposed" victims of the Pinochet regime—even though the "Truth and Reconciliation" commission documented 1,185 cases among 3,197 total victims of human rights abuses during the dictatorship.

During the six-month study period, neither *El Mercurio* nor *La Tercera* addressed poverty among the Mapuche, who are twice as likely to live in extreme poverty as is the average Chilean.[271] In fact, *El Mercurio* did not run any articles on any positive aspect of Mapuche life, such as the bilingual, bicultural hospital staffed and run by the Mapuche, where physicians provide both Western and traditional forms of medicine. The article was available to *El Mercurio* on its internal story file at no cost, having already been published by *El Diario Austral de Temuco*, part of *El Mercurio*'s chain, in January of 2000. *El Mercurio* did, however, run an article on supposed corruption at that hospital. *La Tercera* also published an article on the hospital after the study period.[272]

It is beyond the scope of this book to "get to the bottom" of the conflict between the Mapuche and the forestry companies. Whether the Indians have the right to the land because they were there first or if Chile is better served by the loggers who use the land instead of letting it lie fallow is not our concern. This section only seeks to establish that: 1) there is an issue of sufficient public interest to merit news coverage, and 2) Chile's newspaper duopoly has taken a one-sided approach that does not take into account the viewpoints of the seven percent of citizens who are native peoples.

As for as the significance of the issue, *El Mercurio* called the Mapuche question President Lagos's "gravest conflict."[273] When there is conflict between groups of citizens that has resulted in the use of force (coercion on the part of the state and property damage on the part of citizens), which has only resulted in a stalemate, it behooves news organizations to supply information that can help bring the sides together.

However, in the duopoly's rush to treat the Mapuche as "the enemy," it missed the opportunity to distinguish between Mapuche of different organizations or locales, which vary widely. Many are peaceful. A few fight the forestry companies, while some are content with them. Nonetheless, news organizations simply refer to the group as "the Mapuche."

This treatment impedes an understanding of the problem. Historians say there never was a "Mapuche nation" as such. Instead, the 20 or so independent communities adopted different approaches to Spanish occupation. Today, each group has a different perspective and goals in the conflict. If there is one thing that the Mapuche and forestry supporters and detractors agree on, it is that *this aspect is precisely the factor that makes prospects for negotiated settlements difficult and winds up prolonging the conflict.* No matter whether one sides with the foresters, the Mapuche, or neither, this is significant information.

El Mercurio does give space to authors who revisit history to the detriment of the Mapuche. An op-ed column in *El Mercurio* lists the iron tools and other advances that the Spanish conquest brought the Indians:

Ideas such as good and evil, punishment and reward were introduced. Justice in place of vengeance, monogamy and the condemnation of homosexuality, which was a common practice, were all imposed with time.

An accompanying photograph of a reenactment of an Indian gathering ran with the caption: "The Indians of old were the principal actors [*protagonistas*] in their own domination."[274]

On another occasion, Sunday's *El Mercurio* gave a favorable review of a book by a Benedictine priest that claims to set the record straight about the slavery of Indians in colonial Chile. The review quotes a passage of the book that cites the writings of another clergyman:

Franciscan priest Antonio Sors recalls the sale of some Indians who live in captivity to labor in the homes of the Spanish. "They keep these little Indians so as to raise them like children and not as slaves, and since Christian piety is so compassionate with these miserable people, they are indoctrinated and taught the mysteries of our Holy Faith ... ."

The review reserves its criticism for the final paragraph:

Father Guarda doesn't ignore the hardships under the Spanish crown but also recalls another, perhaps unknown view: that of a humane Christian treatment—to the author's point of view—where the Catholic sacraments contributed to an atmosphere "of Christian charity" between two practically antagonistic cultures.[275]

Furthermore, *El Mercurio* dusts off Cold War language to give a reddish tint to the Mapuche. The article "Mapuches Justify All Forms of Struggle" (March 3, 2000) paraphrases Latin-American Marxist movements who justified a combination of armed struggle, class struggle, and electoral politics.

"Foreign Funding Divides Mapuches," (February 28, 2000) also echos the claims of Latin American oligarchies that *campesinos* were content on the *fundo* and rose up only when financed by Cuba or Russia. *El Mercurio* and *La Tercera* are constantly on the lookout for Mapuche bands that are "infiltrated" by "leftist extremists" or aging guerrillas who miss the smell of gunpowder.[276]

El Mercurio applies photographic techniques it learned during the Cold War. Juxtaposition of an image and an article creates an association in the mind of the reader—even if the two are unrelated. *El Mercurio* used this technique to associate Allende with unrelated pictures of violence as a prelude to the coup. Similarly, the article, "Mapuche Poverty is a Challenge for B. Belmar," is about the task facing the new housing vice minister as she works among the Mapuche. *El Mercurio* ran the article with a 23-day-old photo of a burnt-out pickup truck, which was connected to the housing issue only by its caption: "Episodes like this firebombing of three Mininco forestry guards … are of the sort that the future intendant of the region, Berta Belmar seeks to avoid."[277]—even though violence is not the primary concern of the housing ministry.

Self-inflicted wounds

That burned-out truck in the photograph had been hit with a Molotov cocktail in an ambush. One of the rangers, working for a private security firm, was burned seriously enough to require hospitalization. "Mapuche Ambush Leaves Three Wounded," said the February 20th *El Mercurio* headline—although police and company officials said in the article that it will be difficult to make any positive identification because the attack occurred at night and because the injured men only caught a glimpse of the attackers.

The paper's second-day article (February 21st) broke completely with *El Mercurio*'s normally sober tone, running a sensational headline that quoted one of the victims: "They Hit Me with a Stick when I Got out [of the truck] in Flames." The article was accompanied by color photographs of the burn victim. The guilty are described as members of the Mapuche community.

Two days later, *El Mercurio* buried the most significant of the stories about the ongoing conflict during the six-month study. Two forest rangers working for a private security company denounced their employer for ordering them to set forest fires so as to justify their continued presence. The story found its way to the front page of the February 23rd issue of *MTG*, a free newspaper previously known as *Metro* when it was given away to Santiago subway riders.

One of the guards was interviewed by all the national news networks that day including Meganoticias of Channel 9, whose owner, Ricardo Claro, has substantial forestry interests. The television networks broadcast second-day stories with reaction, including one on members of Congress who called for an investigation. It became the top story of the week.

The story was picked up by *La Tercera*—but two days later, on February 25th, with the curious headline: "Mapuche conflict: former forestry guards incriminate themselves for attacks." Although the guards themselves take the rap, this clever headline still allows the attack to qualify as "Mapuche conflict." The story was given no play in *El Diario Financiero*, a business daily in which Copesa holds a majority of the shares.

El Mercurio sneaked the story into an article on the last national news page headlined: "Indian Violence Causes Split among Mapuches," which led with an accusation that some Mapuche were beaten by other members of the community for refusing to participate in violent acts. (*El Mercurio* gives no source for that information.) An oblique, third-hand reference to the guards' story was buried in paragraph nine.

While other media covered a press conference by congressmen who lent credence to the security guards' story, *El Mercurio* published none of it. The February 25th forestry industry headline was "Rise in National Export Prices" for copper, fish meal, and forestry products.

Such obfuscation qualifies *El Mercurio* as "a bad newspaper," according to its former managing editor, Arturo Fontaine, who says the "mentality" at *El Mercurio* dictates that writers bury certain stories.[278]

Capital

A journalistic voice from beyond the *El Mercurio*-Copesa duopoly is a slick, four-color, pro-business magazine called *Capital*. An article in *Capital's* August 1999 issue looked at forestry through the eyes of Mininco's public relations manager but also interviewed three Mapuche: One works for Mininco and says he likes it; another says he wants to throw the foresters out; the third does not want to say either way.

Nearly every side gets to take a lick at the other in this article: The Mapuche say the foresters steal their land. The foresters say the Mapuche steal their wood. One Mapuche says that the Indians are being robbed of their culture. Another Mapuche says forestry jobs are more important than culture: "It is impossible to preserve the culture if there is nothing for the cook pot."

Why does this simple display of diverse opinions about an issue of public interest stand out so starkly from all the articles examined? "The duopoly is strange. It does not take the [composition of the] social fabric into account," said Héctor Soto, managing editor of *Capital*. "Chile is richer and more diverse than its press."[279] Why is *Capital* so different from other publications?

El Mercurio has historical ties to forestry. In the 1960s, the Edwards family controlled *El Mercurio*, Banco A. Edwards, and companies whose combined value was 20.8 percent of Chile's total corporate investment, making Edwards the third most important combine in the country.[280] Edwards was in the process of vertically integrating its operations with investments in forestry, graphic arts inks, printing, and publishing before Allende began to nationalize, a process that was interrupted in 1973.

Once the military had consolidated its power, the general manager of *El Mercurio* S.A.P., Fernando Léniz, paid a visit to the junta to ask permission for the afternoon paper, *La Segunda*, to circulate once again. It just so happened that the junta was in the market for a minister of the economy and hired Léniz on the spot. He became the first civilian in the cabinet.[281]

Léniz had become *El Mercurio*'s general manager in 1970, when Agustín Edwards lured him away from his post as manager of production at Compañía Manufacturera de Papeles y Cartones (CMPC), *la papelera*, the attempted nationalization of which welded the business community's opposition to Allende. CMPC supplies over half of the newsprint used in Chile.

During Léniz's brief term as economy minister (1974–1975), the military set its first three economic priorities: privatization, deregulation, and the exploitation of mineral, sea, and forest wealth.[282] Léniz, Chicago Boy Michael Kast, and Pinochet's son-in-law, forestry engineer Julio Ponce, subsidized as much as 75 percent of the cost of planting trees. The nearly 26,000 hectares that were planted in 1974 under military Decree Law 701 rose to 92,000 annually before the end of the dictatorship in 1990.[283]

Once edged out of the economy ministry, Léniz eventually became president of the wood industry association, Corma, and director of the Chilean Match Company. In 1999, he also was a vice president of Compañía Sudamericana de Vapores, whose current president, Ricardo Claro, now owns a former Edwards combine holding company with large forestry investments, Cristalerías de Chile. Because Claro controls Megavisión Channel 9, there will likely not be any positive stories about the Mapuche on its Meganoticias, the third-rated news program in Chile.

Léniz's son, Felipe, is also in the forestry business. He says his company is planting where "land is available and there are no conflicts."[284] Forestal Arauco and Celulosa Arauco are both controlled by Ancaleto Angelini, an Italian immigrant who arrived in Chile in 1948 and set Chile's fishing industry into motion.[285] He now controls energy conglomerate Copec, 76 percent of whose profits came from forestry in 1999, according to *El Mercurio* (February 6, 2000). "Critical Phase for Angelini" says he is harried by fishermen, ecologists, and Mapuches who oppose the $2 billion investment in two cellulose plants in the south.

El Mercurio is concerned that the price for pulp will fall before Angelini, whose personal worth exceeds $2 billion, gets his plants on line. The sprawling Sunday review article does not explain why environmentalists, fishermen, and the Mapuche oppose the plants. *Ercilla*, once edited by Christian Democrat Emilio Filippi, does not plumb the forestry industry either, because it was taken over by the same conglomerate as CMPC. The founders of CMPC were part of the banking conglomerate whose collapse triggered the 1981–1982 economic crisis. *Ercilla*'s competitor, *Qué Pasa*, sides with the forestry industry, which it says is endangered by "increased labor costs, excess regulations and the Mapuche conflict."[286] As a Copesa publication, *Qué Pasa* recognizes private property as one of the "Five Pillars" of *gremialismo,* which we will explore later.

So, *El Mercurio* and Copesa are, respectively, bound to the old aristocracy and the new oligarchy, which is made up of Pinochet collaborators who got rich during the dictatorship. However, *Capital* is not part of either group. Its owners are the Luksic family, which distanced itself from Chile's oligarchs during the UP period by attempting to appease Allende in his nationalization scheme by selling some of their properties without opposition in exchange for the promise that others would not be touched. *The Wall Street Journal* reported that the Chicago Boys considered the Luksic family "traitors" and so cut them out of the lucrative privatizations that followed the coup.[287]

Yet, the Luksic family has a history similar to the Edwards combine when it comes to forestry investments. (In fact, they held investments in Agrícola Forestal Colcura and Forestal Quiñeco as late as 1978.[288]) So, perhaps it is not so much the tradition of investment in forestry that sways a medium's reporting; perhaps it is the medium's attachment to the military government, either through the old aristocracy that promoted the coup or the new oligarchy created during the dictatorship. Perhaps it is the Luksic's "outsider" status that permits them to publish alternative views rather than their lack of affinity to forestry investments.

Yet another factor may be *Capital* editor Soto's claim that the Luksic family does not interfere with his editorial decisions. While this claim may be perfectly valid, it is impossible to prove, especially because this claim is made by many Chilean editors who are clearly beholden to their owners. As we see in the following example, reporters whose media are far removed from any connection to the forestry industry still suffer interference.

Reporter Patricia Verdugo says that even Televisión Nacional's news manager demanded that she change a story that questioned the forestry industry. Her script ended with an ironic kicker wondering why former Esprit CEO Doug Tompkins received so much criticism over his Pumalín Park—which conserves a wilderness area—while the Trillium company got the green light to fell a nearly identical acreage of old-growth forest in Patagonia. Her boss accused her of comparing apples with oranges.[289]

Taken together, the news sources in Chile are lined up on one side of the public policy question of what to do about "The Indian conflict in Chile that looks a lot like Chiapas," as *El Mercurio* quoted a Mapuche sociologist in a headline kicker.[290]

Indian lore

How does *El Mercurio* justify its stance? The editorial writer in charge of the Mapuche-forestry beat is Alvaro Bardón, a Chicago Boy. Bardón said the forestry subsidy never made sense. "Chile's comparative advantage [in forestry] is so great that it doesn't need subsidies." As president of the Central Bank under Pinochet, he says that he stymied disbursement of those subsidies—because they disagreed with his free market philosophy. Today, *El Mercurio*'s only corporate interest in forestry is the purchase of newsprint, said Bardón. The Edwards combine's interest in forestry is not guided by market forces: Edwards has a "romantic" tie to forestry and a "social" relationship with CMPC, he said.

Bardón described *El Mercurio*'s long history with CMPC during an interview at the Finis Terrae University. In steel-rimmed glasses and a short-sleeved Madras shirt, he looked more the part of a graduate student than the dean of the economics department. As for *El Mercurio*'s editorial position on native peoples, Bardón said, "It is in part a defense of private property and of the forestry policy plus a conviction that the 'Ley Indígena' was flawed." The Concertación's "Indian Law" recognized some Mapuche claims to land. Bardón said that only inspired the Mapuche to bring more claims. "There was no problem before [the law]," said Bardón. "The law became an invitation [for the Mapuche] to invade land. Also, [the law is imperfect because it] doesn't turn the land over to the Indians as private property, but as collective land. And no one takes care of communal property."

Bardón said that letting the Mapuche live on the land simply perpetuates their poverty; it is better that they leave. He pulled an *El Mercurio* editorial out of a stack he kept on a nearby table. It read: "Probably, keeping the Mapuche tied to the land like serfs on a medieval plot would take away their mobility and limit their chances of doing other jobs within the region or outside of it—which is one of the real ways out of extreme poverty."[291]

Going native

The Mapuche way of life may seem dated in capitalist Chile. But, the average Chilean apparently finds the Mapuche hip enough to turn them into successful advertising symbols. The images of native peoples used in the fashion industry are neither the noble savages of the cigar-store Indian nor the ignoble savage of the Atlanta Braves—but contemporary Indian faces. As part of their glossy offset circulars, Tiendas Paris department stores included clothing models of obvious native extraction—part of the "world harmony" trend pioneered by Benetton. *El Mercurio*'s Sunday travel guide placed a Colombian Wayúu on its cover.

In addition, an ad campaign for *La Tercera* showed two identical photos of a Mapuche woman in traditional regalia. The upper shot is labeled "Chileans" and the lower "Mapuches." Such an ad promises that a debate is taking place about the true identity of this people on the pages of *La Tercera*. The ad's footer reads: "Everyone can have his opinion. The New Tercera. Your new voice."

THE PROPAGATION OF VALUES

The importance and prestige achieved by this newspaper during its 70 years of life have given rise to a situation of a paradoxical character: Its readers include not only those who share the positions its editorials sustain, but also many of those who are the most ardent adversaries of the doctrines put forth in *El Mercurio* when it comes to politics, economics and social matters. This opposition group, from among the very readers of the paper, has its origin in the reliable information that our pages offer. The reader-adversary is conscious that *El Mercurio* provides a faithful version of the facts, as much as that may differ from the editorial page analysis.

—*El Mercurio* editorial, June 1, 1970

"We Chileans are just racist," is a common excuse for the media treatment of native peoples. "Chile is just a conservative country," is a common explanation as to why the news is so anti-worker. Certainly, Chile is a conservative country. However, the news media that survived Chile's switch to democracy are far more conservative than Chileans themselves. Our studies on labor and forestry show that today's media promote the interests of their owners while excluding the views of others—to which many Chileans would be receptive.

When it comes to labor, the Mapuche, the environment, violent crime, health and retirement plans, or any number of broad economic issues, the important print media are unanimous: The top circulation newspapers intended for the middle and working classes (*La Tercera* and *La Cuarta*) as well as the largest-circulation weekly news magazines (*Qué Pasa* and *Ercilla*) and the predominant agenda-setting medium for the upper class (*El Mercurio*) use their overwhelming power to restrict rather than enrich the marketplace of ideas.

However, there is a schism when it comes to spiritual and moral values. A number of non-economic "moral values" are treated differently in the two halves of the media duopoly. Chile's landed aristocracy, for which *El Mercurio* is written, is very devout. Chile's traditional ruling class also is thankful to General Pinochet and the Chicago Boys, respectively, for the legal imposition of their moral values and for enriching their class as a whole.

Copesa's owners, on the other hand, are of the business class. Their surnames tell you immediately they are not from the landed aristocracy because they are not of northern European or Basque origin. They are often of Castilian, Palestinian, or Eastern European origin, identifying them immediately as *nouveaux riches* and less attached to Roman Catholicism.

Most of Copesa's owners have been former Pinochet economists who also got rich during the dictatorship, which explains their attachment to the Five Pillars (the health and retirement systems, private property, the education system, and the 1980 Constitution) as guarantors of their wealth and philosophy. However, moral values are of no significance to Copesa's owners, some of whom have been divorced.

A former Copesa manager says issues of morality are "intellectual jerk-off"[292]—sometimes literally so. Copesa publications, especially *De Mujer a Mujer,* have published articles such as "The Truth About Masturbation" and "Fantasies and Realities of Bisexuality." The Copesa publications also cover the medical use of marijuana, birth control, adoption, and other non-traditional issues.

Another group of media owners who are attached to the liberal wing of the Church, most of them being Christian Democrats, control two important radio news networks. The PDC is tied to labor, shies away from the Chicago Boys economy, and tends toward tolerance of alternative lifestyles—without venturing far from Roman Catholic philosophy.

So Chile's "establishment" and its press may be divided along the following lines when it comes to moral issues (see Table 3.3):

1. *The elite.* There is a unanimous support for the Chicago Boys economic policies. Their media include: *El Mercurio's* chain of 17 newspapers; Copesa (which includes *La Tercera, La Cuarta, Qué Pasa,* and two radio networks); Radio Agricultura; *Ercilla*; Channel 9 Megavisión, Metrópolis-Intercom cable; and Catholic University's Channel 13. This elite is subdivided into the following two groups:

a. *The old aristocracy.* It is composed of religious fundamentalists who were rich before Pinochet came to power and are typically descendants of the northern European or Basque landowning class. Their contemporary sources of inspiration are Opus Dei, the Legionnaires of Christ, and the *gremialistas.* Examples of their intolerant, integralist views can be found in *El Mercurio's* letters to the editor. The religious right seeks the state's imposition of Vatican morality on all Chileans and unswervingly supports and defends Pinochet to this day.

b. *The new oligarchy.* It is composed of those who became wealthy during the dictatorship. The owners of Copesa and their publications favor the free market as well as freer moral standards, reflecting the last real difference between the libertarian Chicago Boys and the devout Roman Catholic *gremialistas.* The new oligarchy is just as conservative as the aristocracy in labor or Indian affairs. They support Pinochet but allow coverage of the accusations against him.

2. *Liberal Christians.* For our immediate purposes, the Roman Catholic Church's liberal wing overlaps with the PDC, which contributed the swing votes necessary to bring Allende to power, then joined the opposition until the coup. Many members of the PDC welcomed the coup, but soon opposed Pinochet in conjunction with the liberal third of the Church hierarchy.

The PDC finds itself trying to reconcile the traditional view of economics favoring government intervention with post-Chicago Boys Chile. The most pluralistic news sources within the most-trusted medium are Radio Cooperativa and Radio Chilena, both of which are held by liberal Catholics, many of whom are attached to the PDC. They are pro-labor, are suspicious of the tyranny of the marketplace, and promote the values of the Roman Catholic Church, but are tolerant enough to have invited for the first time on radio an openly gay man to participate in a talk show. Christian liberals within the Church still publish *Mensaje*, which is not widely circulated and does not qualify as a general news source.

3. *Centrists.* A few members of the former National Party, National Renovation, and the Radical Party have been able to keep a middle ground in this highly-polarized country. These select few typically welcomed the coup and recognize that Pinochet's economy benefitted them personally but say that he should have returned Chile to democracy sooner and should be tried for human rights abuses. Currently, Radicals control no major medium. Some National Party members work for *El Mercurio.*

4. *Old Left.* Supporters of the UP are numerous but marginalized. It is impossible to say what influence they might have if they had an important medium at their disposal. Today, they control *El Siglo, Puro Chile,* and *La Firme,* none of which is a daily newspaper. Their radio stations were for the most part confiscated and have not returned to the air.

5. *Greens and youth.* This growing group has only been able to muster single-digit showings in presidential elections. It has allied with native peoples but not with labor. The defunct Rock&Pop, *La Nación,* and the early version of *El Metropolitano* spoke to youth and greens but were not owned by them.

Because it is not attached to the above groups, the business magazine *Capital* has taken its own path. It is not a general news magazine, at any rate.

As Table 3.3 shows, Chile's important publications are nearly unanimous in their support of the Chicago Boys neoliberal economy. The only two news sources that take a less-than-enthusiastic view are in radio—the medium least appropriate for economic analysis.

The rest of the mainstream media, except Copesa, back the Vatican's view of religious and moral issues to the point of influencing the government to impose their moral standards through legislation and the use of censorship in the prohibition of certain types of information or behavior that the Vatican finds offensive.

The central questions that this section asks are: Where do the Chilean people fit in this scheme relative to the positions of the Chilean media? Are Chileans, by their own admission conservative, well-served by their conservative news media? Or, do the media more closely reflect the will of their owners with the goal of imposing certain beliefs or moral standards upon Chileans who may feel otherwise?

Table 3.3

Social vs. Economic Liberalism among Major Groups in Chile and Their Media

	Greens/Youth: + tolerance + some state economic intervention		
New Oligarchy: + moral tolerance + Mapuche and labor intolerance + *gremialismo* + free markets (Copesa)	**Liberal Catholics:** + tolerance + some economic intervention (Radio Chilena, Radio Cooperativa)	**Old Left:** + Mapuche and labor tolerance + strong economic state intervention (party organs)	increasing social liberalism ↑
Old Aristocracy: + intolerance + strong state moral intervention + *gremialismo* + free markets (*El Mercurio, Ercilla*)			

← ———— increasing economic liberalism ————

Catholic University professor Eduardo Arriagada warned me not to look down my nose at the social values expressed in Chilean journalism. "The Chilean press could appear to be rightist to a foreigner because Chile is a rightist country," said Arriagada. "Just as the United States has what's politically correct, the equivalent here is that you can't say anything bad about the pope—as with blacks in the U.S., you can't say anything bad about Martin Luther King [Jr.]."[293]

Arriagada argues that because Chile's journalism market is free, the news outlets would be punished in the marketplace if they were out of line with the people's way of thinking. He observes that demand is forcing these media to become more pluralistic, citing *El Mercurio*'s supplements that carry items on non-traditional issues. If more people buy the paper, he says, that drives up the price advertisers will pay, making it good business to be pluralistic.

Arriagada says *El Mercurio* and the other media have no obligation to carry secular or leftist ideas. Their obligation is the satisfaction of the demand of the readers. Chileans have a long tradition of buying the newspaper that agrees with their way of thinking and many Chileans—journalists among them—say they prefer a strong editorial line. "The press is part of the system and is not about to challenge authority," said Arriagada. "NGOs are outside the system so they may not have an expression in the press."

If non-rightists have something to say, Arriagada invites them to start their own newspapers. He points out that the right cannot be blamed for the failure of the left-of-center publications; the "other disappeared" must have died off because of poor business practices or poor journalism. We now address Arriagada's arguments one by one.

The Chilean media have become more pluralistic since the return to democracy.

With the return to democracy and the demise of the "other disappeared," Chile's mainstream media did indeed become more pluralistic. For example, the Communist Party's 2000 presidential candidate got a lot more of her message across in *El Mercurio* than did rightists in the Communist organ, *El Siglo*. In other words, *El Mercurio* is, to some degree, pluralistic.

Parceling out ideological niches is *El Mercurio*'s "calculated pluralism," which means providing for many types of readers without undermining the paper's mission. Arriagada was correct in identifying market demand as the impulse driving the shift in the supply. Table 3.4 shows *La Tercera*'s more liberal views of women chipped away at *El Mercurio*'s female readership—pushing *El Mercurio* to include a greater variety of women's issues, a matter we will examine later in this section.

El Mercurio's pluralism takes place outside the news pages. Women's issues, sexuality, or "new age" thinking are all shunted off into their respective supplements. Conservative elite readers may ignore the magazine *Ya* (in which a runway model may bare a breast on occasion) and turn to Sections A, B and C, which are tailored as always for the moneyed elite.

This is why you will get opposing answers from editors, reporters, readers, and politicians to the question: "Is *El Mercurio* more pluralistic?" "It all depends on which *El Mercurio* you're asking about," said *El Mercurio* columnist Alfredo Jocelyn-Holt, one of the liberal columnists *El Mercurio* added since the return to democratic rule. Jocelyn-Holt likens *El Mercurio* to a supermarket with offerings of all types and tastes. If you want to read hard line, pro-Pinochet, integralist thinking, it is to be found every day among the letters to the editor. If you wished to read a liberal columnist, you turned to him every two weeks—until he was dropped from *El Mercurio*.

However, the opinion columns are the least influential, while the news pages are the most influential, in forming perceptions. Former and current *El Mercurio* staffers and other journalists who were asked about the paper's political tendencies agreed that *news coverage has become more conservative or has stayed the same since the return to democracy.* The supplements are more inclusive, however.

In the 1950s and 1960s, when *El Mercurio* and Congress were located a stone's throw apart in downtown Santiago, lawmakers were known to stop by *El Mercurio*. "The flow of information was diverse and the paper tended

Table 3.4

Daily Newspaper Readership— *El Mercurio* versus *La Tercera*

***Comparison of First and Third Quarters 1998—
In Thousands of Readers***

		El Mercurio	*La Tercera*	*El Mercurio*	*La Tercera*
		Weekday	*Weekday*	*Seven Days*	*Seven Days*
Aggregate	Q1	482	604	1139	862
	Q3	469	649	1152	909
Men Q1–Q3	Q1	243	318	539	436
	Q3	265	329	566	443
	% var.	9.1	3.5	5.0	1.6
Women Q1–Q3	Q1	239	289	600	462
	Q3	205	320	587	466
	% var.	**-14.2**	**10.7**	**-2.2**	**9.4**
ABC-1 Q1–Q3	Q1	202	62	318	79
	Q3	195	75	317	90
	% var.	-3.5	21	-3	13.9
C2 Q1–Q3	Q1	193	195	276	305
	Q3	186	217	219	318
	% var.	-3.6	11.3	5.4	4.3
C3 Q1–Q3	Q1	62	210	114	213
	Q3	58	216	117	224
	% var.	-6.5	2.9	2.6	5.2
D Q1 – Q3	Q1	26	140	102	92
	Q3	30	141	104	88
	% var.	15.4	0.7	2	-4.3

not to take sides," said former editor Fontaine. "*El Mercurio* is today less pluralistic politically, more pluralistic culturally."

While *El Mercurio*'s increased inclusiveness should not be ignored, the following examples demonstrate that *El Mercurio*'s news coverage has not

evolved. For example, *El Mercurio* began to favor Unión Democrática Independiente (UDI) candidate Joaquín Lavín just three days after he entered the presidential race, something old hands at *El Mercurio* say the newspaper had never done before.

It is worth noting that while *El Mercurio's* agenda-setting prowess is unequaled, it is declining. *El Mercurio* has been on the losing side of the three presidential elections since Pinochet. This points either to a shift in the balance toward left-of-center thinking or a shift of *El Mercurio* to the right. In either case, it is out of step with the rest of Chile.

Chilean news media could stay in business only if they meet demand.
If *El Mercurio* is so out of step, why do people keep reading it? Even when *La Epoca* was around, surveys showed that a larger proportion of self-identified liberals read *El Mercurio* than read *La Epoca*. *El Mercurio* remains Chile's only full-service newspaper, meeting the demand for everything from movie schedules to society pages. It also covers the left, middle, and center of Chilean politics, something *La Epoca* and the other "trench" media failed to do.

Besides, Chilean readers who disagree with *El Mercurio's* world view say they know how to read between the lines. "Everyone knows how to 'read' *El Mercurio*," said Luis Ajenjo of Radio Cooperativa.[294] *El Mercurio's* references to the "supposed disappearances" of prisoners during the dictatorship was irritating, but the news at least appeared *somewhere* in *El Mercurio*.

"The news is there," said Mónica González, who would qualify as one of the "reader adversaries" mentioned in the epigraph. "You just have to know where to find it." As in the example of the forest rangers who denounced the arson committed by their security company, if you are willing to read to the end of every story, you can indeed find the news. González is the *Cauce* investigative reporter who is one of the best there is at mining nuggets from *El Mercurio's* nooks and crannies. But, must every reader be an investigative reporter to find out what's going on in Santiago's "newspaper of record"? This is not an acceptable standard.

El Mercurio *serves the "establishment" and is under no obligation to carry other viewpoints. Others who want more coverage are welcome to start their own newspapers.*
In the absence of left-of-center publications, NGOs and left-of-center politicians are more dependent upon *El Mercurio* for their political lives, not less. Because their possibilities of getting positive coverage are fewer, they must curry favor with the Copesa-*El Mercurio* duopoly. Only *El Mercurio* can make or break a politician. No left-of-center publication has been able to chip away at that status.

Chile is a conservative country and Chileans' idea of a "politically correct" discourse is far different from what's permitted elsewhere.

Public discourse in Chile is conservative if judged by the examples below:

• A bus advertisement for a radio station shows a woman's naked rump with dotted lines indicating various "cuts" as on a side of beef. The caption "Pure fillet" refers to the station's high-quality content.[295]

• The names of Dolly Parton and Pamela Anderson may be invoked in a radio advertisement for chicken breasts.[296]

• *El Mercurio* reports on Telefónica vice president Hans Eben's sense of humor: "Not only did he win laughs, applause [...] but [also] acceptance with a [joke] that had a *machista* touch: 'The growing scarcity of brains on the planet means we even have to rely on women.'"[297]

Do Chile's news media merely reflect the society that they inhabit? What if Chileans prefer to live in a conservative, conformist society and do not want their media to be more inclusive?

We could respond that what Chileans want to hear about does not matter because what is fair is fair, and the news media's duty is to protect the rights of the minority against the tyranny of the majority. Besides, there is international consensus behind the idea that pluralism is "good" and exclusion is "bad."

Is pluralism a value so universal that, like democracy, we can simply posit it with no further justification? One of the few Chilean journalists who understands Enlightenment liberalism, *El Mercurio* columnist Jocelyn-Holt, could challenge rhetorically my contention that Chile would be better off today if the media were more pluralistic as in Western democracies. He simply asked: "But, why do we *have to* have it?"[298] Wielding unvarnished "pluralism" risks commission of cultural imperialism, so let's look for a more universal standard.

A journalistic practice that no one defends in any culture is the deliberate distortion of the truth. Veracity is the minimum expectation of all readers and the value most proclaimed by news outlets, including *El Mercurio* in the epigraph. Anything else becomes propaganda or plain old bad journalism.

That leaves a huge gray area in which the medium adjusts the news mix to the taste of the readers. This mix can be accomplished with or without bias. *The New York Times* publishes more news about Judaism than other papers, not because it is pro-Jewish or because its owners are Jewish (its history proves the contrary), but because New York City is the largest Jewish settlement outside of Israel. By the same logic, Midwest newspapers carry more farm news than would interest a New Yorker.

To avoid cultural gray areas, the following standards may be described in black and white terms: 1) Does the medium knowingly abridge the truth in order to promote the owner's agenda? 2) Does the medium's news mix reflect the concerns of the Chilean people?

We will measure *El Mercurio*'s claim of veracity on the news pages using two international news stories. This is desirable because examples of journalistic behavior are difficult to explain in objective terms and doubly difficult to explain to readers in another country. Distortions in the news can only be measured against the events themselves. To describe distortions to readers not intimately familiar with current events in Chile, I would have to ask them to make the leap of faith to believe not only my rendition of the event, but also the coverage of it, my description of its context, and *then* my interpretation of its meaning.

We can stay on more objective turf by examining the handling of two foreign news stories that most foreign readers are familiar with.

The eagle of the Alps

By arrangement with *The Washington Post*, *El Mercurio* reprinted a *Post* profile of Austrian nationalist leader Joerg Haider. *El Mercurio*'s version said the head of Austria's Liberty Party answered the *Post* correspondent's questions in "fluent English." However, the adjective seemed out of place for the *Post*. A check of the original version of the article revealed that *El Mercurio* had indeed added the word "fluent." And, that *El Mercurio* had cut the *Post*'s second and third paragraphs recapping Haider's most controversial statements about the Nazis. Removing the nut graph and global graph obviously changed the story's focus, allowing *El Mercurio* to write a headline that cast Haider as the victim: "Haider Trusts that Austria will Overcome Ostracism." The *Post*'s original headline had cast him as defiant: "Haider Unfazed by West's Protests."[299]

This touch-up of Haider is neither an accident, nor the work of an isolated editor; *El Mercurio* also gave Haider a five-page iconographic profile in its Saturday magazine. The cover headline promised: "Austrian Joerg Haider: The phantom threat." Inside, color photos showed a dynamic Haider skiing and holding a press conference. One full-page shot from belt level showed Haider standing on the shore of a lake, chin up, eyes fixed on the horizon. The photo caption described his good looks as "a cross between Kevin Costner's and Toni [*sic*] Blair's." The article was entitled "The Eagle of the Alps" and was introduced as follows:

Accused of eulogizing the Third Reich, he has the European Union scandalized at the thought that one of its members might retreat to Nazism. However, his constant contradictions make one think that he doesn't keep his talons as sharp as they say, but wears instead a populist plumage that changes according to the occasion.

A sympathetic portrayal of Haider is *El Mercurio* policy. A February 10, 2000, editorial reads:

In the opinion of the European Union and of a portion of the world community, Haider is a Nazi because his father was a member, but the parents of a lot of people over the age of 50 were as well—in an Austria where the majority in 1938 favored German annexation. ... Haider arrived to revolutionize a dormant political scene.[300]

Is this the view of the average Chilean? Of course not. When regional neo-Nazis held their congress in Chile in May 2000, a total of 11 people showed up.

In addition, *El Mercurio* also omits negative stories, such as Haider's resignation from the Liberty Party. *El Mercurio* also failed to rectify its faulty reporting on Colombia's guerrillas.

On May 15, 2000, a Colombian woman was terrorized for six hours while being forced to wear a "necklace bomb" until it exploded, killing her and the explosives expert who was trying to remove it. Bogotá's *El Tiempo* guessed that guerrillas were to blame because terrorizing farmers is a common way to collect "war taxes." Days later, Colombian officials said the *modus operandi* pointed to local extortionists instead of guerrillas. On May 19th, the Associated Press reported that such an extortionist had been captured.

Nonetheless, on May 27th, *El Mercurio* reprinted *El Tiempo's* article, now 12 days old, in its Saturday magazine. Although *La Tercera* published a retraction of its rushed story on June 2nd, *El Mercurio* did not. By May 29th, wire services reported that a Colombian governmental commission discounted guerrilla involvement. Just the same, on June 24th, *El Mercurio's* Saturday magazine published the letter of a reader horrified at the cold-bloodedness of the guerrillas. *El Mercurio* still did not take the opportunity to rectify the facts.

Again, this distortion is not an aberration. One op-ed column defended the Colombian military, saying that the human rights accusations against it are part of a "disinformation campaign" sponsored by the Colombian government's human rights ombudsmen, NGOs, Human Rights Watch, and Fidel Castro, among others: "What is surprising is that all this is picked up in the U.S. Department of State in its annual human rights report without criticism or verification of any kind," said the column.[301]

The terrorism of Colombia's guerrillas is so reprehensible that exaggeration is hardly necessary and barely possible. No purpose would seem to be served, yet *El Mercurio* routinely sacrifices its credibility in the service of a hoary Cold War agenda.

To this end, *El Mercurio* routinely amends wire service copy while leaving in place the Associated Press (AP), EFE, *The Washington Post,* or *The New York Times* credit lines that lead the reader to believe that the article meets standards for veracity. The Associated Press and former *El Mercurio* staffers say the editing and manipulation of wire copy is ongoing and incorrigible. "What can you do about it?" shrugged AP's Chile-Bolivia Director Eduardo Gallardo.[302]

Divorce, Chilean style

Chile is one of three or four countries that do not allow divorce. *El Mercurio* and other media honor the Church's desire to keep it that way. *El Mercurio* also remains silent on Chile's current system of annulments, which take the place of divorce. The married couple simply asks one or more witnesses to swear under oath that some detail in the marriage license is false. The magistrate annuls the marriage and becomes an accomplice in the commission of a socially- and judicially-tolerated fraud.

The annulment used to mean that any children born to this marriage-that-never-happened became instant bastards. These children are often kicked out of the rightmost Catholic schools. The "Ley de Filiación" gave these children the right to claim both parents as well as their share of any inheritance. *El Mercurio* opposed the law on the grounds that it was the first step on the road to a law permitting divorce. If Chile is truly a conservative country, could *El Mercurio* be justified in opposing a divorce law? Hardly: Marriages were annulled with a wink and a nod 6,302 times in 1997, compared with 78,077 marriages.[303]

Those figures do not reflect what the divorce rate would be if divorce were permitted, however. Chileans shy from contracting a marriage they cannot get out of. And, many separated spouses cannot obtain an annulment. Many of these simply move in with someone else. In the end, nearly half of Chile's couples simply cohabit—another story that is not covered in *El Mercurio*.

When the Ley de Filiación went on the books in 1999, *El Mercurio* covered the event in just three articles. One of these, on the personal Finance page, took up the law's possible impact on the reader's inheritance or child support.[304] Is *El Mercurio* justified in restricting coverage of such a law because it affects few people? The Chilean government reports that in 1998, 47.2 percent of all Chilean births were out of wedlock.[305] So, clearly the law is of interest to *somebody*.

Other media owners opposed the law, including the controlling shareholder of Megavisión. It goes without saying that Catholic University's Channel 13 opposed the law and the liberal Catholic Radio Cooperativa and Radio Chilena were not enthusiastic supporters.[306]

Are the news media a bulwark against divorce that Chileans do not want? Some 78 percent of Chileans say their government should permit divorce.[307]

Dying from embarrassment

In 1991, Church officials successfully quashed a government AIDS awareness campaign despite its bland message. The television spots and posters warned that: Having more partners means greater risk; HIV is passed through infected blood or from mother to child; you do not get AIDS from kissing, touching, or sharing space with infected people; AIDS can be avoided through monogamy, abstention, condoms, clean needles, and AIDS testing before pregnancy. The campaign's images were silhouettes of fully-dressed dancers (some with hats, even) all of them standing and in positions that do not suggest sex; one couple is nearly—but not quite—kissing.

What did Church officials object to? They objected to the word "partner." Also, "sexual relations" would have to be replaced by "married life." And the word "condoms" had to go. Santiago's archbishop said the advertisements were an "incitement to sexual libertinism." Apparently Church officials saw things that the public did not; just 10 percent of Chileans objected to the spots, according to a poll.

The Aylwin administration at first stood up to the Church. The spots had been taped, the posters printed, and the air time purchased for $1.3 million when pressure got the project shelved for two months. Once the spots were released, they were not aired on Catholic University's Channel 13. Individual media joined the boycott, including Ricardo Claro's Channel 9. *El Mercurio's La Segunda* interviewed the dean of Catholic University's medical school, who condemned the "hedonist exercise of sexuality."[308] The government withdrew the campaign.

Are these media simply doing the will of the people by bowdlerizing media content in a conservative Catholic country? Channel 11 has been able to beat any rating in Santiago simply by showing more skin, pulling 30 points during an explicit Brazilian soap opera. As Chilevisión's Andrés Israel commented: "*Someone* was watching."[309] Likewise, the Playboy channel was seducing 400 new subscribers a week during the second half of 2000. Besides, 44.4 percent of Chileans said that young people *should* have sexual relations before they are married.[310]

Women and the press

El Mercurio embraces the Catholic condemnation of birth control. Reproduction was not covered in *El Mercurio's* news pages during the study period of August 11, 1999 to March 12, 2000. However, Copesa's *La Tercera* ran news articles such as one on a birth control breakthrough achieved by Chileans.[311]

Abortion is a nonissue among the media of the religious right. The military made abortion a criminal offense without exceptions neither for the health of the mother nor in the case of a malformed, non-viable fetus. When candidate Lagos suggested that permission for such abortions was open to discussion, the Church and media backlash assured that he would not bring up the idea again.

The reader has probably guessed where this argument is going: The media do not reflect the sensibilities of a nation opposed to abortion. Chile's 7.58 million women[312] abort 200,000 times a year,[313] placing Chile's abortion rate among the highest in Latin America—not including the abortions sought by the well-to-do in Miami.[314] This is a trend that dates back to the 1960s.[315] Because no one—neither pro-life nor pro-choice—can be happy with these statistics, it would seem that a public policy discussion is in order. The news media should be the first to broach the subject.

A woman's place

Despite the increased inclusion of women's issues in its supplements, *El Mercurio* does not budge on its news coverage. *El Mercurio* used an advance on the opening of the movie "The Next Best Thing" as a peg to reproach its star for her most recent pregnancy in the headline: "Madonna, Single Mother Again."[316]

El Mercurio published no article on International Women's Day—no run-up calendar of March 8, 2000 events, nor next-day coverage of the activities. The exception to the blackout was an article on labor union women's dismay with the CUT for canceling the 2000 celebration.[317] The coverage of a fissure between the two groups in the absence of other coverage of the two movements gives the coverage extraordinary weight as well as the appearance that the coverage is opportunistic.

While *El Mercurio* did publish photographs of prominent Chilean women attending a Women's Day reception at the Australian embassy, it should be noted that this "Vida Social" section is in reality a paid advertisement that can cost up to $10,000 per page. (Many Chilean journalists mentioned the inclusion of Concertación figures in the "Vida Social" as evidence that *El Mercurio* had become more pluralistic. However, most of those who appear in fact pay for the privilege.) The deception is intentional: "With the goal of preserving the journalistic character" of the set of photographs taken at the event, says the page attached to the rate card, "only one person may appear twice."[318]

In *El Mercurio*, women get their say on Mother's Day. The 2000 celebration served as a hook for comments by prominent women. Once again, the occasion was a vehicle for women who wished to complain about the left: Prominent women were asked to score the three Concertación governments, which they criticized either for tardiness or haste in addressing women's issues.

The unsatisfied demand for coverage of women's issues gave entrée to the free *MTG* newspaper, which published eight news articles on International Women's Day 2000 and did follow-up stories the day after.

Armed forces

On May 19, 2000, the Supreme Court ruled that the forced "disappearance" of a person while under arrest could be considered a kidnaping in progress and a crime not covered under the military's self-declared amnesty, opening the way to bringing charges against Pinochet. *La Tercera* and every other newspaper gave the Supreme Court decision front page play. *El Mercurio* relegated its article to Section C, Page 2: A brief description of the decision was followed by 17 paragraphs in which Pinochet's defenders railed against the decision. There was no opposing viewpoint. The writer used the adjective "absurd" to describe the Supreme Court's conclusions. The accompanying photograph was not of the winning human rights lawyer, but of one of Pinochet's attorneys.

El Mercurio's imposition of *pinochetismo* reaches to all parts of its chain. The editor in chief and managing editor of *El Llanquehue* in the southern city of Osorno were sacked in late 1999 after a headline made light of a setback for Pinochet and his legal team in London. On the same day, an accused murderer captured in Osorno lost in his attempt to block extradition to a neighboring city. *El Llanquehue's* headline borrowed from sports lingo: "They both lost an 'away game.'"

While Copesa cannot be called "*pinochetista*," its publications run favorable articles. *Qué Pasa* ran a spread on the former dictator's health, with diagrams of his daily fitness routine.[319]

Is this coverage in line with the treatment that Chileans desire for their former dictator? Not at all. Repeated public attitude polls show that somewhere between two thirds and three quarters of Chileans believe Pinochet should face trial.[320]

As dictator, Pinochet assured favorable coverage by using the media's government debts to lever pro-military rightists onto editorial staffs, squeezing out editors of the traditional right such as Arturo Fontaine. Pinochet then used public monies to assure friendly ownership of these media. However, in the post-democratic world, Chile's right wing must use subtler means.

The powers-in-fact

The previous section shows that Chile's news media are, to varying degrees, out of step with their readers, listeners, and viewers. How can this be so, if these media are subjected to market forces? Catholic University's Channel 13 simply chooses to drown in red ink rather than defy the Holy See. Meanwhile, Televisión Nacional Channel 7's rating rose past Channel 13's in part because its governing board *requires* that it be pluralistic.

Owners make those choices on their own or under pressures from peers, Fathers Confessor, high-ranking military leaders, politicians, or business connections at the country club—the *poderes fácticos*. The "powers-in-fact" is a term Andrés Allamand made famous in an interview that he granted *El Mercurio* as president of National Renovation (RN), the party of the "traditional right" whose truly democratic principles distinguish it from UDI's *gremialistas*. Allamand was a promising political figure who might well have become president one day—until internecine tussles in the UDI-RN alliance and Allamand's unmasking of the *poderes fácticos* as what he called a "power in the shadows." The mere public mention that such a mechanism exists earned Allamand *El Mercurio's* maximum reprisal: banishment of his name from its pages.

Few public figures have suffered *El Mercurio's* capital punishment. Curiously, the most famous of these are rightist victims of Edwards's personal vendettas, such as Hernán Cubillos, former manager of Publicaciones Lo Castillo and Edwards' former yachting partner. Although Cubillos rose to the rank of foreign minister under Pinochet and later became ambassador to Argentina, *El Mercurio* published no obituary when he died in 2001—apparently in reprisal for an ancient dispute over power or money.

Former communications minister Francisco Javier Cuadra was banned in 1987 after testifying in court that he had neither handed *El Mercurio* photographs of two students, nor fingered them as the agitators behind a disturbance during the pope's visit. *El Mercurio* had apparently taken Cuadra's word for it, published the photo with an accusatory caption—and found itself embroiled in a million-dollar lawsuit in which Cuadra testified—to save his own skin, not *El Mercurio's*.

No politician can survive without appearing on *El Mercurio's* pages and Agustín Edwards knows it. Allamand left Chile and landed an ignominious desk job with the Inter-American Development Bank in Washington. Former *El Metropolitano* editor Enrique Mujica said of his stint at *El Mercurio*, "You even had to be careful when you mentioned power, because my bosses were among the powerful."[321]

The only serious examinations of the powers-in-fact were published in *Cosas* and in *Capital*, magazines that are not owned by the Copesa-*El Mercurio* duopoly. When the former editor of *Qué Pasa* magazine, Bernardita del Solar Vera, launched a series that would examine the *poderes fácticos*, she only got as far as the first installment. She was canned, say editors, for not seeking the permission of Copesa's shareholders first. The article said Chile's business elite "derives its power in part from its cohesion and the uniformity of its conduct and ideas," through an amalgam of ultra-right politics, economics, and Catholic service organizations. Liberals or moderates are not welcome in the world of business and will not have the inside track on lucrative business deals. The reason is simple: With wealth comes the power to sway public policy, and Chile's elite does not welcome fresh ideas that could dilute their public agenda, said the article. "They have formed a club whose weight is such that practically no issue reaches the public agenda without having first passed through its filter."[322]

Other loci of the powers-in-fact are media owners, *gremialistas*, UDI, Pinochet's Chicago Boys, and rightist Catholic service organizations, including Opus Dei and the Legionnaires of Christ. Opus Dei is Spanish and placed its members in Franco's government throughout his four decades in power, garnering resources and privilege, and establishing footholds in education. This "Work of God" emphasizes the leadership of the elite, so it was no coincidence that its founder, Josemaría Escrivá de Balaguer, recently canonized, swooped into Santiago within months of the 1973 coup to conquer souls in journalism, education, and the business community.

Until recently, Catholic University's Channel 13 was controlled by Opus Dei, most famously by former director Eliodoro Rodríguez, who banned even Santiago's cardinal from its studios for having criticized the dictatorship.[323] Opus Dei adherents include *El Mercurio's* former business section editor and 1999–2000 presidential candidate Joaquín Lavín, and it counts among its supporters Ricardo Claro, owner of the third-largest television network and the second-largest cable television operator.

The Legionnaires of Christ is jokingly referred to in Chile as the "Millionaires of Christ" for the wealth of its contributors. It is similar to Opus Dei in its ultra-right interpretations of the Vatican's messages. Its benefactors include Agustín Edwards and Eliodoro Matte, of CMPC, both of whom sit on the board of Finis Terrae University, which is 50 percent owned by the Legionnaires. Another adherent is Javier Vial, one of the *piranhas* who helped strangle both Radio Minería and Radio Portales.

These powers-in-fact are the non-market forces that can determine the flow of information. Yet, how can these media defy market forces in a population that was liberal enough to elect a Socialist to the presidency in 2000?

Nearly every publication is beholden to two markets—circulation (readers) and sales (advertising). Of the two, advertising pays the lion's share of the bills—and all of the profits. The value of most publications' advertising space is predicated upon its circulation. However, advertisers also want to know the publication's penetration among its potential purchasers, which is expressed in the publication's demographic profile. Of course, if those readers have the disposable income to purchase the products advertised, the numerical size of the audience matters little. *Cigar Aficionado*'s potential audience of cigar smokers is an extraordinarily thin slice of the population— but it has the most affluent demographics there are. The quarterly's revenues reached $10 million on circulation of 225,000.[324]

In Chile, the concentration of wealth is high. In addition, there also is a high correlation of wealth with rightist political views. Advertisers do not have to look far to know where the money is. Even if they were not predisposed to promoting rightist views, the Copesa-*El Mercurio* duopoly would be obliged to do so in order to survive. Having the highest circulation in Chile does not bring in ad revenue if the readers are poor, as is the case with *La Cuarta*.

The idea of burying the editorial line to appeal to a larger audience is appropriate to a mass medium, not a niche publication. *The New York Times*, ABC News, or the "Larry King Live" show seek to increase readership or ratings by appealing to more people with a balanced offering, which pushes up their advertising rates. *The Daily Worker*, Pacifica Radio, G. Gordon Liddy, and Rush Limbaugh worry more about serving their loyal audiences. By the same token, an opinion-forming publication such as *The New Republic* seeks to reach the "right" people rather than everyone.

El Mercurio's "niche" just happens to correspond to the wealthiest of Chile's consumers. *El Mercurio* serves the elite well and sells advertising on that basis without having to modify its editorial content to include more liberal readers who are too poor to buy much of anything. (The exception that proves the rule is *El Mercurio*'s Sunday classifieds, which we will take up later.) Other news outlets belong to mass media. Radio Chilena and Radio Cooperativa are more pluralistic and enjoy high ratings. At the same time, outlets having foreign backing, such as *MTG*, Chilevisión-Channel 11, and Radio Activa, have audience appeal, although they stray far from the moral, political, and religious values of the Chilean right.

As long as the media on the right hold the attention of the rich, circulation numbers are meaningless. *El Mercurio* actually *hides* its circulation numbers, as we will see. That is part of the reason *El Mercurio* can make money, while mass media such as Catholic University's Channel 13 and Ricardo Claro's Channel 9 lose money with their conservative content, because their ratings are known. However, although Channel 13 may lose viewers to Televisión Nacional, it will always hold the attention of Chile's moneyed classes. These phenomena are the subject of the next section on advertising.

These factors—along with government subsidies—allow Chile's major media to remain out of step with the bulk of Chileans. The defense of morality and rightist politics is the bailiwick of the old aristocracy. The new oligarchy is uninterested in morality but distorts news coverage to defend its own investment interests.

Reporting for your health

Soon after Pinochet privatized the health care system, Chilean hospitals found a novel way to ensure payment. They began admitting only patients who handed them a blank check—literally. That policy jeopardized the lives of the half of all Chileans who had no checking account. The Concertación ended the odious "guarantee check." However, compliance was not immediate, even at the most prestigious hospitals.

No sooner had the *cheque en garantía* been banned, the populist *La Cuarta* diagnosed a serious case of irony. It reported that none other than a vice president of the Chilean medical association took his mother-in-law into an emergency room the day after the guarantee check had been outlawed. But before the woman could be admitted, she had to leave a blank check at the admissions desk of "a prestigious clinic in Las Condes."[325]

Although *La Cuarta* named the vice president and even his mother-in-law, the clinic remained curiously anonymous. The "prestigious clinic" in the Santiago municipality of Las Condes is where Augusto Pinochet himself is treated: La Clínica de Las Condes. A check of the hospital's board revealed the possible reason for not mentioning the name of the clinic: Hospital board member María Soledad Saieh Guzmán is the daughter of Alvaro Saieh. Her brother, Jorge Andrés Saieh Guzmán, watches over his father's investment from his seat on the board of Copesa, which owns *La Cuarta*.[326]

Biases are rarely so clear, but many other newsworthy events are buried because of owners' financial interests or because they are one of the Five Pillars.

Criticism of that part of the health care system belonging to Copesa's owners is proscribed, of course, as is criticism of the privatized system in its entirety. The private health plans, called *isapres*, are one of The Five Pillars. In fact, *La Cuarta*'s article on the guarantee check was the closest any newspaper came to an oversight of the private health care system during the study period August 11, 1999 to February 11, 2000. *El Mercurio* covered complaints about the guarantee checks, but pointed the finger at a *public sector* hospital, the University of Chile Clinic.[327]

Of course, television was made for the drama of families saddled with debt from unpaid and unpayable medical bills. Catholic University's Channel 13, Megavisión's Channel 9, and Chilevisión's Channel 11 covered stories such as that of a woman dying from breast cancer because she could not afford treatment. However, television treats these as human interest stories, not as symptoms of a sick medical system.

Sometimes, high-rolling advertisers may call the shots in the newsroom. In the United States, tobacco's effects on public health was rarely television news until cigarette ads were banned from the tube. In Chile, health care and retirement plans privatized during the Pinochet era were among the top advertisers as they jostled for a share of a lucrative market. The preponderance of their spending influenced the news even at Televisión Nacional, an SOE. Because of the congressional mandate that TVN survive without subsidies, TVN is just as dependent upon advertisers as any other medium.

Although politicians have great weight at TVN, they do not have as much pull as the advertisers. "I can avoid the call from a senator or a government official. Or, I can take the call and listen for a while until they get tired," said former TVN reporter Patricia Verdugo. "But the call you can't avoid taking is from the sales office." And yes, the sales office is allowed to tell reporters what to cover in Chile.

Health was Verdugo's beat. Her 1994 investigation resulted in the closure of a loophole in the regulations governing the private Instituciones de Salud Previsional—*isapres*—created in 1981. Workers contribute seven percent of there earnings to the *isapres*. For the highest-paid workers, that seven percent gets them full coverage with no deductible—and there's cash left over. What happened to that overage? Until Verdugo's investigation, the *isapres* just chalked it up as windfall profits. Because of her reporting, the government insurance oversight body places that extra cash into a fund that covers catastrophic illnesses.

Verdugo also discovered that the *isapres* were making prompt reimbursements to the private hospitals—while falling behind in payments to the public hospitals. The government now requires the *isapres* to make timely payments to all hospitals. Although Verdugo's reports saved millions for the very government that cut her paycheck, she said TVN reporters were ordered to ease up on health care reporting.[328] This occurred, despite the fact that a government study shows that Chileans' number one concern is health care.

Serious health care reporting was not abandoned for a lack of motivated reporters. Verdugo simply got frustrated with TVN and quit because there was no firewall between the newsroom and the business office. "You can do a lot for the good of the people," said Verdugo. "But the power of these [health care providers] is such that they can [effectively] censor these investigations."

The AFPs

The private retirement plans called AFP (for Administradores de Fondos Prevsionales) are another creation of the Pinochet government, one of The Five Pillars, and an industry that has attracted investments by Copesa's owners. They replaced Chile's government-run social security system, founded in 1925, ten years before the U.S. Social Security Administration and the first in the Americas.

Social Security collects 15 percent of American workers' wages and transfers the monies to retirees of the previous generation. The AFP is an alternative to such "pay-as-you-go" plans by avoiding the inter-generational transfers. The money the AFP pays out at retirement is the money you invested over the course of your working life—only you receive more of it through the miracle of compound interest. Where is the money in the meantime? Invested in the stock market, real estate, or wherever the privately-held AFPs feel is best.

It is beyond the scope of this book to pass judgement on the AFPs. However, any journalist, economist, or public policy analyst would not question the need for constant vigilance over a system that deducts 10 percent of your pay and whose assets in 2001 equal 54 percent of GDP in a volatile, highly-liquid mass.

There is serious debate surrounding Chile's AFPs. While the U.S. Social Security system is often criticized for its inefficiency, it spends 1 percent of its funds on administration. The AFPs charge the worker a 2.5 percent commission. When politicians brought this up for discussion, *La Tercera* defended the industry in an article headlined: "Chilean AFP commissions: among the lowest in the region."[329]

El Mercurio confidently predicts "Chileans Will Retire with 100% of 2020 Salary," in a headline over an article that cites only AFP officials.[330] However, two Finance Ministry economists say half of pensioners will retire poor enough to require government assistance.[331] That deflates the principal argument for privatized pensions: alleviating government spending. There is plain evidence that many workers will not retire without government help: Some 200,000 workers ceased contributions in 1999 because they were unemployed.[332]

Copesa also paints a rosy picture. Most of its owners were heavily invested, until Alvaro Saieh bought out Juan Carlos Latorre and Sergio de Castro's portions of the AFP Provida in exchange for a larger share in Copesa in the late 1990s. Saieh became owner of 51 percent of Corp Group, owner of Provida, which then controlled 32 percent of the AFP market. Other Corp Group investors included Saieh's business partners from the Banco Osorno:

Fernando Awad, Odde Rishmahue, and Juan Pablo Díaz, as well as Carlos Abumohor, also of Copesa. Saieh is the single largest AFP investor in Chile.

El Mercurio backs any Chicago Boy initiative, such as the AFP.[333] But even the media supposedly independent of the private sector, such as TVN, could not risk losing the mass of advertising monies spilt in the competition for the accounts of workers.

The only articles critical of the AFP during our study period were non-news items. *La Tercera* carried an op-ed rant by a minor presidential candidate: "The AFPs are a fraud."[334] *El Mercurio* published an editorial by Alvaro Bardón that chastised the AFPs for touting their yearly gross earnings before deducting their commissions, giving workers the impression that their retirement accounts had grown 2.5 percent more than they had.

The head of the association of AFPs is Guillermo Arthur, one of Pinochet's ministers of labor and pensions and is one of the few sources *El Mercurio* consults about the AFPs. The vice president of the association of *isapres* is Fernando Léniz, former *El Mercurio* general manager and Pinochet economy minister.

Table 1.2 in Chapter 1 showing listeners' faith in radio also shows the public's greater faith in the press compared to the AFPs and *isapres*, indicating that the public might be better served if reporters were left to do their jobs.

Copesa's interests

In addition to the ban on reporting on The Five Pillars, Copesa's owners do not permit reporting on their own businesses.[335] Therefore, Copesa avoids covering Chile's largest steel manufacturer, its largest AFP with one-third of the market, the largest provider of cheeses, sausages, and cold cuts, several banks, a dizzying array of real estate and investment companies, a hospital, universities, and a cemetery.

Construction investments by the owners of Copesa may explain the inordinate amount of attention that *La Tercera* pays to Chile's infrastructure, warning motorists of the penalties for circumventing toll booths[336] and listing municipalities that hold up housing developments.[337] De Castro and Miguel Angel Poduje are keen bidders for government contracts. *La Tercera* carried an op-ed column by Poduje suggesting that the government increase subsidies for low-income housing as a way to spark the sagging economy. The writer was identified as a former cabinet minister.[338] However, Poduje was not identified as part-owner of Copesa, nor as a business partner in a construction company with de Castro—the intellectual leader of the Chicago Boys, who disparaged the Keynesian stimulation of economic growth through government spending. Nor was he identified as having held the housing and urban planning portfolio under Pinochet, when the administration wrote off thousands of low-income subsidized mortgages in a failed attempt to buy the winning votes in the 1988 plebiscite.

During the dictatorship, it was a lot easier to make money.

The theft of the century

In the 1980s, Carlos Cáceres appointed fellow *gremialista* José Yuraszek to privatize Chilectra. Yuraszek encouraged his workers to buy shares in their electric company and to place them in shell companies. Workers got Class "A" stock in the new holding companies, which sounded good—except that the Class "B" stock, held by Yuraszek and his friends, had the voting rights. Each of the voting "B" shares was worth 740 times a worker's "A" share when Yuraszek sold out to Spanish investors—for $480 million.

One of the non-*gremialista* Chicago Boys, Juan Villarzú, called this "the theft of the century."[339] *La Tercera* and *El Mercurio* defended Yuraszek through his trials and acquittals, with follow-up analysis saying that the government "went after" Yuraszek because he is considered a *gremialista*. Indeed, this was a *gremialista* scheme. It was a fellow *gremialista*, Cáceres, who named Yuraszek to privatize Chilectra during the time both were working at Oficina de Planeación (ODEPLAN) under the *gremialista* Chicago Boys.[340] More important, Yuraszek was already a business partner with Copesa's owners, in the construction of a downtown office building called Santiago 2000. The beneficiaries of this and many other privatizations donate liberally to the UDI, the *gremialistas'* political party, which is close to Chile's media duopoly. *El Mercurio* called Yuraszek's avoidance of judicial punishment "an important triumph."[341] *La Tercera* and *El Mercurio* amended "theft of the century" to read "deal of the century" in their articles.

While minister under the Frei government, José Miguel Insulza made an offhanded remark about the beneficiaries of Pinochet's privatization piñata (of which Yuraszek was only one of many), *La Tercera* published its only article that during the year-long study period gave the appearance of an in-depth investigative piece. Insulza had stepped on the prominent toes of Yuraszek and of Carlos Alberto Délano, who headed Joaquín Lavín's presidential campaign. The resulting three-page Sunday business section article with sidebars and graphs uninterrupted by advertisements gave the private sector's spin to the privatizations.[342]

These *gremialista* alliances hail from their Catholic University days. "In fact, we used to sit together in the lunchroom. The group included [Joaquín] Lavín, [Sebastián] Piñera, Carlos Alberto Délano, Alvaro Donoso, Cristián Larroulet, among others."[343]

Journalistic protection of businessmen is nearly seamless. "You can criticize even some politicians," said journalism professor and former *El Metropolitano* managing editor Juan Ignacio Brito. "But you can't criticize businessmen." It skirts the idea of questioning the right to private property.

Private property[344]

We have no evidence that *El Mercurio* has a list similar to Copesa's "Five Pillars." But neither did *El Mercurio* disagree with Copesa during the six-month study period from August 10, 1999 to February 10, 2000, especially when it comes to the last of Copesa's Five Pillars—the sanctity of private property. As *El Mercurio* sees it, Chile's 50-year slide toward socialism began with the 1925 Constitution, which placed the public interest ahead of individual rights to exploit private property. That was reason enough for the *gremialistas* to replace the Constitution of 1925 with the Constitution of 1980. The primacy of private property takes some extreme forms when it affects news coverage.

El Mercurio and *La Tercera* did not cover the naming of the national copper company (CODELCO) president as "Copper Man of the Year" by New York's Copper Club in 1999. The "Ankh Award" is the industry's highest honor for managerial excellence. No Latin American had won the award because South American mines have historically been run by foreigners. Were it not for the duopoly blackout, the award might have been a point of national pride in Chile, which is so frequently identified with copper.[345] Similarly, when Chile's postal service files its year-end report, the duopoly does not recognize what is likely the most efficient and least corrupt mail service in Latin America, but instead characterizes it as producing meager profits.

El Mercurio *and politics*

El Mercurio was disdainful of all political parties (including those of the right) during the events leading up to the coup. It did not miss them during the dictatorship and today clearly favors UDI's *gremialismo* as an alternative to party politics. The paper avoids alienating (as much as possible) readers of the center-right and the RN in particular. But when it must choose, *El Mercurio* supported UDI's Carlos Bombal for the Senate seat in western Santiago over Allamand of RN. *El Mercurio*, then, never raises the issue of laws that favor UDI's climb to power.

Fairness in congressional representation is not a principle of Guzmán's 1980 Constitution. It includes seats for nine non-elected senators, which are appointed by the armed forces, the Supreme Court, and others. Likewise, the Constitution's skewed electoral system was meant to prevent the greater number of voters on the left from electing both Senators to represent any one district. For one party to win both senatorial seats under this system, the number of votes cast for each of those candidates must be more than double the number of votes cast for any other candidate. For example, Guzmán himself defeated Ricardo Lagos for the right to represent Santiago's western district with this mechanism in the 1989 election. Concertación candidate Andrés Zaldívar was the top vote getter, winning a Senate seat with 31 percent of the vote. However, Lagos's 30 percent lost to Guzmán's 17 percent.[346]

This so-called "binomial" voting procedure was an alternative to denying suffrage to poor Chileans. Guzmán argued that 19th century democracy worked in the absence of universal suffrage. Chile is too underdeveloped for party politics, he said, which is what led to the breakdown in 1973. He justified this position by arguing soberly that Chileans who are not committed to the neoliberal program will look to the state sector to resolve their problems.[347] The day after Christmas in 1981, *El Mercurio* published Guzmán's arguments in "El camino político," an article that proved central to Pinochet's ideology and seminal for the *nueva institucionalidad* of the *gremialistas*.

Neither *El Mercurio* nor *La Tercera* question the lack of transparency in campaign financing. "Campaign financing can't be touched," said former TVN reporter Patricia Verdugo.[348] Unlimited campaign contributions and the news blackout on public debate of the issue—as well as the binomial districts and institutional senators—favor UDI. Despite the concentration of its membership among the elite, UDI has become the second-biggest vote-getter in Chile. This is a product of UDI's extraordinary media campaign spending financed by undisclosed means. Much of UDI's funding comes from former Pinochet operatives who benefitted from the Chicago Boys' privatization piñata.[349] De Castro himself funneled monies through Siglo XXI to back Hernán Büchi's aborted 1989 presidential candidacy.[350]

By the end of Aylwin's transitional term, the five parties on the right, including UDI and National Renovation, joined forces for a presidential bid. The campaign was run by the five party presidents with four high-powered fund raisers: Johnny Kulka, Jorge Prado, Sergio de Castro, and Fernando Léniz.[351] Not only did three of these four men serve Pinochet, three had at one time worked for *El Mercurio*: Kulka and Léniz as general managers and de Castro as Agustín Edwards's personal assistant. *El Mercurio* editorial board member Jovino Novoa flirted with the idea of becoming the candidate of the right, which would have brought the newspaper close to qualifying as its own political party.

Chicagonomics

The duopoly places the Chicago Boys' neoliberal economy beyond reproach. However, Chile is today dependent upon the export of raw materials for nearly 90 percent of its foreign currency earnings. Mining, forestry, and fishing bring in the hard currency, leaving Chile as exposed to gyrations in world commodity prices as any developing country—a matter that doesn't get much press. As a result, the publications duopoly vaguely blames Chile's current slump on the 1997 Asian crisis. Specifically, the Asian crisis lowered the demand for copper, which accounts for 40 to 45 percent of Chile's foreign export earnings, which cannot be recovered with value-added manufacturing exports that Chile does not offer. *Business Week*, *The Washington Post*, and *The Economist* made the connection between copper prices and the downturn.[352] The Chilean media did not.

El Mercurio is at least as strict as Copesa when it comes to the AFPs, calling debate out of bounds even on the floor of the Senate "[i]n what is now a habitual practice among officials who do not completely understand the essence of the private pension system." The editorial belittles not politicking but the careful considerations of Senator Alejandro Foxley, an accomplished economist. As long as Pinochet's Chicago Boys own Copesa and write editorials for *El Mercurio*, serious debate about their economic policies cannot take place.

THE POWER OF ADVERTISING

Television, radio, and print media have different advertising regimes due to their differing audience measurements—each distorting the market in its way. First, the lack of a circulation auditing bureau helps *El Mercurio* and its chain of newspapers keep the upper hand in advertising revenues. Second, radio networks use an inaccurate audience measuring system that favors the top networks over newcomers. Third, television's PeopleMeter is at once a menace to journalistic criteria and the most rational of the audience measurement systems. We will deal with each medium in turn.

The advertising pie

In Chile, newspapers are king as radio is in Colombia and as television is in Brazil. Geography and historical accident mean different populations favor different media, and disproportionate amounts of advertising spending follow. As Table 3.5 shows, Chile is unique among Latin American countries in the proportion of ad revenue dedicated to newspapers, which garner 35 percent of all ad spending. In Colombia, newspapers receive less than half of that proportion.

Chilean newspapers owe their success to *El Mercurio* and the nationwide chain of newspapers it built up during the dictatorship. However, *El Mercurio*'s take of ad revenue is difficult to justify. A circulation auditing bureau lasted from the mid-1970s until the 1981–1982 economic crisis, but it collapsed when *El Mercurio* withdrew. Since then, *El Mercurio*'s circulation is the best-kept secret in Chile. Through its regional newspapers, *El Mercurio* lobbied successfully against a provision in the 2001 Press Law requiring circulation disclosure. In a reversal, *El Mercurio* has signed on to an agreement to form a circulation bureau, to be established by 2004.

There can only be one reason why *El Mercurio* would want to keep its circulation a secret: *El Mercurio* is selling its advertising space for more than it's worth. While *El Mercurio*'s daily circulation in Santiago hovers around 60,000, it claims that each newspaper passes through nearly six pairs of hands, inflating its reach by 30 percent. *La Segunda* bases its ad rates on the claim that nearly eight people read each issue. The real question, then,

Table 3.5

Advertising Spending in Latin America, 1997

	Television	*Newspapers*	*Radio*	*Magazines*	*Outdoor*
Argentina	49%	25%	8.3%	10%	7.6%
Brazil	61%	23.7%	4%	9%	1.9%
Chile	**42.7%**	**35%**	**11%**	**4.5%**	**6.4%**
Colombia	60%	16%	18%	6%	N/A
Mexico	76.6%	8.6%	10.6%	4.3%	N/A
Peru	63.9%	12.2%	16.2%	3.6%	4.1%
Uruguay	47.9%	25.5%	16%	N/A	10.6%
Venezuela	65.8%	27.6%	1.6%	1.6%	3.4%
Central America and Ecuador	55.9%	28%	11%	4%	0.6%
Regional Average	59.6%	28%	8.3%	7.3%	2.7%
Total per medium	$9387.5	$3478	$1311	$1142	$430

Source: J. Walter Thompson, cited in Sergio Godoy. Gestión de radio y televisión (1999).

becomes: How can *El Mercurio* continue to sell its advertising for more than it is worth?

Even though *La Tercera* and *La Cuarta* outpace *El Mercurio* in circulation, they receive 14 percent and 2 percent of newspaper advertising revenue, respectively, while *El Mercurio* receives 70 percent.[353]

Ricardo Avello, deputy research director at Copesa, said the disposable income of *El Mercurio* readers is partly responsible. So is tradition—advertisers who always relied on *El Mercurio* continue to do so. Copesa set about changing that tradition. Copesa brass chose the 100 top advertisers and invited one to lunch each week over a two-year period. The result: Both *La Tercera* and *La Cuarta* doubled their advertising revenues. Avello says a certain classism prevents the market from becoming rational: Advertisers will not receive complimentary subscriptions of the sensationalist *La Cuarta* in their offices. Advertising executives say that *La Cuarta* and *La Tercera* are not making money for Copesa. Avello contends that the newspapers operate in the black.[354]

Copesa also inflates reach. *La Tercera*'s circulation is neck-and-neck with *El Mercurio*'s, while Copesa claims each issue is read by more than four people and that each issue of *La Cuarta* is read by more than two. *El Mercurio* takes in one-third more ad revenue than is justified by its reach, while one-fifth of *La Tercera*'s take is not justified. *La Cuarta* and *La Hora* each exaggerate by 10 percent. On top of such prevarication, the Edwards conglomerate controls advertising information through its Publicaciones Lo Castillo, which publishes the annual advertiser's guide to the media market as well as a large selection of guides to various industries.

What Avello would really like *La Tercera* to conquer is classified advertising. *El Mercurio* has a virtual monopoly, which in turn drives the high Sunday circulation even among the poor who seek employment and the middle-class Chileans who buy used cars. Classifieds do not logically belong in *El Mercurio*, because the rich do not look for jobs or used cars in the newspaper. *El Mercurio* has an accessible and agile system for placing classified ads by telephone or in person at any of its affiliated newspapers around the country. The 70 percent of newspaper ad revenue that accrues to *El Mercurio*'s Santiago newspaper does not include classifieds, which represent $1.3 million of revenue every week in *El Mercurio*.[355]

PeopleMeter

In 1992, PeopleMeters were installed in 350 Santiago homes to relay real–time information on what families are watching to advertisers and networks. News directors complain that maintaining their viewers' attention during newscasts amounts to an intrusion of the business office into the newsroom. News programs drift toward sensational coverage and have adopted the annoying habit of moving sports coverage into the midst of newscasts to keep the attention of sought-after young men.

Despite the fact that only Santiago is measured, the PeopleMeter has done much to rationalize advertising rates. However, radio and newspaper media are not keen to repeat the success. Television advertising rates actually *dropped* once the PeopleMeters were installed—one more justification for *El Mercurio*'s hermeticism and for established radio networks to conduct inaccurate audience surveys.

Squelching radio

Radio has itself to blame for a lack of data. Just as *El Mercurio* takes full advantage of being the incumbent, large Chilean radio networks do the same. The system conducts random audience surveys in Santiago on a quarterly basis, every six months in medium-sized cities, and yearly in smaller markets, if at all. The survey quizzes listeners as to what they heard the previous day in 15-minute increments. Because memory is highly perishable, such a survey favors big names: A listener is more likely to remember a known show or spot than to recall having heard one for the first time.

The results are not released for three months, so that producers of a summertime pilot may not even know how well they did until after the contract has run out and the show is off the air. Muddying the waters even further are the "rolling quarterly" results that are posted: The most recent three-month result is combined with the previous result. The rationale: It yields a larger sample.

It is difficult to convince broadcasters to create a system of audience surveys that is either fairer or more technically advanced. The Chilean potential market of 16 million people is small—perhaps too small, given the cost of surveying listeners of the 1,000 stations that are currently licensed. A better survey implies taking a larger sample more frequently, which costs more than broadcasters are willing to pay. Because the best-rated networks are on top due to the fact that the current system put them there, they have no intention of changing it. "The current system favors us," said Luis Ajenjo, president of Chile's top network, Radio Cooperativa.[356]

Irrational actors

A concept essential to the neoliberal claim to scientific precision is the reduction of the human animal to the status of "rational actor" within the economy, meaning that he will seek the best product or service at the lowest price. As such, his behavior cannot only be predicted but quantified. However, the behavior of advertisers who avoid purchasing ads in the most efficient media for ideological reasons cannot be reduced to a formula.

During the past decade, advertising spending has indeed become more rational than it was during the dictatorship, said Pedro Labbé, marketing director for Radio Cooperativa. He sold advertising during the Pinochet years and watched political bias contribute to the demise of the resistance publications just as it hurt Cooperativa. Labbé said certain advertisers did not place spots on Cooperativa due to its opposition to the dictatorship and its attachment to the Christian Democratic Party. "An advertiser is human," said Labbé. "[He says:] 'This isn't rocket science and there are 20 other outlets for my message.'"

Labbé says that for lack of a circulation audit, it's impossible to assess how much damage advertisers did to the resistance publications and how much blame rests with lackluster sales staffs. Poor sales also plagued the right, Labbé points out: Radio Minería, in the hands of the *piranhas* who supported Pinochet, lacked enough advertising revenue to keep itself afloat.[357]

Radio Cooperativa's president, Luis Ajenjo, says the elite purchase or boycott of advertising space is an act of solidarity within the ruling class. "Marxism may be discredited as a social analysis, but in Chile, the class struggle is alive and well." Ajenjo said that the business community puts up a united front against the left: "The [*gremialistas*] and Opus [Dei] are very strong in the business community. It's not normal that all [Chilean] capitalists are of one political and social position." Before coming to Radio

Figure 3.1

Vergara scandal doesn't sell soap

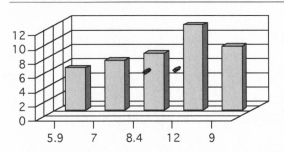

- ☐ **"Dia a Dia" Ratings from June 1–7, 2000**
- • **Sanitary napkin and cough syrup withdraw**
- ◦ **Flour withdraws sponsorship**

Source: *MTG*

Cooperativa, Ajenjo was the business manager of *La Epoca.* In the absence of audit figures, however, he cannot prove his sense that rightist advertisers contributed to the disappearance of opposition media.[358]

However, a contemporary example demonstrates—with the accuracy of the PeopleMeter—that Chile's powers-in-fact are still guided by ideology rather than acting "rationally" when purchasing advertising. When the story broke on June 1, 2000, that TVN host Ivette Vergara's son was not her husband's, the rating of her noontime talk show, "Día a Día," doubled (see Figure 3.1), which in the United States would be considered "normal." What would not occur in the United States was that three of the show's four sponsors would pull their advertising at the very moment the rating was on its way up. Manufacturers of a baking flour and a cough syrup quietly withdrew their ads. The Nova brand announced that it was withdrawing its advertising because the scandal could sully the image of its sanitary napkins.[359] Little wonder: Nova is owned by CMPC, of the Matte family, which sponsors the Legionnaires of Christ. Of the four products that sponsored Vergara's show, only her deodorant stuck by her when she needed it most.[360]

Unfortunately for Vergara, her program was sponsored by Chilean companies. The only publication in Chile to point out the inverse relationship between ratings and advertising was *MGT*, a foreign-owned newspaper.[361] Because foreign money does not care about Chilean politics, morals, or customs, it helped to rationalize advertising and brought a professionalism to the industry. Use of the PeopleMeter has unveiled a disparity between Chilean programming and what Chileans want to see, which is the topic of our next section.

Unlucky 13

Toward the end of the dictatorship, Channel 13 was the only network not directly controlled by the military, and its top rating provided Catholic University with millions toward its operating budget. But today, Channel 13 is losing money. While TVN-7 made cuts in 1991, Channel 13 did not reorganize until 2000, cutting salaries for all but its stars by 20 percent. Channel 13's conservatism has kept it in good stead among Chileans with large disposable incomes. However, TVN-7 has surpassed Channel 13 in overall ratings and news hour ratings.

Channel 13 captured viewers by running "Bay Watch" discretely at 10:00 P.M. However, the bright spot of the UC-13 lineup was a quirky Colombian soap, "*Yo soy Betty, la fea.*" "I am Betty, the Ugly One" is an unlikely title for a Latin American *telenovela*—which usually has to do with rich men and beautiful women living off the family fortune. Standing the standard soap opera formula on its head is what "Betty" is all about.

Betty comes from a lower middle class family. She studied hard and landed a job with a Bogotá garment maker, not through family connections and certainly not by being the prettiest candidate, but on merit. Betty was a hit all over Latin America whose emergent middle classes saw themselves portrayed in their struggle for admittance into an economic system based on privilege. So, everybody rooted for Betty—including lots of UC-13 viewers.

However, just as "Betty" outpaced TVN-7's top soap, UC-13 felt compelled to do some editing. Bedroom scenes were cut without damaging the story line. However, later episodes included plot elements that could not be cut, like the marriage of the company's fashion designer—to another man. As ratings rose, however, Church moralists did not protest.

"Commercials and confessions don't mix," said Catholic University professor Oscar Godoy.[362] The university may have to sell its television station—unless the pope blesses fornication or Chileans swear off sexy soaps. Godoy and Javier Vial estimate UC-13's worth at less than $100 million, down from $500 million just five years ago.

Megavisión

UC-13's moral dilemma also spanks impresario Ricardo Claro, owner of Megavisión and a moralist legend in Chile. The *pinochetista* stunned competing bidders with his $11 million offer for the Channel 9 concession in 1989. Instead of pandering to the public, Claro has spent his way into second place in overall ratings by purchasing Mexican soaps, yielding the largest losses of any network. Foreign investor Televisa of Mexico reduced its 49 percent share to 37 and eventually to zero as a result.

Cable Guys

Claro has become the face of the cable television industry as he has been the face of a lot of things in Chile. His investments are far-flung, including the marine shipper Compañía Sudamericana de Vapores, Santa Rita wines, and Cristalerías, which has large forestry holdings. His face is frequently photographed with Pinochet's and others of Chile's ultra-right. He makes no bones about his CIA connections, including two of its former directors, the late William Colby and George Bush.

Although Pinochet offered him the ambassadorship to the United States, Claro preferred to work behind the scenes as a special envoy to China. Under the cover of a trade mission to China, Claro's real task was to secure the Chinese vote against Chile's expulsion from the United Nations. He accompanied Foreign Minister Hernán Cubillos and Roberto Kelly—on leave from the Edwards combine—on a second trip to China. Claro's other diplomatic mission kept him in Chile arranging the 1976 Organization of American States (OAS) meeting in Santiago. There, Claro says, he struck a blow for freedom of the press, talking Pinochet into granting entry visas even to journalists working for media that had criticized the dictator or his regime.[363]

Claro is a power-in-fact—he is more comfortable being the puppeteer than being on the stage. He says his role in the newsroom and other businesses is exaggerated. "I'm an authoritarian, which does not mean I'm arbitrary," said Claro who admits he has an image problem. "My grandmother used to scold me for the scowl on my face. She told me: 'You're turning out to look like a judge on the criminal bench.'"[364]

The face of Ricardo Claro does not smile, especially when talking about cable TV. As self-appointed censor, Claro yanks movies that he feels unfit—up to 296 times in a single month—from HBO Olé, Cinecanal, Cinemax, Fox, TNT, Space, Entertainment USA, and Isat, which are all carried on Metrópolis-Intercom.[365] Consumer organizations have threatened to sue, because subscribers who signed up to see HBO are not getting what they paid for. Claro is unmoved: "*I* have the same right as the magazines and newspapers to have an editorial policy. Let people say what they will."[366]

Claro pulled HBO's transmissions of "Winchell" and replaced it with "Dave," "Henry and June" was replaced by "The Odd Couple," "Harold and Maude" by "Crazy People," and "Havana" by "Earthquake." "Deceived" and "A Little Romance" were both replaced by "Someone to Watch Over Me."[367] HBO Olé is by far the most popular cable channel in Chile.

Claro says he was only complying with the law, which applies the same standards to cable as it does to broadcast television. Claro is accused of going even beyond the CNTV requirements, which, like any censorship regulation, reside in the eye of the beholder. He cut an entire Argentine channel,

América 2, because of one of its shows, "D a 2," a "let's talk about sex" format with movie clips, sexologists, and psychotherapists. More curious still was his termination of Gems Televisión, a channel for women that included then-First Lady Marta Larraechea de Frei and writer Isabel Allende. Claro let the contract expire at year's end in 1999 after attempting to terminate the contract unilaterally two years earlier, arguing lack of viewer interest. *El Metropolitano* reported Gems' ranking at 14 out of 76 channels.

The defection of subscribers to rival VTR has not dissuaded Claro. Metrópolis-Intercom's market share fell to 36 percent, while VTR's rose to 57 percent. That prompted Spain's Telefónica to sell its 40 percent share to Claro for $270 million. The other 60 percent of Metrópolis-Intercom is owned by Cristalerías de Chile, which Claro controls, and Liberty Media Corp.[368] The purchase ended Claro's lawsuit to prevent Telefónica from offering Internet connectivity over television cables or anything but telephone lines. Claro now plans to invest in the Internet.

News and civil society

Alejandro Guillier is the bearded anchor who delivers the news leaning on his elbow, as though the Channel 11 news desk were an extension of your kitchen table. Guillier works at Radio Chilena in the mornings and brings the warmth of radio to the cool medium during the evening news. He appears in a medium shot that includes his hands and a pen, replacing the talking head preferred by dictatorships. His discourse captures the informality of sportscasters or meteorologists. These changes make him the only television personality to successfully create a post-dictatorship television language for Chile.

He says the foreign owners give him greater latitude than Chilean investors would. Hicks, Muse, Tate & Furst formed Ibero American Media Holdings with Cisneros of Venezuela to invest throughout Latin America, Spain, and Portugal. Ibero American owns six radio networks in Chile besides Chilevisión and coordinates sales through a common sales office. Guillier says of the multinational ownership: "They're on your back a lot less."[369]

Since the return to democracy, he has watched the elite take over the media: "They've replaced real debate with a debate in the media. Everything is reduced to [sound bites of] less than 40 seconds and that isn't debate. The country is left with nothing but the image. We are [now] a country of images." (As with some of television's best, Guillier has a healthful suspicion of the medium.) Guillier says his journalists are partly to blame, because they cannot conceive of covering a story without first interviewing a key actor—a politician or a businessman. The end result is that there is no room for enterprise journalism and little room for the average Chilean unless he is the victim or perpetrator of a crime.

Guillier's observations can be demonstrated statistically (see Table 3.6). Politicians and legislators enjoy the lion's share of appearances as the chart indi-

Table 3.6

Concentration of actors on Chilean news programs.

seconds accrued	# of persons portrayed	politicians and legislators	social, labor and business leaders
1000–9000	62	13	4
900–999	8	2	1
800–899	7	0	1
700–799	13	2	1
600–699	15	5	1
500–599	20	2	3
400–499	39	6	5
300–399	69	9	5
200–299	124	17	16
100–199	361	41	39
0–99	9444	226	891

Table 3.7

Chileans' assessment of the frequency of people seen on news shows.

Actors:	too much	not enough
politicians/legislators	45%	7%
ministers	33%	9%
sports figures	31%	19%
president	30%	11%
labor and business leaders	24%	25%
businessmen	22%	19%
mayors	21%	27%
clergy	17%	25%
artists	15%	27%
citizens	2%	67%

Source: Secretariat of Communication and Culture, 1996.

cates. Of the 62 persons who filled more than 1,000 seconds of news airtime, 13 of these were politicians and legislators, while just 4 were leaders in civil society, according to a government study. This has not gone unnoticed by the average Chilean, who rarely sees herself depicted in the news and would like to see more of her concerns addressed in the news, according to the same study (see Table 3.7).[370]

Why such emphasis on politicians' opinions? The state has historically promoted Chile's economic, social, and cultural growth. Journalists have internalized this and seek politicians and others at the top of the hierarchical society. Almost by definition, the dictatorship had the answer for everything and newsrooms organized their beats accordingly. Exacerbating all of the above is the reduction of public debate to the political realm.

If Guillier is so concerned about this, why not change it? With no important soap-opera lead-in for his newscast and a small budget, his is the least-watched of the four national news shows. The penultimate rating is held by Ricardo Claro's Meganoticias on Channel 9. It has joined number two Catholic University's "Teletrece" on Channel 13 on the same side of Chile's polarized society.

So, if Televisión Nacional's "24 Horas" holds the top rating, why doesn't *it* reverse the trend of giving the politicians all the good sound bites? Because the Senate approves the president's slate of TVN board members, the nominees must be politically apportioned. Board members represent the interests of their political "constituencies." This mechanism maintains a balance in political terms. However, TVN is so distracted by this political football that it would be hard to give more attention to NGOs, environmentalists, or anyone else who does not have representatives in Congress—that is, civil society. Citizens do not have a representative on the TVN board nor an ombudsman, either of which would dilute the influence of politicians.

So, there is no mechanism for balancing things political with the items that may concern citizens but which do not happen to be on the political agenda. That leaves agenda-setting to *El Mercurio* and the powers-in-fact, who have their own NGOs to promote their agendas.

Drug wars

The "natural" order of a *gremialista* society is based on the assumption that "People don't know. And when the people don't know, they can't criticize." *El Mercurio* uses its agenda-setting power to shut citizen input out of policy debate and to corral debate in the legislative arena. Once there, the "political class" monopolizes the discussion and the solution.

El Mercurio's channeling mechanism consists of positing the terms of the debate by publishing the opinions of legislators, business leaders, and Church officials.

In a study of newspaper stories covering debate on an anti-drug bill, *El Mercurio* makes 119 mentions of politicians during the study period while mentioning only 3 members of Chilean civil society (see Table 3.8). This penchant for quoting government officials extends even to foreign governments whose representatives are mentioned far more than members of Chilean civil society. And, *El Mercurio* is even more likely to mention foreign members of civil society than Chilean citizens.

El Mercurio mentions rightist legislators (RN and UDI) 40 times during the drug debate, while it mentions Concertación legislators 11 times—although the Concertación dominates Congress, the presidency, and the cabinet. However, politicizing the drug problem is not as significant as *El Mercurio*'s preordained solution: law enforcement and prison. *El Mercurio* promotes the ideas of 20 judges and prosecutors while mentioning only 3 rehabilitation workers. This tendency is replicated within the executive branch: There are no mentions of health or education ministry officials while justice dominates.

Likewise, in *La Tercera*, politicians were mentioned 67 times while 9 members of civil society were mentioned. *El Metropolitano* managed a slightly more balanced 24 mentions of government officials and 3 members of civil society.[371]

Civic peace

Agustín Edwards sees drug abuse as part of a generalized climate of lawlessness that has prevailed since the return to democracy, beginning with the kidnaping of his son by terrorists in 1991. Edwards founded his own think-tank and advocacy group, Paz Ciudadana (Civic Peace), in 1992. Paz Ciudadana ignores white collar crime and focuses on neighborhood drug trafficking and street crime, advocating ever higher penalties while ignoring any of the social or economic factors leading to criminality, such as unemployment or inadequate education. Edwards has commitments from Copesa to give play to Paz Ciudadana's findings in *La Tercera, La Cuarta,* and *Qué Pasa*.[372]

El Mercurio's anti-crime campaign also takes the form of a series called "Victims of the Violence," where victims describe the crimes and their wounds—both physical and emotional—at the hands of muggers, thieves, and drug dealers. The series appears under its own logotype every other day, on average. In addition, *El Mercurio* gives blow-by-blow coverage of police busts, student protests, and labor unrest. (This is one of the few places a common Chilean will appear in *El Mercurio*.) For statistical backup, *El Mercurio* calls upon Paz Ciudadana.

The foundation has an eye for contradicting the government's statistics. During the period May 11–14, 2000, after the Interior Ministry released its

Table 3.8

Mentions of Actors During Debate of Drug Bill

Drug Articles August 19, 1999 to April 17, 2000		La Tercera	El Mercurio	El Metropolitano
Total # of articles		29	31	11
Executive	Current	21	40	19
	Former	2	2	0
Legislative	Concertación	12	11	3
	RN and UDI	6	40	2
Judicial	Judges and prosecutors	5	20	0
	Police	21	6	7
Total Chilean government		67	119	24
Foreign Government Officials		3	28	3
Total Chilean & Foreign governments		70	147	27
Civil Society	Chilean	9	3	3
	International	1	16	19
Rehabilitation	Governmental	3	1	0
	NGOs	9	2	0

Study conducted by the author using the same methodology as in the labor reform study.

crime statistics for the first quarter of 2000, both *El Mercurio* and *La Tercera* accused the government of a "cover-up" that "minimized" crime and "disguised" a rise in crime. *La Tercera* ran such news articles and editorials each of the following four days.

The publications based their accusations on the fact that the government statistics mentioned only reported crimes, while Paz Ciudadana's statistics were based on surveys among Chileans to assess total crimes. Paz also accused the government of comparing quarterly crime statistics to the previous quarter without either adjusting for seasonal differences or comparing to the same quarter one year ago, which would have shown an increase between the periods.

Paz Ciudadana, *El Mercurio,* and *La Tercera* cover crime as a phenomenon of poor neighborhoods. "Puente Alto is a lawless land," says a *La Tercera* headline. *El Mercurio* says, "Drugs are Sold in One of Every Four Houses," in the poor neighborhood of Cerro Navia without explaining how such a market could possibly sustain itself. (If one out of every four houses sold Avon cosmetics or snow-cones, *someone* would go out of business.) *El Mercurio* uses the term "*microtráfico*" to describe street corner dealers. However, no article mentions money laundering or the use of drugs in upper-class neighborhoods.

El Metropolitano shot back with a series of articles on white collar crime, a color map of wealthy neighborhoods where you can score drugs, and the article "The illusion of crime statistics" that debunked the notion that crime is a product of the poor.[373] Unfortunately, few read *El Metropolitano.*

As in other countries, Chile's poor are arguably more law abiding than the rich. While 19 percent of Chileans would hook up cable without paying if they got the chance, 50 percent of wealthy respondents said they would do the same. Sixty percent of Chileans admitted they would fix a traffic fine if they could, while 100 percent of the wealthy would.[374]

Eugenio Tironi, a political communications strategist who donates his time to Paz Ciudadana, justifies its view, saying correctly that violent crime is more of a worry among those who live in poverty than among the rich.[375] When asked why Paz Ciudadana ignores criminal activity of the rich, such as embezzlement or laundering the drug receipts, he said: "If you want that, you'll have to go to another foundation."[376]

Policy is determined by the Paz Ciudadana Board of Directors:[377]

José Yuraszek—absolved of white-collar crime while in charge of the privatization of Chilectra. He was named to that job by fellow *gremialista* Carlos Cáceres. **Carlos Cáceres**—Pinochet finance minister, interior minister, and president of the Central Bank who helped draft the 1980 Constitution, while lobbying to restrict voting rights to property holders. Universal suffrage threatened to turn Chile into another United States, he said, "whose political parties make it impossible to exercise freedom of choice."[378] Cáceres inherited the leadership of *gremialismo* from Jaime Guzmán. **Edmundo Pérez Yoma**—The yachtsman and Frei administration defense minister is the brother of Francisco Pérez Yoma, head of Copeva, the construction company that built leaky homes for 25,000 families with public subsidies. About the time the leaks were discovered, Housing Minister Edmundo Hermosilla received a show horse as a gift from Copeva and felt compelled to resign. **Mónica Jiménez de la J.**—PDC activist. **Gonzalo García**—Pinochet-era undersecretary of the Interior and Matte family communications strategist who is credited with keeping the family's name out of the Mapuche conflict. **María Pía Guzmán**—Renovación Nacional Congresswoman. **Roberto Edwards**—Agustín's brother. **Martín Subercaseaux**—supporter of Legionnaires of Christ and member of the Finis Terrae University board, both of which he shares with Agustín Edwards. He also is on the Finis Terrae faculty and was the creative mind behind the presidential campaigns of *gremialistas* Büchi and Lavín. **Enrique Montero Marx**—Pinochet's longest-tenured Interior Minister, engineered Pinochet's nomination for an unsuccessful additional eight-year term. The air force general is now *El Mercurio*'s legal advisor. **Francisco José Folch Verdugo**—Edwards private secretary who served on Pinochet's "Bustamante" committee that established private universities.

During the study period August 1999 to August 2000, neither *El Mercurio* nor Copesa publications disclosed the interlocking relationship between *El Mercurio* and Paz Ciudadana or the pact among Copesa, Edwards, and Paz Ciudadana when citing the think-tank as a source of information in their news stories.

It is common to hear Chileans mention that their country must be the most violent in Latin America. (It is, in fact, one of the most pacific.[379]) Many Chileans have actually commented to my Colombian wife: "In Colombia, things can't possibly be as bad as this!" (Over the decades, Colombia has arguably proven itself to be the most violent country in the world.) Media guru Tironi said that it is beyond the power of the news media to induce such an exaggerated perception of violent crime in Chile.[380] However, neither Tironi nor anyone else had an alternative explanation of how this came to be.

A UN study shows that while 78 percent of Chileans felt that it was "very probable" that they would be mugged, only 17 percent said that they had been. Likewise, while 61 percent said it was "very probable" that their homes would be robbed, 6 percent were.[381] Other studies have identified the news media as the source of the public perception.[382]

Whether the publishing duopoly is responsible for this level of distortion is not as important as asking why it contributes to it. Suspicious minds, some of them from high on the mastheads of *El Mercurio* publications, say the idea is to create a yearning for the dictatorship. *El Mercurio* eulogized "tranquility" during the dictatorship in the wake of the turbulent UP years. In any case, criminality did *not* rise dramatically with the end of the dictatorship.[383]

At the very least, creating the perception of lawlessness reflects badly upon the Concertación administrations.

Raising the specter of violence was key to Pinochet's 1988 plebescite campaign against a return to democracy. Today's use of sober-sounding statistics is more sophisticated.

Certainly Paz Ciudadana has elevated crime on the presidential agenda after the drubbing the administration receives on the issue. Lagos agreed to toughen the criminal code at the request of Paz Ciudadana. He was rewarded with a color photograph on the front page of *El Mercurio*, posing with a man wearing a dog mask and trench coat and looking very much like anti-crime dog McGruff. The caption identified the canine detective with his arm around the president as Don Graf, the new mascot of Paz Ciudadana.[384] However, there was no disclaimer saying that Don Graff was Edwards's dog.

The domination of rightist think-tanks parallels the concentration of the media. During the dictatorship, liberal thinkers often took jobs with Latin American Faculty of Social Sciences (FLACSO), Work and Employment Project (PET), Transnational Studies Institute (ILET), Latin American Economic Research Corporation (CIEPLAN), the Ford Foundation, and other refuges. Many of these folded or shrank after the return to democracy and for the same reasons as the "other disappeared" media: Foreign funding dried up and many staffers went on to government jobs.

This left a void into which the right moved, with the Liberty and Development Institute (ILD), a free-market think-tank founded by Hernán Büchi, a Pinochet cabinet member, *gremialista*, rightist presidential candidate (briefly) in 1989, and who sat on the board of Copesa in 2000. ILD studies receive a lot of ink in Copesa publications. One study covered in *Qué Pasa* showed that TVN gave Concertación politicians a greater number of seconds in sound bites than it did the rightist coalition—without a disclaimer of the relationship between the magazine and the think-tank.[385] Paz Ciudadana director Carlos Cáceres is president of ILD.

Eliodoro Matte founded the Center for Public Studies (CEP) which frequently plumbs public opinion with the help of Adimark, whose owner, Roberto Méndez, is a board member of Paz Ciudadana.

Losing presidential hopeful Joaquín Lavín founded Action Chile as a charity organization that specialized in collecting donations for projects in poor neighborhoods. Lavín's supporters donate money with the knowledge that Lavín, as the current mayor of Santiago, will be on hand to cut the ribbons (and the newspaper duopoly will be on hand to publish the photographs) as a way to garner votes among the poor in preparation for a second attempt at the presidency.

However, opponents of the powers-in-fact fail to see the "concentration of the media" as problematic. Andrés Allamand himself dismissed *El Mercurio* and Copesa's subsidies by saying: "That's normal." To the State Bank swaps to keep *El Mercurio* out of the hands of the Concertación, he responded:

"Who on the left could have run it?" To Bardón's million-dollar loan to Finis Terrae University, Allamand says: "So what?" And to Bardón's seat on *El Mercurio*'s editorial board along with Montero, Passicot, Errázuriz, and other Pinochet collaborators, he asks rhetorically: "What's wrong with that?" There is a complacency among Chileans that Allamand summed up by saying: "That's the way things are in Latin America."[386] Things certainly are that way in Latin America and in Southeast Asia as well, where tightly-knit oligarchies hamper free markets and undermine democracy.

In this chapter, we have seen that *gremialista* media owners violate journalistic standards and dictate news content through hierarchical editorial management that impedes journalistic integrity, innovation, and quality. "*El Mercurio* editorializes not just on the editorial page but in the headlines and [the rest]," said EMSAP's former general manager Fernando Léniz.[387]

Chile's media owners form the epicenter of the powers-in-fact that are arguably more powerful than the government itself. As the Chilean dean of American University's law school, Claudio Grossman observed, "In Chile, the government is in the opposition."[388]

However, there still is some hope for the future of Chilean journalism, which will be addressed in the final chapter.

Chapter 4

News Today and Tomorrow

Economic totalitarianism leads—necessarily and inevitably—to political totalitarianism.

—El Mercurio, March 18, 1972

New technologies and foreign investment bringing unadulterated news to Chile have forced slight changes in the duopoly's treatment of the news. Several Chilean projects threaten to change the way news is managed, but face formidable obstacles as well as co-option by the duopoly through investment and expanded use of calculated pluralism.

THE FUTURE OF PRINT MEDIA

The 2001 Press Law eliminated legal restrictions on foreign ownership of media, except when the investor's domicile country places limits on the permissible proportion of foreign ownership; in those cases, Chile will then impose reciprocating restrictions. News directors must still be Chilean, according to the Press Law, while ownership and changes of ownership will be public information.

El Mercurio's corporate by-laws will maintain their built-in protection against outside interference: Although family members of Agustín Edwards hold all the shares, any shareholder must prove his or her citizenship, and non-Chileans may not own more than 15 percent of *El Mercurio*. El Mercurio S.A.P.'s articles of incorporation are curious in light of the newspaper's promotion of free market capitalism: "The board's objective is to keep all of the corporate assets in Chilean hands, considering the influence that the company's publications can have on a national level."[389]

Just the same, *El Mercurio* could face challengers as Chile's agenda-setting publication, but they would need lots of backing.

Clarín

One can only guess how much cash would be necessary to challenge *El Mercurio*. Perhaps $50 million would furnish a physical plant with enough journalists, presses, and equipment to produce a one-stop, must-read newspaper. Another $50 million could produce the supplemental magazines. In addition, the owners might have to endure $100 million in losses over a decade to sway dyed-in-the wool Chileans toward a more liberal newspaper, for a total of $200 million.

The only project with that kind of cash would be *Clarín*. Should Victor Pey win his arbitration at the World Bank, the most optimistic estimated award that included full restitution of his buildings, presses, and lost earnings could total $200 million. He might have to spend it all—perhaps posthumously—to challenge *El Mercurio* with no guarantee of success.

However, the Concertación shows no sign of relenting in its opposition to a reincarnation of Pey's newspaper.

Le Monde

Representatives of France's liberal newspaper, *Le Monde*, make periodic trips to Chile to meet with a group of investors about the possibility of attracting a liberal-minded readership. To avoid the biases traditionally created by Chilean media owners, *Le Monde* would require that Chilean investors be from varied political viewpoints—without being themselves politicians. That is tricky to impose, given the thick alliances in Chile between money and political power and the influence of the powers-in-fact. Prospective investors are José Said, who can boast of holding investments with George Soros, and Fernando Léniz, a former general manager of *El Mercurio*.[390]

Le Monde would also require investment by a large number of small shareholders who would ostensibly represent the interests of the readers. This scheme could condemn *Le Monde*-Chile to the same affliction as Televisión Nacional, where attention to political balance overwhelms the full array of public interests. Also, this model does not protect *Le Monde* from the irrationality of Chile's advertisers.[391]

One important contribution these newspapers might make would be a home for some of Chile's great journalists who are currently not working. No national medium has an "investigative unit." Several journalists (not all of them unemployed) said they dreamed of producing a newspaper similar to Argentina's *Página 12*, whose stock and trade is investigative reporting. The most onerous legal obstacles to such a publication were rescinded by the Press Law. However, journalists continue to be cowed by similar provisions in the Criminal Code.

Some new media are broadening incrementally the freedom of expression in Chile.

The Clinic

At first glance, *The Clinic* does not look to be a serious blow for freedom of expression, what with its photos of politicians' faces pasted onto the bodies of women and its satiric headlines. A recent example: When the Church and the Lagos government had a spat over the approval of the "day-after pill," *The Clinic* headline read: "Government and Church Agree on a Day-After Communion Wafer."

The writing can be howlingly funny or as crude as its photomontages, but there is a method in its madness: *The Clinic* has redrawn the line of what one can get away with in Chile. The tabloid is distributed from one end of Chile to the other and routinely sells 35,000 copies. "The success is not because of quality," editor-investor Patricio Fernández admits. "It's because a similar product doesn't exist." *The Clinic* was launched in 1999, while Pinochet was under arrest in a London clinic, hence the name in English.

Among essays that range from wry to ribald is sharp political satire that seems to "dishonor" public figures of all stripes in a way that would be damned hard to prove in a court of law. That may explain why *The Clinic* has not been dragged into court, or why Lavín campaign manager Carlos Alberto Délano resorted to insulting Fernández while Alan Cooper, who was involved in the botched attempt to kidnap General Schneider 30 years ago, hit him in the face after an article that made fun of Jaime Guzmán. *The Clinic* spatters mud in all directions, says Fernández, so no politician has attacked *The Clinic* because he then would become the newspaper's foil.

The paper's layout belies the fact that Fernández studied art history in Florence. He returned to Chile as an art critic for *Las Ultimas Noticias*—which fired him once *The Clinic* hit the streets. Papers of the media duopoly do not cover the doings of *The Clinic*, although (or maybe, because) its circulation per fortnightly issue tops the daily circulation of *La Segunda*. Fernández is already seeing a profit from the $4,000 investment he and a partner made.[392]

Fernández says *The Clinic* points in the direction other media will have to go because it has filled a need to laugh and shock in the tradition of *Clarín* or *Puro Chile*. As with those pre-coup scandal sheets, readers included intellectuals, irreverent college students, and the poor who like a good chuckle—anyone but "the establishment." Fernández says *The Clinic* could even spin off publications that would target groups of readers—with investigative journalism or thoughtful essays—without sacrificing its outsider status.

One obstacle inherent to satirical publications is that potential advertisers are sometimes doubtful that readers take their ads seriously. *The Clinic* often lets advertisers test their effectiveness for free.

Another publication that started out underground is now above ground.

MTG

The newspaper duopoly made novel use of the 1980 Constitution, which precludes government investment in new media without approval of the legislature, to kick *Metro* out of the Santiago subway. *Metro* was founded by a multinational that pays the cities of Stockholm, Prague, and a dozen other cities for exclusive rights to give away their newspapers in the underground. National Press Association lawyers argued that amounted to state support for the medium. *El Mercurio* broke its ban on labor coverage and ran front-page interviews with the union of newsstand operators who moaned publicly that *Metro* would put them out of business. Privately, they said *El Mercurio* put them up to it.

The courts nullified the deal and forced *Metro* to change its name. Copesa then relaunched its failing afternoon paper, *La Hora,* to be distributed free wherever *MTG* (née *Metro*) was. Newsstand owners have not gone out of business, because the free newspapers expanded the universe of newspaper readers, who were nearly non-existent on subways before *Metro/MTG*. That universe has expanded by 18 percent—which is a good thing because 78 percent of Chileans do not read newspapers at all, said *MTG* editor Rodrigo de Castro. De Castro wrote for *Análisis* and spent part of the dictatorship in Italy learning the journalism trade.

MTG claims to distribute 120,000 issues five days a week and has plans to print 200,000 copies of a 32-page issue by 2002. Editor de Castro attributes the acceptance to the newspaper's neutrality, which is strict even by U.S. standards. There are no editorials. Opinion columns must be submitted by individuals, not representatives of political, religious, or peak organizations. Neutrality comes in part from the heavy use of wire services—which also cuts costs and at the same time makes the newspaper dry. However, the paper is not shy about picking up a scoop when it can. These scoops may come from journalists working for establishment media that have spiked their stories, a positive form of *coleguismo*.

De Castro said that it is not the paper's political balance that brought on the duopoly's lawsuit but rather *MTG*'s encroachment into advertising spending. The duopoly newspapers give deep discounts to the advertising agencies, who turned their backs on *MTG*, said de Castro. That backfired when *MTG* created a system of direct sales to small businesses such as travel agencies and auto dealerships that cannot afford to advertise in a nationally-distributed newspaper, said de Castro: "[The ads] are for the middle class [customers] from the middle class [owners of the small businesses]."

The bite-sized articles (100–500 words) that are ideal for subway riding give *MTG* the appearance of *USA Today*. It is a buffet of varied items that are readily accessible. "It's really a printed version of an Internet newspaper," said de Castro.[393] That's about as subversive as news gets in Chile.

The Internet

In countries that enjoy democracy but suffer from media concentration, the Internet has democratized the flow of information to the benefit of those outside the mainstream, such as religious cults, spelunkers, hate groups, or Studebaker owners. Members of these groups may now contact each other inexpensively over a broader territory, uniting a larger number of people than was previously possible. In Chile, where the concentration of media does not reflect the views and concerns of the majority, the World Wide Web has the potential to command a swath of mainstream Chileans.

Chinese and Singaporean officials know the futility of attempting to block web content at the borders. The Chilean right is finding it far easier to restrict the content at the source. Ricardo Claro, owner of Megavisión and Metropolis-Intercom cable, has already announced his intention to invest heavily in Internet services that would draw web users away from sites such as El Mostrador.

El Mostrador has made significant strides in providing mainstream news coverage on the web, albeit of a limited nature due to budget constraints. Taking advantage of the speed of the Internet, El Mostrador has published stories that the duopoly then is forced to pick up. For example, El Mostrador made the private retirement system's 2000 performance its top story the same day the Superintendent of AFPs reported the industry's paltry 4.4 percent earnings. *La Tercera* may not have covered the report at all, because its owners are large AFP investors. Once El Mostrador posted the report, *La Tercera* ran it two days late, on Friday, at the end of a column of "economic briefs," and below a report on American Airlines's 2000 year-end earnings figures.

El Mercurio covered the story too, but later and without much play. All three media reproduced lightly edited versions of the AFP superintendent's press release. The absence of further analysis could be chalked up to the reporters' wishes to avoid accusations of bias, to avoid a *telefonazo*, or to avoid work. In this case, however, the media's differential treatment resulted from the story's placement, which is determined by the editors, not the writers.

El Mostrador managing editor Federico Joannón is a lawyer, as is a majority of the nine shareholders. They hold nearly equal shares but represent varied points of view, "including the right," boasts Joannón. Their mission is simple: "We were bored with the press in Chile," said Joannón in his office.[394] The downtown rabbit warren is reminiscent of the offices of the "trench" magazines during the dictatorship.

It is surprising how little their million-dollar investment buys when it comes to setting up a news organization. However, keeping costs down lets Joannón predict a break-even point by the end of their second year in business—not a pipe dream with 50,000 visits a day. That is more hits than *La Tercera*'s and *El Mercurio*'s on-line publications get combined—and El Mostrador's ad rates are cheaper per eyeball, says Joannón. Advertisers already include airlines, banks, and insurance companies. El Mostrador sells content to portals and has an in-kind agreement with the BBC. How far El Mostrador can go depends in part on how many Chileans have access to computers. There may be a million in Chile today.

Besides taking a slice of the advertising pie, El Mostrador is forcing changes in Chile's staid media.

El Mercurio *On-Line*

Readers who frequent *El Mercurio* on-line may have the impression that the previous chapter of this book exaggerates *El Mercurio*'s lack of pluralism. Actually, *El Mercurio* on-line is clearly more liberal and inclusive than the print version. The intrusion by El Mostrador and by websites outside of Chile has caused a revision of editorial policy at www.emol.cl.

"Former dictator Augusto Pinochet" may appear at www.emol.cl in recognition of the futility of editing out the "D" word since it appears everywhere else on the web. In effect, *El Mercurio* treats www.emol.cl like another supplemental magazine, only more so, allowing it to cover more contemporary ideas that would offend its core readership of stodgy aristocrats who largely stick to the print version. This is simply the latest example of calculated pluralism through the segmentation of *El Mercurio*'s readers.

Websites of the duopoly are slow in posting breaking news. For the most part, they rely on the newspapers' reporters who file on the newspapers' deadlines. Not being attached to a print newspaper, El Mostrador has a never-ending news cycle. El Mostrador was the only web-based medium to handle correctly the May 20, 2001 death of 26 prisoners during a fire in the northern city of Iquique. Prison officials initially blamed the fire on a riot—perhaps to cover up the fact that they had delayed the firefighters' access. *El Mercurio* on-line wrote the official story and left it posted during the entire following day as did PrimeraPagina.com and latercera.com. However, by 10:00 P.M. on the 21st, El Mostrador's own story said that the blaze had been attributed to an unauthorized cooking fire, not a riot. Although *El Mercurio* on-line had access to Agence France-Presse and Orbe stories that questioned the official version at various times on the 21st, *El Mercurio* stuck with the story that blamed rioting inmates rather than point to a failure of the authorities to admit to firefighters.

El Mostrador has revived radio's largely-abandoned system of using correspondents in distant cities, in the process frequently scooping the radio networks, which in Chile have become notoriously slow.

RADIO

A spin across the 35 stations on Santiago's FM dial may yield as many as 10 stations playing songs in English. This is only the most obvious testament to foreign influence in Chilean radio. Eleven of the top radio networks in Chile are owned by two foreign consortia: investors SER and Caracol from Spain and Colombia, respectively; and Ibero American. The investors are forming "networks of networks" in preparation for the day that multinationals will make buys for all of Latin America from, say, Miami.

In the process, foreign investors have accelerated the concentration of the media—albeit for financial reasons, not ideological ones. They buy up local stations, lay off the news staffs, and use the frequencies to relay satellite signals emitted from the studios in Santiago. Some 89 local stations, many with newsrooms, were closed in 1999 alone.[395]

Closing local newsrooms is devastating for local news coverage, of course, but it also eliminates the possibility of true network coverage. Nearly gone are the days when reporters at affiliated stations filed reports with the network, which could then broadcast them as national news. The local independent stations also are cut out of advertising, 99 percent of which is sold to national advertisers by the national networks—all of which are based in Santiago. As local stations close, low-power community stations are springing up, although they are hamstrung by the prohibition against the sale of advertising.

Foreign radio owners use successful formats that mate contemporary rock and Caribbean music with highly animated deejays whose bosses do not care a fig about Chilean morality. Radio's most successful show, "El Chacotero Sentimental," did not play music but was instead a lonely hearts open mic. Callers got the chance to unload their personal baggage on the sympathetic host, Roberto Artiagoitía, a/k/a Rumpi, who has since taken his show to the "W" network, owned by Caracol's CRC. Because most of the talk is of the love-and-sex variety, the show's faithful developed their own language of euphemisms and metaphors to describe the intimate details of their lives. It is debatable whether Chilean networks would have been interested in such libertine talk, but it was not an issue for Ibero American.

Unfortunately, foreign investors do not care much about Chilean news, either, since a stable of journalists is more expensive to feed than a deejay and an engineer. The Colombians, who have crack news teams back home, have made some inroads into local news gathering. Not only would it be hard to outdo Radio Chilena, it would be even harder to make money at it.

All news, all the time

The brightest spot in radio news is Radio Chilena's conversion to a 24-hour news format. "SóloNoticias" hired on 100 journalists to recreate true network reporting from the provinces. Between morning and evening drive time newscasts, the slack hours are filled by talk shows, which are punctuated by breaking news and updates. Radio Chilena sold off its music network, Aurora, for $10 million as a way to finance the all-news format.[396] "SóloNoticias" needs to speed up its delivery of breaking news and concentrate on business news if it is to compete with the increasing rapidity of Internet news. The stakes are higher than just turning a profit, however.

Futures file

Taken together, these news projects and technologies may challenge the duopoly and may be better allies to journalists than their own association. The aim of the College of Journalists and ethics panels is to further the professionalism and prestige of the press and journalists by fostering "responsibility" within the press corps. If anything, the Chilean news media could benefit by being *less* responsible—to the powers-in-fact, politicians, their parties, and *telefonazos*, less responsible to business combines and mostly, less responsible to the "politics of consensus" sought by the Concertación.

Prior to the coup, civil society and businesses looked to the government for solutions. Then, the Chilean polity was atomized and alienated from government during the dictatorship.[397] Since the return to democracy, Chileans committed to furthering freedom of expression lobby quietly for reforms but make few demands. For example, journalists are more shy about risking jail time than they were during the dictatorship. If a high-profile journalist landed in jail today, she would become a focus of public pressure. It was quiet lobbying that ended film censorship, although protest would have accelerated the process.

Film censorship

The Interamerican Human Rights Court of the Organization of American States found that Chile must lift its ban not only on "The Last Temptation of Christ" but on all censored films—which *El Mercurio* called a "recommendation" but was reported as an "order" in *La Tercera* and El Mostrador. The Court gave Chile "a reasonable period" to change its censorship laws and Chile will eventually comply because "you can't block the sun with just one finger," as the Spanish proverb goes. Chilean cable companies bound by CNTV censorship have a competitive disadvantage against satellite operators, which are not.

Technology, markets, and foreign investment will eventually force more openness in Chilean communications in general, led by the entertainment industry. The importation of a broader range of movies or erotic films is an advance (of sorts), but what about the all-important news coverage of economic and political issues? Foreign investors' detachment from Chilean internal politics is a qualified plus for Guillien's Chilevisión-Channel 11 news, whose rating has climbed from three to eight points.

However, foreign investors are not willing to lose money to promote a viewpoint as are some Chilean media owners. Nor will foreign media receive the subsidies, bailouts, free licenses, or protections that every one of today's major Chilean media have at some time enjoyed. Foreign investment has liberalized content but has shuttered newsrooms. If foreign media are not interested in news because it is not lucrative, the news duopoly and the rest of the right will control news content indefinitely unless Chilean media challenge the duopoly.

Alternative media are needed and with deep pockets. The cost of not doing this could be greater, however. The media duopoly is controlled by the same people who sponsored and squelched criticism of the economic crisis of 1981–1982. The elite's ownership of the news media furthers its own narrow interests, while at the same time insulating the oligarchs, the Chicago Boys, and their policies from scrutiny. That may hinder Chile's economic expansion. Perhaps it already has.

"The End of the Chilean Model?" was a cover story for the Latin American Dow Jones business magazine published in Santiago, *América Economía*, at the time Chile entered its economic slump in the late 1990s. However, that question has not been raised in Chilean media. Control of business information benefits incumbents and creates monopolies. In concert with Chile's rigid class structure, restrictions on upward mobility and individual initiative exacerbate class and ethnic cleavages in Chilean society. *Gremialistas,* who share Guzmán's fear that the poor, having no commitment to Chile's economic system will wind up voting for leftists, should know that the answer is to encourage them to participate in the system, not to take away their rights to vote. Small business is the foundation of innovation and the creator of jobs in wealth-producing societies. However, Chile's economy is dependent upon corporations that export raw materials and speculate in finance.

Restricting information and debate is the common goal shared by Chile's market fundamentalists and religious fundamentalists. A government that is separate from religion and disinterested in business affairs is the only entity that can assure equality before the law, equal access to information, and a tolerance of opposing ideas. The common interest of the religious and market fundamentalists in Chile is to prevent the citizenry from deciding upon a set of social principles democratically through their state apparatus.

OPEN SOCIETY

At present an uneasy alliance prevails in politics between market fundamentalists and religious fundamentalists. They are united in their opposition to big government but they have quite different objectives in mind. Market fundamentalists object to government intervention in the economy; religious fundamentalists oppose the liberal standards imposed by the state. Market fundamentalists are against international cooperation for the same reason that they dislike big government: They want to give business a free hand. Religious fundamentalists are against it for the opposite reason: They resent the threat global markets pose to their intrinsic values. It is amazing how the two disparate groups have been able to reconcile their differences. I expect that they will find it increasingly difficult to do so the more progress they make in achieving their objectives.

—George Soros in *The Crisis of Global Capitalism: Open Society Endangered*[398]

The allegory of rocketing La Moneda could not have been clearer: The state would be dismembered and rebuilt. The destruction of a national symbol and the suicide of a president is normally a moment of loss—even to those who deem it "necessary." *Qué Pasa*'s headlines were gleeful: "Here come the Hawker-Hunters!" Construction of the demolished state according to the *gremialista* concept of "subsidiarity," which restricts the role of the state, leaves to the private sector the ownership and regulation of nearly everything, with especial emphasis on the news media.

This *nueva institucionalidad,* which took nearly a generation to establish, is so firmly ensconced that a decade of democracy—an even longer tradition in Chile—has been unable to make fundamental modifications. Although 19th century Chile was on a liberal path, industrialists of the right found ideological bases for promoting the liberal economy while limiting other liberal values. A new elite has carried on that tradition. Convinced of their moral and economic righteousness, they are willing to impose their beliefs upon the bulk of Chileans who may feel otherwise.

With the emergence of the opposition press during the latter years of dictatorship, Chile's press represented a greater variety of views and was better suited to the needs of a democracy than are the media of today. Opposition publications that sprung up during the dictatorship died afterwards, leaving the pro-military media largely unchallenged. During the transition to democracy, military saber-rattling prevented elected administrations from making democratic reforms, enabling the consolidation of the "authoritarian enclaves" in the Constitution and the entrenchment of the right. Although the most repressive press laws have been removed from the books, it is unlikely to have much of an effect upon those media whose owners are dedicated to promoting anti-democratic political and economic ideas. These ideas are far to the right of the center of gravity of Chile's polity, which has elected governments from the left of center. These elections should not be misconstrued as a weakness of the right but as a strength: The current government is hamstrung—on one side by the right and on the other by its own timidity before the media duopoly and the powers-in-fact.

UDI's *gremialistas* are the only viable political force to have emerged from Latin America's military dictatorships. Futhermore, the anti-democratic forces of *gremialismo*, UDI, religious fundamentalists, market fundamentalists, and Chile's media owners have actually grown in power and influence during the past decade of democracy. At a time when other political leaders, such as José María Aznar and Carlos Menem have renounced their ties with dictators Franco and Perón, respectively, the Chilean right has not distanced itself completely from Pinochet.

The Chilean authoritarian right took advantage of state resources and the government-imposed near-monopoly over periodicals and speech to position itself to impose a post-Pinochet *nueva institucionalidad*. Under the banner of "free markets," the Chilean right has been able to wield the power of the private sector with at least as much force as the three Concertación administrations, thus limiting the field of action of Chile's elected leaders. The result has been a power shift from the mass politics of the 1960s, in which the aggregated interests of the citizens were satisfied through the state apparatus, which was crushed under Pinochet. Gone with it is Chile's closed, statist economy and paternalistic welfare system. Gone as well is the state's ability to create an even playing field—among economic, social, or political actors.

While the *nueva institucionalidad* reduces the state's role, it does not leave those functions unattended. In fact, it shifts them into the private sector. "The Five Pillars" of Chile's *nueva institucionalidad* (the 1980 Constitution, privatized education, *isapres*, AFPs, and private property) places control of these critical functions in the private sector. With the exception of private property, these are all *gremialista* creations. Today, Pinochet's collaborators among the Chicago Boys and *gremialistas* control many of these institutions through ownership. And they control the information the public reads, sees, and hears about them.

Chile's economic outlook is filtered through the *gremialista*-Chicago Boy media duopoly, which dispenses business advice. The man who publishes this business advice is Agustín Edwards, possibly Chile's most spectacular business failure, having reduced his family's empire to a $100 million debt. He managed this despite his unique access to Pinochet or any of his policy makers. Edwards's ineptitude is rivaled by Chicago Boy Javier Vial and may soon be joined by Chicago Boy leader Sergio de Castro, whose business empire is now shaky.

The media duopoly defends the likes of José Yuraszek, Miguel Angel Poduje, and Alvaro Saieh, supposed proponents of "free market capitalism," none of whom has gotten rich without the state: Vial had the inside track on lax banking regulations; Saieh and Jorge Ross built fortunes on Central Bank buy-backs of international debt;[399] de Castro bid on governmentally-guaranteed concessions; Poduje begged for government-subsidized housing contracts in *La Tercera*; Yuraszek "privatized" Chilectra. *El Mercurio* grew the fastest during what was nearly a government-protected monopoly during the dictatorship. "*El Mercurio* was never a free-market enterprise," said Vial. "They always had a monopoly and tried to be the only newspaper."[400]

El Mercurio uses its market position to question the very value of democracy on its pages. "Is Democracy Liberty?" asks the headline of one of *El Mercurio*'s op-ed pieces from the Future of Freedom Foundation. In it, Jacob Hornberger argues that the Bill of Rights was attached to the U.S. Constitution because "Americans knew that democracy does not mean liberty and that historically democracy has been a threat to liberty."[401]

This argument echos Hayek, who wrote that democracy is no more essential to liberty than it is to a foreigner who may enjoy liberty even while living in a country where he is not entitled to vote. Guzmán argued against universal suffrage because it can result in the tyranny of the majority. His solution: minority rule. The disenfranchised may still be free, under Hayek's logic; they simply become foreigners in their own land. The imposition of such a social order is not being accomplished through an open public debate. It is being decided by the powers-in-fact and promoted by the owners of Chile's print media.

The *gremialistas* found it unnecessary to deny suffrage to those without property. Today, Joaquín Lavín is trolling the slums for their votes. The "authoritarian enclaves," the military, control of the media, and Concertación acquiescence are sufficient to prevent citizen participation and any erosion of "The Five Pillars" of the system. Obviously, the business leaders are beyond the criticism of the news media. Even when the State Security Law made criticism of office holders a breech of national security, Chilean journalists found it easier to criticize politicians than business leaders. This is because the media duopoly has a disdain for democratic expression through party politics while the private sector has immunity from criticism. There is reason for concern about a society without checks and balances.

George Soros warns that the rigidity of "market fundamentalists" could be the end of the Open Society as Karl Popper envisioned it: It was the very rigidity of Marxism and fascism that led to their demise. The free flow of information and ideas forms the basis for political stability and economic expansion since neither the state nor an oligarchy is efficient at allocating resources and deciding what people should have.[402]

Soros warns us about capitalists who deify the free market but are agnostics when it comes to societal values of democracy and tolerance. However, neither the quotation that opens this section nor the book where it is found addresses Chilean democracy. For Soros, the "capitalist threat" to the Open Society is simply the collateral damage of *laissez-faire*. However, Chile's rightist elite is engaged in a kind of social engineering descended from Spanish fascism that seeks to impose *gremialismo* upon a society that is nominally a democracy.

Joaquín Lavín is a *gremialista par excellence*. There is every indication that he will win in 2005, given his near-win in 2000, the lack of obvious

Concertación candidates, and given the exposure he will gain by christening the projects funded by his private-sector backers in the meantime. The ribbon cuttings in needy neighborhoods will garner him votes among the poor, a strategy UDI has followed since the party was founded in 1983, says party president Pablo Longueira.[403]

As president, Lavín would enjoy a press holiday surpassed only by Silvio Berlusconi, the media magnate who owns, or, as prime minister, controls, all of Italy's television networks. He enjoys the backing of Copesa publications, of course, given his Chicago Boys and *gremialista* loyalty: "I am in public service because of Jaime Guzmán," Lavín recently told *La Hora*.[404] His Opus Dei activism shields him from criticism from Ricardo Claro's Megavisión. And as former business and economy editor at *El Mercurio*, he would be favored by "the dean." He would nominate members to the CNTV board, name its director, and name the editors of *La Nacion*.

A Lavín presidency would usher the return of Pinochet's Chicago Boy collaborators, who have indicated no willingness to admit to their mistakes. Alvaro Bardón, for example, still insists that de Castro *should not have budged from the 39-peso per dollar exchange rate.*[405] These men are convinced that it was factors beyond their control that caused their downfall. "The problem is not that the world conspired by its economic slowdown to make things more difficult for Chileans than for others, but rather that the Chicago Boys turned out to be bad economists," Sidney Weintraub wrote in 1984 in *The Wall Street Journal*. "The Chicago Boys were so certain that their economic model would succeed that there has been no real economic debate in Chile for the past 10 years."[406] With the business community and the news touting the Chicago Boys, there has been no debate during more than a decade of democracy, either.

During the dictatorship, there is no record that Edwards used his influence with U.S. officials to denounce murder and torture by the state, made no speeches to the Inter-American Press Association (IAPA) about the lack of democracy in Chile, and did not abet the CIA in toppling Pinochet. Instead, Edwards hosted IAPA in Santiago and brought Pinochet to the meeting. Likewise, Pinochet's Chicago Boys left no record that they urged an improvement in the human rights situation to promote Chile's business interests, or that they denounced Pinochet at international conferences or multilateral banks. Instead, they hid behind the pretext that their economic science is value-neutral.

Media owners tied to the UDI-*gremialista* authoritarian movement see themselves as defenders of the *nueva institucionalidad,* Guzmán's name for *gremialismo* without Pinochet. Lavín's apostasy from Pinochet—by saying that he should stand trial—was not mere campaign rhetoric. *Gremialistas* believe that the *nueva institucionalidad* is more important than Pinochet. Lavín's move was as shrewd as it was Machiavellian.

El Mercurio remains faithful to the *capitán general.* But Copesa, Lavín, and the *gremialistas* understand that a trial would have benefitted the UDI. Making a scapegoat of Pinochet and allowing his legacy to be heaped with the thousands of lives that he destroyed would expunge UDI and its *nueva institucionalidad* of its past collaboration with the regime. In any case, Lavín has come a long way since 1991, when he defended UDI's decoration of Pinochet with the Jaime Guzmán medal, saying: "He deserves it more than anyone."[407]

Under three administrations, Chile's Concertación of Parties for Democracy undercut the mass, participatory democracy of the 1960s, leaving in place not only the enclaves of Guzmán's "authoritarian, protected democracy but also the concentration of media. Long-range projects such as establishing media outlets from scratch are difficult for the Concertacíon, which that has been struggling to stay in power. The French call such alliances "cohabitation," which shares the aversion to long-term planning with the living arrangement from which it takes its name: Partners who are living together "for now" are less likely to take on a mortgage than those who have a more permanent commitment. One thing that might force parties of the left to focus would be a win by the right.

In keeping with Chilean tradition, newspapers pop up around election time and disappear soon after. As Lagos's lead over Lavín nearly vanished in 1999, *El Nuevo Fortín Mapocho* was revived as an eight-page weekly, capturing some of the populism—at a popular 20-cent price—if not the tendentiousness of the original. It closed down soon after the Concertación was safely returned to the presidency. Director Manuel Salazar said the Concertación pays real attention to "concentration of the media" when it is out of power: "The best thing that could happen to journalism in Chile would be a Lavín victory."[408] Such circumstances might do more to revive more ephemeral party organs than to establish media such as El Mostrador and *MTG,* which are not attached to parties, did not spring up as a response to an electoral need, and thus have longer life expectancies.

There is more to Salazar's observation than a hyperbole or nostalgia: Toward the end of the dictatorship, journalism was more pluralistic and better suited to democracy than is Chilean journalism today. The existence of the resistance publications indicates that Chilean journalists have sufficient talent and courage to play a role in the promotion of democracy.

Notes

1. Fernando Léniz, interview by author, Santiago, Chile, 2001.

2. Hernaní Banda, news director of Radio Portales 1968–1969, 1975–1976, and 1983–1985, interview by author, Temuco, 2000.

3. Iván Cienfuegos, former managing editor of *El Sur de Concepción*, interview by author, Temuco, 1999.

4. Alberto Gamboa, former *Clarín* editor, interview from Catholic University archives.

5. James R. Whelan, *Out of the Ashes: Life, Death and Transfiguration of Democracy in Chile, 1833–1988* (Washington, D.C.: Regnery Gateway, 1989), 455.

6. Radio Magallanes's Leonardo Cáceres, who took in Allende's final message, interview by author.

7. Carmen Ortuzar Meza, "La Prensa antes y después del '70" (Universidad Católica, Santiago, 1972).

8. Juan Gabriel Valdés, *Pinochet's Economists: The Chicago School in Chile* (Cambridge: Cambridge University Press, 1995).

9. Gonzalo Vial Correa, *Una Transcendental Experiencia Académica* (Santiago: Fundación Facultad de Ciencias Económicas y Administrativas Pontificia Universidad Católica de Chile, 1999), 82–84.

10. *Ibid.*, 115.

11. Harry G. Johnson, *On Economics and Society* (Chicago: University of Chicago Press, 1975).

12. Marcelo Pollack, *The New Right in Chile: 1973–97* (New York: St. Martin's Press, 1999), 46.

13. George Soros, *The Crisis of Global Capitalism: Open Society Endangered* (New York: Public Affairs/Persus, 1998), 41.

14. Vial Correa, 155–181.

15. Valdés, 225.

16. Mirko Macari, "Simplemente Jaime," *El Sábado* (March 31, 2001). *El Mercurio's* Saturday magazine quoted Guzmán's 1962 letter on the occasion of the 10th anniversary of his murder.

17. Pollack, 31–33.

18. Pollack, 30–36.

19. Pollack, 33–50.

20. Renato Cristi, *El Pensamiento Político de Jaime Guzmán: Autoridad y Libertad* (Santiago: Editorial LOM, 2000), 12.

21. Arturo Fontaine Aldunate, *Los Economistas y el Presidente Pinochet* (Santiago: Zig Zag, 1988), 103–104.

22. Léniz, interview by author, Santiago, 2001.

23. Vial Correa, 194.

24. Carlos Huneeus, *El Régimen de Pinochet* (Santiago: Editorial Sudamericana, 2000), 336–339.

25. Macari. The senator quoted is Jaime Gazmuri.

26. Vial, interview by author, Santiago, 2001.

27. *Qué Pasa*, "El Enigma de Rudolf Hess," 19 June 1974.

28. *Qué Pasa*, 22 September 1973.

29. Lenka Carvallo G., "El Alma de la Economía," *El Mercurio*, 1 April 2001.

30. *Ibid.*

31. Vial, interview by author, Santiago, 2001.

32. *Ibid.*

33. *El Mercurio,* 19 April, 1981, quoted in: Renato Cristi, *El Pensamiento Político de Jaime Guzmán: Autoridad y Libertad* (Santiago: Editorial LOM, 2000), 46.

34. Valdés, 29.

35. *El Mercurio,* 15 April 1973, quoted in: Renati Cristi and Carlos Ruiz, *El Pensamiento Conservador en Chile* (Santiago: Editorial Universitaria, 1992), 115.

36. Kelly, interview by author, Santiago, 2001.

37. Fontaine, 16–17.

38. Christopher Hitchens, "The Case Against Henry Kissinger," *Harper's Magazine*, February 2001.

39. *Ibid.*

40. The Edwards combine printer, Lord Cochrane, was a shareholder in *PEC*.

41. Mary Helen Spooner, *Soldiers in a Narrow Land* (Berkeley and Los Angeles: University of California Press, 1994), 26.

42. Orlando Sáenz, quoted in Mónica González, *La Conjura* (Santiago: Ediciones B, 2000), 138–139.

43. *El Mercurio* published a vehement front-page denial of the information published in *Covert Action in Chile*, the 1975 U.S. Senate Intelligence Committee Report. In an interview with the author, Léniz denied that the paper had accepted CIA monies.

44. Claudio Durán, *El Mercurio: Ideología y Propaganda 1954–1994* (Santiago: Academia de Humanismo Cristiano de Chile, 1995). In addition: Guillermo Sunkel, *El Mercurio: 10 Años de Educación Político-Ideológica 1969–1979* (Santiago: ILET, 1983).

45. Eduardo Silva, *The State and Capital in Chile* (Boulder, Colorado: Westview Press Inc., 1996), 44–45.

46. *Ibid.*

47. *Ibid.,* 47.

48. Ross, interview by author, Santiago, 2001.

49. Léniz, interview by author.

50. Silva, 4.

51. Fontaine quoted in González, 323.

52. *Ibid.*, 14–20.

53. González, throughout.

54. González, 119.

55. Quoted in González, 118–119.

56. Silva, 71; Fontaine; *Diccionario Bibligráfico de Chile* (Santiago: Editorial Universitaria, 1985), 14–20; and Andrés Sanfuentes, Alvaro Bardón, and Hermógenes Pérez de Arce, interviews by author, Santiago, 2000.

57. Sebastian Edwards and Daniel Lederman, *The Political Economy of Unilateral Trade Liberalization: The Case of Chile* (Boston: National Bureau of Economic Research, 1998).

58. Kelly, interview by author, Santiago, 2001.

59. González, 184–85. González reproduces a secret June 1, 1973 memorandum that circulated among military coup plotters.

60. The Spanish word for "brick" is *ladrillo,* which is a derisive term for a weighty, dense book, although the Chicago Boys use the term with self-deprecating humor.

61. For a more complete examination of the Chicago Boys' *gremialista* ideology, see: Ken Dermota, *Chile Inédito* (Santiago: Ediciones B, 2002), Chapter 1.

62. Actas de la Honorable Junta del Gobierno, December 11, 1974. Quoted in Carlos Huneeus, *El Régimen de Pinochet* (Santiago: Editorial Sudamericana, 2000), 399–400.

63. Simon Collier and William F. Sater, *A History of Chile, 1808–1994* (Cambridge: Cambridge University Press, 1996), 365.

64. Javier Martínez and Alvaro Díaz, *Chile: The Great Transformation* (Geneva: United Nations Research Institute for Social Development, 1996), 56.

65. Silva, 85.

66. From Central Bank figures on the Gross Domestic Product.

67. Iván Cienfuegos, managing editor, *El Diario Austral de Temuco*, interview by author, Temuco, 2000; Gonzalo Picó Domínguez, interview by author, Santiago, 2000.

68. Filippi, interview by author, Santiago, 2000. Filippi's second in command, Abraham Santibáñez, said that Mujica sold Ercilla overnight without giving the journalists a chance to purchase it. See *Análisis*, "Prensa en Dictadura," 23 April 1987.

69. Pérez de Arce, interview by author, Santiago, 1999. Pérez currently sits on *El Mercurio*'s editorial board.

70. The Dirección Nacional de Comunicación Social (DINACOS) was part of the Secretario General de Gobierno. The secretary is a member of the president's cabinet who acts as government spokesman and manages communications media policy. We will refer to him as the "communications minister."

71. Dinges, interview by author, Washington, D.C., 2001.

72. Paulina Salcedo Guzmán, "Cambios de los Medios de Comunicación y Sus Efectos en el Público" (thesis, Pontificia Universidad Católica de Chile, 1991).

73. Mayor Carmen Grez banned *Cosmopolitan, APSI,* and a science magazine similar to *Nature*, called *Conozca Más*, for reasons that are unclear. Grez was mayor of Providencia, the upscale section of Santiago.

74. Otano, interview by author, Santiago, 1999.

75. Leigh quoted in Eduardo Segovia, *La Historia Secreta de "Cauce"* (Santiago: Pehuén Editores, 1990), 94. The book was commissioned by *Cauce*'s former owners.

76. Segovia, 98–99.

77. The photograph for *Cauce* issue number 10 was credited to Brazil's *Manchete*, where it had originally been published.

78. Osvaldo Hernán Rivera Riffo, director of DINACOS, letter to Jorge Lavandero on official state letterhead, 11 May 1984.

79. Jorge Lavandero, *El Precio de Sostener un Sueño* (Santiago: LOM Ediciones, 1997), 126–134.

80. Lavandero, interview by author, Santiago, 1999.

81. Dinges, interview by author, 2000.

82. Otano, interview by author, 2000.

83. Patricia Collyer, "Así Dejaron La Moneda," *Análisis,* March 26–April 1, 1990.

84. Filippi, interview by author, Santiago, 1999.

85. Fernando Ossandón and Sandra Rojas, *El Primer Impacto* (Santiago: Universidad de Chile, 1989), 104–108.

86. Aldunate is quoted in *La Segunda,* 31 August 1998.

87. Avello, interview by author, Santiago, 1999.

88. Lavandero, interview by author, Santiago, 1999.

89. Eugenio Tironi, interview by author, Santiago, 2000.

90. Cited in Claudia Lagos and Mariela Ravnal, "Cronología de la Libertad de Expresión en Chile" (working paper, University of Chile's Freedom of Expression Program, 2000).

91. Manuel Salazar, former national editor of *La Epoca,* interview by author, Santiago, 1999.

92. Braithwaite, interview by author, Santiago, 1999.

93. Segovia, 89.

94. Jorge Berazaluce Donoso, interview by author, Santiago, 1999.

95. "La 'Imagen'," *Qué Pasa,* 19 June, 1974.

96. Huneeus, Chapter VI.

97. Whelan, 617–620.

98. Huneeus, 364–366.

99. For discussions of the Chacarillas speech, see Huneeus, 364–366; Alfredo Jocelyn-Holt, *El Chile Perplejo* (Santiago: Planeta, 1998); and Pollack, 63.

100. Cristián Bofill, "La Historia Oficial del Nuevo *Qué Pasa,*" *Cuadernos de Información* 8 (Santiago: Pontificia Universidad de Chile, 1993). Bofill was then editor in chief of *Qué Pasa* and would later edit *La Tercera.*

101. *La Segunda,* editorial, 28 August 1998.

102. See Silva (1996); Patricio Rozas and Gustavo Marín, *El Mapa de la Extrema Riqueza: 10 Años después* (Santiago: Ediciones Chile-América, 1989), 35–36; Ascanio Cavallo, Manuel Délano, and Manuel Salazar, *La Historia Oculta del Régimen Militar* (Santiago: Ediciones Antártica, 1990), Chapter 34; and Spooner, Chapter 6.

103. Fontaine, 156–158.

104. Cavallo, Délano, and Salazar, 381.

105. Silva, 144.

106. Spooner, 180–181.

107. For a detailed account, see Martínez and Díaz.

108. Huneeus, Chapter IX.

109. The averages were taken from Central Bank of Chile figures.

110. See Ricardo Ffrench-Davis, *Entre el Neoliberalismo y el Crecimiento con Equidad* (Santiago: Dolmen Ediciones, 1999), 24. Ffrench uses 1977 pesos until 1985, and 1986 pesos during the period of 1985–1998.

111. The figures are from Central Bank.

112. *Ibid.*

113. Martínez and Díaz, 4.

114. *El Mercurio*, 30 August 1989.

115. *Estrategia*, 24 July 2000, citing Central Bank figures.

116. Manuel Délano, Alberto Luengo, and Manuel Salazar, *Para Entender al Decano* (Santiago: Ediciones Ainavillo). The undated study was sponsored by Investigación y Acción Comunicacional. All of the financial figures cited from this work were taken directly from *El Mercurio* S.A.P. financial statements or elaborated from them.

117. *"¿Quiénes Controlan 'El Mercurio'?" APSI*, 21 February 1984, 18–19. In this article, *APSI* reports that *El Mercurio* gave the State Bank 51 percent of its shares as collateral and that the CMPC guaranteed a second loan. However, *APSI* does not cite its source and there is no indication from other sources that this was so.

118. Fontaine, interview by author.

119. Spooner, 9.

120. Spooner, 218–219.

121. "Curiosidades de '*El Mercurio*'," *Análisis*, February 24–March 2, 1987.

122. Gonzalo Picó Domínguez, interview by author, Santiago, 2000.

123. Readers may be curious about the names Chileans have given their newspapers. *El Mercurio* called its afternoon paper *La Segunda*, as in "The Second" edition of the day, implying that it was more complete because it included the previous day's news plus news from the morning it was published. So, naming a newspaper *La Tercera* implies that it is even more complete, because "The Third" edition was then published in the evening (although it is now a morning paper). *La Cuarta* stretches this logic beyond its limit because it is a morning paper. It is simply "The Fourth" newspaper to hit the streets.

124. Picó and Cienfuegos, interviews by author.

125. Picó, interview by author.

126. Banda, interview by author, Temuco, 1999.

127. María Cristina Lasagni, Paula Edwards, and Josiane Bonnefoy, *La Radio en Chile* (Santiago: CENECA), 104.

128. Secretaría General de Gobierno, Available at www.segegob.cl/secc/estudios.

129. Cooperativa's corporate owner is Compañía Chilena de Comunicaciones.

130. Cooperativa had stations in Antofagasta, La Serena, Valparaíso, Concepción, Temuco, and Puerto Montt plus four short wave licenses, according to Lasagni, *et. al.*

131. Labbé, interview by author, Santiago, 1999.

132. Tarud, interview by author, Santiago, 2000.

133. Venegas, telephone conversation with author, July, 2000.

134. Tarud, interview by author, Santiago, 2001. When asked if Tarud's version of events were correct, Vial said: "Could be. I don't remember."

135. Lasagni, *et al.*, 65–67.

136. Lasagni, *et al.*, 73.

137. Tarud, interview by author.

138. Délano, Luengo, and Salazar, 16.

139. *Ibid,* 39.

140. Silva, Chapter 6.

141. Délano, Luengo, and Salazar, 47–48.

142. *Diccionario Biográfico de Chile*; and Fontaine, 139, 148, 159, 172.

143. Délano, Luengo, and Salazar, 42–43.

144. The names of de Castro and Kulka are added in the margin of the company's articles of incorporation on file at the Conservador de Bienes (Recorder of Deeds) in Santiago. The year is clearly 1989. The date appears to be June 19th. It is signed by notary Andrés Rubio and filed as Fojas 16225, number 8173.

145. Délano, Luengo, and Salazar, 47–49.

146. Roberto Silva Bijit, "¿Dónde se Habrá Metido la Democracia?" (Quillota: Editorial El Observador, 1985), cited in Délano, Luengo, and Salazar.

147. Bardón, interview by author, Santiago, 2000.

148. This is Price Waterhouse's undated statement to Fifth Criminal Court.

149. Andrés Benítez, "Gerente de 'El Mercurio': 'La Empresa No Ha Recibido Créditos en Condiciones Especiales'," El Mercurio, 26 November 1991.

150. All exchange rates are from Chile's Central Bank as reported in Estrategia (July 24, 2000).

151. Bardón, interview by author, 2000.

152. Letter listing 22 clients dated January 2, 1984. A memo instructing the destruction of the letter was sent the following day. Additional information on economic groups can be found in Fernando Dahse, Mapa de la extrema riqueza (Santiago: Editorial Aconcagua, 1979).

153. Capital, "¿Resucita El Clarín? [sic]," April 2000. The definite article is often included erroneously in Clarín's name. It has no connection with the Argentine newspaper of the same name.

154. This is from a review of documents provided by the Ministry of State Properties.

155. Spooner, 187.

156. Rafael Otano, Crónica de la Transición (Santiago: Planeta, 1995), 20.

157. Diego Portales, María Eugenia Hirmas, Juan Carlos Altamirano, and Juan Pablo Egaña, Televisión Chilena: Censura o Libertad (Santiago: ILET, 1988).

158. Cavallo, Salazar, and Sepúveda, 563–564.

159. María Eugenia Hirmas, "The Chilean Case," Television, Politics and the Transition to Democracy in Latin America, ed. Thomas E. Skidmore (Washington: The Woodrow Wilson International Center for Scholars, 1993).

160. Sanfuentes, interview by author, Santiago, 2000.

161. Bardón, interview by author, Santiago, 2000.

162. Manuel Guzmán Vial, statement to Fifth Criminal Court, December 27, 1991.

163. Inspector General's Statement to Fifth Criminal Court, April 30, 1990.

164. Andrés Sanfuentes, State Bank President, statement to Fifth Criminal Court, November 8, 1990.

165. Ibid.

166. According to documents on file at the Judicial Archive, de la Cuadra Fabrés is a shareholder (along with principal shareholder Roberto Edwards Eastman, through Inmobiliaria Los Nogales) in Editora de Publicaciones, which holds shares in Paula Comunicaciones. He sat on the bank's board in 1989, according to records filed with the Banking Superintendent.

167. Lord Cochrane S. A., 1999 annual report to SVS. The Edwards combine is a shareholder in Lord Cochrane through two companies controlled by Roberto Edwards, Inversiones Los Nogales, and Editora de Publicaciones S. A. U.S.-based R.R. Donnelley owns 78 percent. For a more complete catalogue of Chilean media owners' assets see Ken Dermota, Chile Inédito (Santiago: Ediciones B, 2002).

168. Sanfuentes, statement to Fifth Criminal Court, November 8, 1990.

169. Manuel Guzmán Vial, statement to the Fifth Criminal Court, January 9, 1992.

170. Arturo Selles, of Langston Clark y Cia, Ltda. Coopers and Lybrand, which audited State Bank records, statement to the Fifth Criminal Court on January 17, 1990.

171. Inspector General, statement to the Fifth Criminal Court, April 30, 1990.

172. Sanfuentes, statement to Fifth Criminal Court, November 8, 1990.

173. Sanfuentes, interview by author, 2001.

174. Senén Conejeros, interview by author, Santiago, 2000. Conejeros was the State Bank's public relations director 1990–1998.

175. Benítez (1991).

176. Sanfuentes, interview by author, 2001.

177. Bardón statement to the fifth criminal court.

178. "Presidente Enviará Ley de Prensa en la Semana," *La Epoca,* 3 July 1993.

179. Hales, interviews by author, Santiago, 1999 and 2000. At the time, Hales was a candidate of a leftist coalition.

180. Mosciatti, interviews by author, Santiago, 1999 and 2001.

181. Sebastian Brett, *The Limits of Tolerance* (New York: Human Rights Watch, 1998).

182. Quote found in Felipe Portales, 50–51.

183. Portales, 40–47.

184. Huneeus, 327–88.

185. Portales, 41–42.

186. Otano, 152–160, and 306–314.

187. "Niegan Asistencias en Senado," *El Mercurio,* 15 May 2000, along with television news reports of UDI and RN responses.

188. Pérez de Arce, interview by author, 1999.

189. Enrique Mujica, former *El Metropolitano* managing editor, interview by author, Santiago, 2000.

190. Otano, 244. Otano credits a non-aggression pact between *El Mercurio*'s managing editor Juan Pablo Illanes and Aylwin communications chief Eugenio Tironi, both graduates of Saint George high school.

191. Margarita Serrano, "La Reception a Pinochet Pudo Haber Sido Más Prudente," *La Tercera,* 12 March 2000.

192. Estela Cabezas, "Tensa Semana Se Vivió en los Pasillos de la Estación," *La Tercera,* 30 November 2000.

193. Verdugo, interview by author, Santiago, 2000. Also see Otano, 329–330.

194. *Qué Pasa,* 14 January 1995.

195. Cuadra, interview by author, Santiago, 1999.

196. Felipe González, *Leyes de Desacato y Libertad de Expresión* (Santiago: Universidad Diego Portales, Centro de Investigaciones Jurídicas, 2000).

197. Stephen Baker, "Taming the Wild, Wild Web," *Business Week,* 4 October 1999.

198. Matus, interview by author, Miami, 1999.

199. Felipe González, 20.

200. Paula Afani, Héctor Rojas, Pablo Vergara, and José Alé. "Las Réplicas del Escándalo de la Ex Jueza Olivares," *La Tercera,* 14 May 2000.

201. *El Mercurio* on-line, August 29, 2000. www.emol.cl.

202. Constitución Política de la República de Chile de 1980, Chapter III, Article 19.

203. *Ibid.*

204. Spooner, 147. Spooner cites the minutes of the council meetings.

205. Pollack, 76.

206. The author's *América Economía* article on the difficulties in obtaining the Ley de Probidad prompted two letters from readers. One wondered why I hadn't consulted www.gobierno.cl. However, the web page did not list the law. The second letter, from *El Diario Oficial*, wished that I had brought this to their attention earlier.

207. Ramírez, interview by author, Santiago, 1999.

208. Patricio Bernedo and Paulo Ramírez, "Transparencia Informativa en Instituciones del Estado" (Research obtained from the authors). Bernedo is a professor of the Catholic University of Chile.

209. *Chile Sustentable*. Published at www.greenpeace.org.

210. Bardón, interview by author, Santiago, 2000.

211. Ricardo Lagos, *La Concentración del Poder Económico* (Santiago: Editorial del Pacífico, 1961).

212. For a thorough, step-by-step investigative method, see: Ken Dermota, *Manual de Investigación Periodística* (Santiago: Ediciones B, 2003).

213. Bernedo and Ramírez.

214. Lagos, 142.

215. Alfredo Matte, ARCHI secretary-general, interview by author, Santiago, 2000.

216. Lorena Rubio C., "Estiman que Codelco Obstaculizó Investigación de Caso Alto Cachapoal," *El Diario Financiero*, 8 June 2000.

217. The author performed a store-by-store comparison of prices of the dictionary at a dozen retail bookshops in Buenos Aires and in Santiago, which showed that the variation in prices was consistent.

218. Media magnate Ricardo Claro was the teaching assistant who reviewed Lagos's book when it was in thesis form at the University of Chile. Claro then qualified the work as "not very serious." He still does.

219. Lucía Castellón and Miguel González P., "Autoregulación de la Etica Periodistica en Chile," *Reflecciones Académicas* (Santiago: Universidad Diego Portales, 1999), 87–99. González is the secretary of the Ethics Council.

220. Miguel Gonález P., "¿Qué Dice el Consejo de Etica?" *Reflexiones Académicas* (Santiago: Universidad Diego Portales, 1995), 27–50.

221. Fontaine, interview by author, Santiago, 2000.

222. Colegio de Periodistas, "Fallos del Tribunal de Etica y Disciplina del Colegio de Periodistas," *Reflecciones Académicas* (Santiago: Univeridad Diego Portales, 1998), 133–148.

223. The members of the board serve eight-year terms. The president names the director without the Senate's approval. Half of the board is replaced at the beginning of each presidential term.

224. Author interview with Hales, Santiago, 1999.

225. John Bartlett, *Familiar Quotations* (Boston: Little, Brown and Company, 1968), 418. Bartlett said that the quote is usually attributed to Voltaire (François Marie Arouet).

226. Bernardo Subercaseaux, University of Chile philosophy professor, interview by author, Santiago, 2000. The university is now 70 percent self-sufficient.

227. Alicia Olivia, "El 'Yo acuso de los academicos'," *Análisis*, 24–30 March 1987.

228. From the comptroller's report quoted in "Canal 11: Lo que Vale el Show," *Cauce*, 1983.

229. Sergio Godoy, Catholic University professor, interview by author, Santiago, 1999 and 2000.

230. Roberto Meza, "Polémica Sobre *La Nación*," *La Nación*, 5 January 2000.

231. According to Huneeus, the Army supplied 46 cabinet ministers and the Chicago Boys supplied 31. Gremialistas supplied 26, the Navy 22, former Alessandri adherents 20, independents 17, Air Force 15, Carabineros 13. My count of 17 Edwards combine staffers includes those who were at some time on the payroll. If friends of Edwards, his publications' guest columnists, or political sympathizers with less formal relationships were included, this number would be much higher. This count does not include Edwards personnel who wielded enormous power at the Central Bank and the State Bank. See Huneeus, 305–313.

232. "Reformas Laborales," *El Mercurio*, 23 November 1999.

233. As inadequate as the English word "objective" is for describing one of journalism's ideals, the alternatives in Spanish are no better. Parada is not saying that "objectivity" has fallen into disuse in favor of another term, but that the whole concept has fallen by the wayside.

234. Parada, interview by author, Santiago, 1999.

235. See Collier and Sater, throughout; Whelan, 36–41; and Brian Loveman, *Chile: The Legacy of Hispanic Capitalism* (Oxford: Oxford University Press, 1988).

236. Arturo Valenzuela and Pamela Constable, *A Nation of Enemies* (New York: W. W. Norton and Company, 1993).

237. Peter M. Siavelis, *The President and Congress in Postauthoritarian Chile* (University Park: Penn State Press, 2000), 91.

238. Alejandro Guillier, 1999 Diego Portales University forum.

239. José Tomás Rebeco, telephone conversation with author, Santiago, 2000. Visión Nacional has since been killed by *El Mercurio*.

240. Mac Hale, interview by author, Santiago, 1999.

241. Fontaine, interview by author, Santiago, 2000.

242. Mac Hale, interview by author, Santiago, 1999.

243. Bardón, interview by author, Santiago, 2001.

244. Luis Alberto Ganderats, "Asbesto: No Hay Enemigo Chico," *El Metropolitano*, 10 December 1999.

245. Homero Ponce, former *La Tercera* labor reporter, interview by author, Santiago, 1999.

246. Olivares, interview by author, Santiago, 1999.

247. Ponce, interview by author.

248. The editor wishes to remain anonymous.

249. Patarrieu, interview by author, Santiago, 2000.

250. Avello, interview by author, Santiago, 1999. Avello is now *Copesa*'s research director.

251. *Ibid.*

252. Rafael Otano and Guillermo Sunkel, *Libertad de los Periodistas en los Medios* (Santiago: Centro de Investigaciones Jurídicas of the Diego Portales University, 1999).

253. See Huneeus, Chapter VII.

254. Patricio Arriagada, Report prepared for the Corporación de Promoción Universitaria (1983).

255. E.H.F. (Edwin Harrington), "Plan para Destruir a la U. de Chile," *Cauce*, 1984.

256. Léniz, interview by author.

257. *Qué Pasa*, "Dos Universidades a la Competencia," 3–9 December 1981, 13–14.

258. Cavallo, Salazar, and Sepúlveda, 30.

259. Ximena Pérez Villamil, "El Poder de la Fe y la Fe del Poder," *Capital*, July 2000.

260. Sellas statement.

261. Carolina García de la Huerta, "El Nuevo Saieh," *Capital,* June 2000.

262. "Círculos de Poder Palestinos," *El Mercurio,* 28 March 1999; Hugo Fazio, *El Mapa de la Extrema Riqueza* (Santiago: Ediciones LOM, 1997).

263. Arriagada was invited to offer a dissenting opinion to Otano and Sunkel who presented their article at the Diego Portales University, in 1999. Some of Arriagada's thoughts are taken from that response. Others are from an author interview, also in 1999.

264. Arriagada, presentation.

265. Ramírez interview by author, Santiago, 1999.

266. José Benoga, *Historia de un Conflicto: El Estado y los Mapuches en el Siglo XX* (Santiago: Planeta, 1999).

267. "Noticias que Hacen Noticia," *Qué Pasa,* 25 September 1999.

268. María Angélica Venegas, "Arden 200 Há de Bosques En Plena Zona Mapuche," *El Mercurio,* 26 January 2000.

269. Marcela Alam, "Nicolasa Quintremám acusa a Endesa de etnocidio," *La Tercera,* 28 January. 2000.

270. Alvaro Medina, "Chile Rechaza Informe de EE.UU. sobre Realidad de Mapuches," *La Tercera,* 29 February 2000.

271. Encuesta Casen, 1996, quoted in *Qué Pasa,* 20 October 1999.

272. *La Tercera,* 5 January 2001.

273. Pilar Molina, "Lagos y Su Conflicto Más Grave," *El Mercurio,* 2 April 2000.

274. Sergio Villalobos, "Araucanía: Errors Ancestrales," *El Mercurio,* 14 May 2000. The "error" of the title refers to historians who do not recognize that the native peoples benefitted from Spanish domination.

275. Paola Segovia, "¿Mapuches Pacíficos?" *El Mercurio,* 10 May 2000. The book, *La Historia de la Iglesia en Valdivia,* was written by Gabriel Guarda.

276. Victor Osorio, "La (des) Información y el Conflicto Mapuche," *El Metropolitano,* 20 January 2000.

277. "Pobreza Mapuche Es Desafío para B. Belmar," *El Mercurio,* 4 March 2000.

278. Fontaine, interview by author.

279. Soto, interview by author, Santiago, 2000.

280. Ricardo Lagos Escobar, *La Concentración del Poder Económico* (Santiago: Editorial del Pacífico, 1961), 140–142.

281. Fontaine, 60–61.

282. Whelan, 923.

283. Rayén Quiroga Martínez and Saar Van Hauwermeiren, *Globalización e Insustentabilidad* (Santiago: Instituto de Ecología Política, 1996), 62.

284. *El Diario Financiero,* 22 September 1999.

285. *Estrategia,* 14 October 1996.

286. "Ciclo Expansivo," *Qué Pasa,* 24 December 1999.

287. Jonathan Friedland, "The Family Empires—Chile's Luksics: Battle-Tested and on the Prowl," *The Wall Street Journal,* 1 December 1995.

288. Fernando Dahse, *El Mapa de la Extrema Riqueza* (Santiago: Editorial Aconcagua, 1979), 65.

289. Verdugo, interview by author.

290. Rodrigo Barria Reyes, "Canciller Mapuche," *El Mercurio,* 19 March 2000.

291. Bardón, interview by author, Santiago, 2000.

292. Copesa editor (who wishes to remain anonymous), interview by author.

293. Arriagada, interview by author.

294. Ajenjo, interview by author, Santiago, 2000.

295. Radio Tiempo agreed not to renew the bus advertisement after the governmental National Women's Service (Sernam) complained to the Advertising Ethics Self-regulation Council. Station owner Ricardo Bezanilla refused to take down the ad, saying, "This is a matter of free expression."

296. Super Pollo radio spot aired in Santiago, June 2000.

297. "Fraces para El Bronce," *El Mercurio,* 24 October 1999.

298. Jocelyn-Holt, interview by author, Santiago, 2000.

299. William Drozdiak, "Haider Unfazed by West's Protests," *The Washington Post,* 10 February 2000; "Haider Confía en que Austria Superará Ostracismo," *El Mercurio,* 11 February 2000.

300. "El Fenómeno Haider," *El Mercurio,* 10 February 2000.

301. Miguel Posada, "Colombia y Washington," *El Mercurio,* 26 January 2000.

302. Gallardo, interview by author, Santiago, 2000.

303. Instituto Nacional de Estadísticas, *Compendio Estadístico* (Santiago: Instituto Nacional de Estadísticas, 1999). A recent high of 6,405 annulments was reached in 1993, and a low of 6,195 was reached in 1996.

304. Andrea Villena M., "Los Hijos También Pueden Exigir," *El Mercurio,* 23 October 1999.

305. Sergio España, Secretario General de Gobierno research director, interview by author, Santiago, 1999.

306. "[The law] is a step backwards," said the president of Radio Cooperativa's board, Luis Anjejo, in an interview with the author, Santiago, 2000.

307. "Fundación Futuro," *Qué Pasa,* 8 January 2000.

308. All information on the AIDS campaign is from Rafael Otano, "La Guerra de los Profilácticos," *APSI* 410, 14–17 January 1992.

309. Israel, head of sales for Ibero American Radio Chile, interview by author, Santiago, 1999.

310. Information from the Fundación Futuro survey of greater Santiago 1998, cited in Pedro Pablo Herranz, Andrea Rutman, and Gonzalo Vega, "Consumistas, estresados y optimistas," *Qué Pasa,* 8 January 2000.

311. Patricio Abusleme, "Expertos Chilenos Crean Método Anticonceptivo," *La Tercera,* 6 December 1999.

312. Instituto Nacional de Estadísticas, *Compendio Estadístico* (Santiago: Instituto Nacional de Estadísticas, 1999), 77.

313. *24 Horas,* Televisión Nacional, 16 March 2001.

314. Clifford Crauss, "Abortion Debated in Chile, Where It's Always a Crime," *The New York Times,* 9 August 1998.

315. Leonard Gross, *The Last, Best Hope: Eduardo Frei and Chilean Democracy* (New York: Random House, 1967), 167. In 1966, there were 129,000 abortions in Chile—one for every two live births. In a 1962 survey, 26 percent of women in Santiago admitted having had illegal abortions.

316. J. Sperling Reich, "Madonna, Madre Soltera Otra Vez," *El Mercurio,* 5 March 2000.

317. "Trabajadoras Celebran en la Calle 'Día de la Mujer'," *El Mercurio,* 9 March 2000.

318. "Tarifas Crónicas Sociales," rate card, provided by *El Mercurio.*

319. Javiera Moraga and Andrea Rutman, "El Diagnóstico Actual," *Qué Pasa,* 22 July 2000.

320. The information is from the Centro de Estudios Públicos survey results of June 1999: 69 percent were in favor of a trial for Pinochet, 19 percent opposed, and 12 percent had no response.

321. Mujica, interview by author, Santiago, 1999.

322. Andrés Azócar, Pablo Gazzolo, and María Eugenia Larraín, "El Peso del Dinero," *Qué Pasa*, 10 June 2000.

323. Otano, 285.

324. Scott Donaton, "Where There's Smoke, There's Shanken's Star," *Advertising Age*, 11 March 1996.

325. "Como Mucho: Pidieron Cheque en Garantía a Vice del Colegio Médico, *La Cuarta*, 25 October 1999.

326. The information is from the company's annual report for 1999, which is filed with SVS.

327. "Resurgen Críticas a Cheque en Garantía," *El Mercurio*, 11 February 2000. The article mentions three cases of complaints at the University of Chile and one at a private hospital.

328. Verdugo, interview by author.

329. "Comisiones de AFP Chilenas: entre las Más Bajas de la Región," *La Tercera*, 2 December 1999.

330. *El Mercurio*, 5 February 2000.

331. "Sólo Una de Cada 10 Personas Jubiliará con Pensión Mínima," *El Metropolitano*, 21 January 2000. The headline refers to the AFPs' rebuttle of the Finance Ministry. Both views were included.

332. Edgardo Ortega, "AFP Bajan Comisiones y Proyectan Buen Año 2000," *El Metropolitano*, 23 December 1999.

333. Pinochet Labor Minister José Piñera, a neoliberal Harvard economist, was adopted by the Chicago Boys who also adopted the AFP.

334. Tomás Hirsch, "Las AFP Son un Fraude," *La Tercera*, 27 October 1999.

335. Anonymous (former editor), interview by author. The official Copesa source for this information was the author's interview with research director Ricardo Avello, Santiago, 1999.

336. Claudio Canales, "Preocupación por Rutas Alternativas a los Peajes," *La Tercera*, 8 February 2000.

337. "Municipios Frenan Negocios Inmobiliarios," *La Tercera*, 2 June 2000.

338. Miguel Angel Poduje, "Reactivación con Emoción," *La Tercera*, 19 July 2000.

339. "Juan Villarzú: Antecedentes de Su Carrera," *El Mercurio*, 12 January 2000.

340. For detailed accounts of the privatization, see Hugo Fazio, *Mapa Actual de la Extrema Riqueza* (Santiago: Editores LOM, 1997), 210–218; and Huneeus, 472–485.

341. Ricardo Leiva, "'Operación del Siglo'," *El Mercurio*, 13 January 2002.

342. M. Cristina Goyeneche G., "Quiénes Son los Dueños de las Empresas Privadas," *La Tercera*, 7 November 1999.

343. *La Tercera* quotes an anonymous source in "Las vidas cruzadas de Sebastián Piñera y Joaquín Lavín," 10 June 2001.

344. For a more thorough look at property ownership in Chile, see: Ken Dermota, *Chile Inédito* (Santiago: Ediciones B, 2002).

345. A Copper Club member said privately that CODELCO president Carlos Lima was "one of the industry's brightest leaders" and called the news blackout "a shame." The Copper Club's 600 members include the industry's top executives.

346. Siavelis, 35.

347. Arturo Valenzuela and J. Samuel Valenzuela, "Party Opposition under the Authoritarian Regime," *Military Rule in Chile*, eds. J. Samuel Valenzuela and Arturo Valenzuela (Baltimore: The Johns Hopkins University Press, 1986), 193–194.

348. Verdugo, interview by author.

349. Pollack, 128–138.

350. Pollack, 169–170.

351. Otano, 338–339.

352. "Supermodel Angst," *The Economist*, 30 July 1999; Anthony Faiola, "Latin Turmoil Deepens," *The Washington Post*, 13 July 2001; and "Goodbye Copper, Hello Recession," *Business Week*, 29 March 1999.

353. The data were provided by the Chilean Association of Advertisers (ACHAP).

354. Avello, interview by author, Santiago, 1999.

355. The study was conducted by the author and Marcela Nagel at the University of Chile, using advertised classified rates that were not discounted.

356. Ajenjo, interview by author, Santiago, 1999.

357. Labbé, interview by author.

358. Ajenjo, interview by author.

359. "Auspiciadores se Alejan de Ivette Vergara," *El Metropolitano*, 6 June 2000; "Brusca Baja de Avisadores Sufre Programa de TVN," *El Mercurio*, 8 June 2000; and "Se Retira Auspiciador de Día a Día," *La Tercera*, 6 June 2000.

360. "Rating Promedio del Programa Conducido por Ivette Vergara en TVN," *MTG*, 8 June 2000.

361. *MTG*, now *Publimetro*, is owned by the Modern Times Group of Stockholm.

362. Godoy, interview by author, Santiago, 2000.

363. Ximena Pérez Villamil, "Ricardo Claro," *Capital*, August 1999.

364. *Ibid.*

365. Brett, 162. The study counted the number of times the words "feature film" appeared in the Metrópolis-Intercom subscriber guide for March 1998 in place of a title scheduled by the content providers. The number of titles censored would be fewer than 296 because an individual film may be transmitted several times per month.

366. Pérez Villamil.

367. "Diputado Acusa de 'Censura' a Metrópolis-Intercom,' *La Tercera*, 19 July. The orignal list was elaborated by Congressman Antonio Leal.

368. Newspaper reports.

369. Guillier spoke at a forum on press freedoms at Diego Portales University, Santiago, in 1999.

370. Departamento de Estudios Secretaría de Comunicación y Cultura-DESCC (executive branch communications study), 1996 and 1967. www.segegob.cl/secc/estudios.

371. The study was conducted by the author.

372. Tironi, interview by author.

373. "El Espejismo de las Cifras del Delito," *El Metropolitano*, 19 April 2000; and "Hombres de Cuello Blanco," *El Metropolitano*, 17–18 November 1999.

374. Fundación Futuro, 1998, in a survey conducted in metropolitan Santiago.

375. Tironi, interview by author.

376. Tironi, interview by author.

377. Information from April 6, 1995 minutes of board meeting held at the offices of *El Mercurio*, on file at the Judicial Archive.

378. Spooner, 147. Spooner quoted the minutes of the council meetings; the translation is hers.

379. Chile has the lowest homicide rate in South America, with 2.9 per 100,000 population. The United States has 11 and Colombia, 80, according to the United Nations Demographic Yearbook.

380. Tironi, interview by author.

381. United Nations, *Desarrollo Humano en Chile* (Santiago: Programa de las Naciones Unidas para el Desarrollo, 1998), 130.

382. Enrique Oveido, "Percepción de Inseguridad en la Ciudad. Entre lo Imaginario y lo Real. El Caso de Gran Santiago," Alberto Concha Eastman, Fernando Carrión, and Germán Cobo, eds., *Ciudad y Violencias en América Latina* (Quito: Programa de Gestión Urbana, 1994), 277–312. The report was sponsored by the United Nations and the World Bank.

383. Instituto Nacional de Estadísticas, *Compendio Estadístico* (1970–2000), Table 1.8.2 entitled "Aprehendidos por Carabineros, por Causal de la Detención." Arrests *per capita* remains flat.

384. *El Mercurio*, photograph, 30 April 2000.

385. *Qué Pasa*, 6 May 2000. There is little reason for there to be equity in the total duration of sound bites because the Concertación is the party in power in the Executive branch of the government and in Congress.

386. Allamand, interview by author, Washington, D.C., 2001.

387. Léniz, interview by author.

388. Grossman, interview by author, Washington, D.C., 1999.

389. *El Mercurio* S.A.P. Articles of Incorporation, as amended April 29, 1997 and filed in the Archivo Judicial.

390. Ximena Pérez Villamil, "Prensa Movida," *Capital*, March 2000. Also listed are Vicente Caruz and Oscar Guillermo Garretón.

391. Godoy, Catholic University professor and Chilean participant in conversations with *Le Monde* investors, interview by author, Santiago, 2000.

392. Fernández, interview by author Santiago, 2000. In the interest of full disclosure, the other investor in *The Clinic*, Pablo Dittborn, is, through Ediciones B, the publisher of the Spanish-language version of this book. The section on *The Clinic* was written in its current form without the author's knowledge of this relationship and before the publisher contacted the author.

393. DeCastro, interview by author, Santiago, 2000.

394. Joannón, interview by the author, Santiago, 2000.

395. Communications Minister Claudio Huepe (University of Chile, 2000).

396. Abel Esquivel, Radio Chilena programming director, interview by author, Santiago, 1999; and "Pura Información," *Capital*, July 2000.

397. Valenzuela and Valenzuela.

398. Soros, 231–232.

399. See discussions of 1980s "Chapter XIX" debt buy-backs in Fazio, 343–345. Chile's Central Bank paid face value to investors who had purchased on the international market Chilean foreign debt, which was at the time trading at 60 percent of face value. Ross said that he used his proceeds to build a paper pulp plant in an interview with the author.

400. Vial, interview by author, 2001.

401. Jacob G. Hornberger, "¿Es Democracia Libertad?" *El Mercurio*, 4 December 1999. Hornberger wrote as president of the Future of Freedom Foundation, a libertarian group similar to the Cato Institute.

402. Soros; and Karl Popper, *In Search of a Better World* (London: Routledge, 1994).

403. *La Hora*, 30 March 2001.

404. Pollack, 129.

405. Bardón, interview by author, 2000.

406. Sidney Weintraub, "The Chicago Boys Were All Wrong in Chile," *The Wall Street Journal*, 3 February 1984.

407. *La Nación*, 11 November 1991, quoted in Portales, 135.

408. Salazar, interview by author.

Index

About the Author

KEN LEÓN-DERMOTA is an Editor for Agence France-Presse, in Washington, D.C. He is the author of *Chile Inedito* (2002), and has contributed to *Business Week*, National Public Radio, and *The Christian Science Monitor*.